Sustenance

WRITERS FROM BC AND BEYOND
ON THE SUBJECT OF FOOD

Sustenance

WRITERS FROM BC AND BEYOND
ON THE SUBJECT OF FOOD

EDITED AND WITH A FOREWORD BY
RACHEL ROSE

PHOTOGRAPHY BY
DEREK FU

anVIL
PRESS

2017

Anvil Press Publishers Inc.
P.O. Box 3008, Main Post Office
Vancouver, B.C. V6B 3X5 Canada
www.anvilpress.com

Library and Archives Canada Cataloguing in Publication

        Sustenance : writers from BC and beyond on the subject of food / Rachel Rose, editor.

ISBN 978-1-77214-101-6 (softcover)

    1. Food--Literary collections. 2. Gastronomy--Literary collections.
3. Canadian literature (English)--British Columbia. 4. Canadian literature (English)--21st century. I. Rose, Rachel, 1970-, editor

PS8237.F6S87 2017   C810.8'03564   C2017-906610-2

Printed and bound in Canada
Cover design by Rayola.com
Inside design by Derek von Essen
Unless otherwise noted, all photography by Derek Fu
Represented in Canada by Publishers Group Canada
Distributed by Raincoast Books

The publisher gratefully acknowledges the financial assistance of the Canada Council for the Arts, the Canada Book Fund, and the Province of British Columbia through the B.C. Arts Council and the Book Publishing Tax Credit.

To those in our community who nourish:
with words, with deeds and with food.

Table of Contents

Sustenance
WRITERS FROM BC AND BEYOND ON THE SUBJECT OF FOOD

INTRODUCTION

As an anthology, *Sustenance* is unique. Unpublished writers, some of whom are in elementary school, stand shoulder to shoulder with some of the best writers in Canada and abroad. In these pages, famous chefs share recipes, and Project Chef kids cook together at our local schools. Buddhist monks and nuns teach us how to eat with mindfulness and without bloodshed. Refugees share their longing for lost homelands and their grief at not belonging, as well as resilience and recipes from home. Immigrants grateful for the prosperity Canada has brought them write hymns about farming in the Fraser Valley, hymns tinged with the fraught task of becoming Canadian in their own eyes and in the eyes of those who came before them. Words of pain and hope from within our fractured literary community sing on these pages, as we collectively struggle to find a way through our own complicated inheritances.

When I became Poet Laureate, I knew I wanted a project that would engage those outside of the poetry community as much as those within it. Writing inspired by food invites us all to the table. When neighbouring politicians insisted that we must build walls to keep out Mexicans and Muslims, I wanted, as Poet Laureate, to do the opposite. I wanted to build a table. When we build walls, we do so out of fear and anger. When we build walls, we can't see the people we exclude. But when we build tables, we sit eye to eye in the sacred relationship of guest and host, mutually obliged and interdependent.

As we recognize Canada's 150th Anniversary, and create and publish an anthology on the unceded homelands of the *Musqueam, Squamish,* and *Tsleil-Waututh* First Nations, we also are compelled to recognize the history of this place. Whoever we are, however long we've called this place home, we have an opportunity to contemplate what it means to be living in a City of Reconciliation, and how we can make the spirit of reconciliation manifest in ourselves, individually and collectively.

Together we have written provocative work about the environment, class, motherhood, women's roles, immigration, and occupation, and together we have written work that celebrates our strengths in a way that connects us. We are a city of diverse cultures, belief systems and economic backgrounds, a city of great wealth and grinding poverty. But, as *Muscogee* (Creek) Nation poet Joy Harjo reminds us, "The world begins at a kitchen table. No matter what, we must eat to live."[1] All of us carry memories of those first foods we ate, the foods that taste like home. All of us have something to say about food.

Knowing that I wanted to reach as many people as possible, I invited participation from other accomplished poets and teachers, each recognized by their own communities as contributing in important ways. Often sporting their legacy turquoise T-shirts that proclaim POETRY IS NECESSARY, the Poetry Ambassadors have worked with generous hearts to engage with people in Vancouver, giving workshops and gathering poems and pieces for *Sustenance*. I am grateful to them all: Hartley Banack, Adèle Barclay, Juliane Okot Bitek, Jillian Christmas, Elee Kraljii Gardiner, Fiona Tinwei Lam, Jami Macarty, Ngwatilo Mawiyoo, Lynda Prince, Annie Ross, Renée Sarojini Saklikar, Karen Shklanka, Kevin Spenst and RC Weslowski. Many thanks as well to Sarah Taliha and Karim Alrawi for correcting the final Arabic proofs of Raed Aljishi's translation of my poem, "Cooking Lesson: *Kebbeh.*"

Sustenance is about giving back to those in need and supporting those who feed us locally. But it is only an invitation, and its success will be measured only to the extent that those connections, those new shoots, are cultivated and grow strong. I invite you to read this book, and to take the risk of connecting with someone outside your social group. Make soup; make amends; make new friends. Allow yourself to be uncomfortable and do it anyway. Bake Thomas Haas' chocolate sparkle cookies for someone you hardly know. Find a way to forgive, just a little. Read Thomas Larson's essay, "Kneaded," and feel your spirits expanding with the yeast of it. Read Mark L. Winston and Renée Sarojini Saklikar's meditation on apples and honey and find strength in the renewal of the seasons reflected in religious ritual and the work of beekeeping.

The table is symbolic, but symbols matter. Writers will be donating their honoraria to the BC Farmers Market Nutrition Coupon Program. Every book sold will provide a local refugee or low-income family with fresh, locally grown produce through these vouchers, and at the same time will support BC farmers. Nothing is simple; even the act of feeding people is fraught and complicated— but this project is, simply, a love letter to the city in which I was born. All the writers here, many of whom also struggle to make ends meet, have generously donated their work to create community and to sustain others.

Sustenance is also a reminder to myself, and to all of us, that we never know when the seeds of kindness and connection will germinate, and what they will become. It was more than ten years ago when my family and I first began to volunteer with Shar Yu, a widowed mother of six children, and a refugee from Myanmar (Burma). Our job was to help her and her children settle in and deal with the many challenges of Canadian life. We delivered food, drove people to medical appointments, did a joyful and stressful Christmas gift drive, and gathered people who wanted to help, like Dr. Ian Macdonald, who visited and assisted several of the hundreds of new arrivals struggling with diabetes and malaria. I invited the wonderful stylist from Volution, Jennyfer LeClaire, to spend a day at their apartment building in Surrey, where dozens of the families had been resettled. That day, Jennyfer volunteered to cut and style people's hair, which was probably the most popular welcoming initiative ever.

I won't forget those hours as I bent over the sink of a small bathroom apartment in Surrey, in the projects where all the refugees were housed, sudsing the scalps of people I'd only met a few minutes ago. A crowd of hopeful teenagers jostled around Jennyfer, hoping for a cool new haircut.

No matter what we did, we were always fed. As soon as we showed up, Shar Yu, or a neighbouring woman, would start the ginger and garlic frying. It is a very intimate thing, to wash the hair of strangers and to be invited into their kitchens to eat. To be the host is also intimate: to welcome newcomers to eat at your table, and to invite their kids to bounce on your trampoline. None of it was comfortable; all of it was worthwhile.

I have watched Shar Yu's family struggle, persevere, and enter the work force. I've watched two of Shar Yu's daughters graduate from high school, and one from college. I met hundreds of other refugee families from Burma, and I became close to another family, Paw Thi Blay and her children. We've attended *Karen* New Year's celebrations, and one heartbreaking funeral. We have been given hand-woven sarongs and many gifts as well as meals—but most of all, we've been willing to take a chance on each other, on connecting. I think it was at Shar Yu's table and at Paw Thi Blay's table, where every child who entered the door was made welcome and fed, as we were, that the seeds of this book were planted. I am so grateful to them for all I have learned about generosity and community.

We now have refugees coming from Syria, but also from many other areas of conflict around the world: Eritrea, Iraq, Congo, Columbia. The needs of new arrivals are great; the connections and friendships made can be transformative. (If you are interested in learning more about volunteering, you can call Mount Pleasant Family Centre, Circles of Care and Connection Program and use the program manager's number 778 372 6552.)

Each of you, holding this anthology in your hands, has a place at the table. I invite you to make your community and your city more compassionate, more joyful, more ethical. May you find sustenance within these pages, and the inspiration to make new connections within our city. I close with a poem I wrote after visits and interviews with two women, Ayat and Yasmeen, both recent refugee arrivals from Syria, as they patiently tried to explain to us how to cook *Kebbeh*. «•»

Cooking Lesson: *Kebbeh*

RACHEL ROSE

I would not wish to welcome you with rain, Ayat,
with this bitter wind, Yasmeen. But here we are,
one young son banging plastic nails into a plastic board,
turning it over to hammer the other side.
Isn't that life? All noise and repetitive energy,
and so we turn and begin again: the work song of mothers
at the stove, at the table, at the cradle.

Today I drove through hard rain to meet you.
I came empty-handed, asking for your recipes,
which Sarah translates, which Lynda writes down. We cannot speak
directly to each other, though the eyes take measure,
the hands. Let's avoid the war for a moment, politely, like ladies,
let's look the other way. Six women in a community
kitchen: every story we tell is a door to another story.

Thank you for teaching me the art of *Kebbeh*,
though I'm not sure I'll ever understand
your lesson on how to prepare bulgur, how to use pomegranate molasses
to add depth and sweetness. *We used to watch wars in other countries*, you say.
Soak the bulgur, drain it and let it dry, then add pepper—
suddenly it happened in our own country.
Children as young as this one don't know the sound of bombs,
they aren't afraid of anything. Blend the mixture either in a machine
that is not to be found in Canada, or with the hands.
Cook the meat separately, *though in Aleppo we eat it raw.*
Do you have any Canadian friends yet? I ask,
and you both shake your heads.
We came here as refugees; we will stay refugees.

When the mixture is ready, add flour.
Press the meat into the centre, then deep fry in oil.
We used to cook all together. When we made Makoubeh,
we turned it over with many hands. Now we cook alone.
Yes, now you cook like Canadian women, each in her lonely kitchen.
Yes, like that. We lost everything.
My parents are still there. My cousin's cousin's family,
all of them killed. We can never go back.
Dice a pound of onions, cook them in a shimmer
of oil, cumin, seven spices—Oh, here's your baby pressing his mouth
against the side of your face, he wants to be fed,
the windows stream rain. *Crying*
has become a habit; we do it every day.

This wind is a daughter knocking at the door
of a bomb shelter. Let her in. Let me hold your hands
as the tears begin; even Sarah, the translator, is in tears.
Add them to the onions, simmer until all is translucent,
until the moisture is out, the baby asleep, villages dreaming
under their soft blankets of gas, pomegranates split on the bush,
grinning their blood-toothed grins.

No, I would not wish to welcome you here with rain, Ayat,
with this bitter wind, Yasmeen. But welcome all the same
to my homeland, where many are hungry but not for food,
welcome to the cold shelter of this stolen place, welcome with songs
of rivers and ancestors, of boats that brought us here
and boats that sank on the voyage. One day
may you have a garden and the blessing of grandchildren,
may you run out of tears. Welcome.

Rachel Rose has won poetry, fiction, and non-fiction awards, including a 2016 Pushcart Prize, and a 2016 nomination for a Governor General's Award. Recently a fellow at The University of Iowa's International Writing Program, she is the Poet Laureate of Vancouver. Her non-fiction book, *The Dog Lover Unit: Lessons in Courage from the World's K9 Cops*, is forthcoming from St. Martin's Press/Thomas Dunne Books (http://rachelsprose.weebly.com/) in 2017.

Raed Anis Al-Jishi (poet, translator; Qateef-Saudi Arabia) has published 13 books. He was recently a fellow at the University of Iowa's International Writing Program.

درس طبخ: كبة

لم أكن أتمنى أن أرحب بك وقت المطر ، يا آيات،
ولا مع هذه الريح العاتية يا ياسمين. ولكن ها نحن ذا،
أحد الأبناء الشباب يطرق مساميرَ بلاستيكية في لوح بلاستيكي،
يقلبّه ليطرق الجانب الآخر.
أليست تلك هيَ الحياة؟ كلها صخب و طاقات متجددة
وهكذا ندور ونبدأ من جديد : أغاني الأمهات
وهنّ يعملن قرب الموقد، الطاولة وعند المهد.

اليوم، قدتُ خلال المطر العنيف لألتقيكن.
أتيتُ خاليةَ الوِفاض، أسألَ عن وصفاتكن،
التي ترجمتها "سارة"، ودونتها "الندا". لا نَستطيعُ الحديث
مباشرة مع بعضنا البعض، ولكنّ الأعينَ تتدبر الأمرَ،
كالأيدي. دعونا نتجنبُ الحرب للحظة، بكل أدب، كسيدات،
دعونا ننظر إلى جانب آخر.
مجموعة من ست نساء
بالمطبخ: كل قصة نقولها هي بوابة لقصة أخرى.

شكرًا لكنَّ لتعليمي فن إعداد "الكبّة"
رغم أنني لست متأكدة من كوني سأستوعب يومًا
درسكما في كيفية تحضير البرغل، وكيفية استخدام دبس الرمان
لزيادة الكثافة والحلاوة.
قلتما: لقد اعتدنا على مشاهدة الحروب في دول أخرى.
-انقعي البرغل، أفرغي الماء عنه حتى يجفَّ، ثم أضيفي الفلفل.
-وفجأة حدثت ببلدنا.
لا يعرف الأطفال الصغار كهذا الطفل ما صوت القنابل،
لا يخافون من أي شيء.
امزجي الخليط في آلة، آلة لن توجد بكندا ، أو اخلطيه باليد.
اطبخي اللحم بشكل منفصل، مع أننا في حلب نأكله نيّا .
سألتكما : ألديكن أي صديقات كنديات حتى الآن ؟
وكلاكما هززتما رأسيكما.
لقد جئنا هنا لاجئتين؛ وسنظل لاجئتين.

-عندما يجهز الخليط أضيفي الطحين.
اضغطي اللحم إلى المركز ثم اقليه في الزيت المحمي
-كنّا نطبخ جميعًا. عندما نحضّر المقلوبة
نقلبها بأياد عدة. الآن نطبخ بمفردنا.
-نعم، الآن تطبخن كنساء كنديات، كل واحدة بمفردها في مطبخها.
- نعم هو كما قلتِ. لقد خسرنا كل شيء.
مازال والداي هناك، أبناء عمومتي
قتلوا كلهم، لن نستطيع العودة أبدًا.
-قطّعي رطلين من البصل، اطهيه على زيتٍ مُحمى ،
أضيفي الكمون و البهارات السبع – أوه، ها هو طفلك
يضغط فمه على جانب وجهك، يريد أن يرضع
النافذة تقطر من المطر. البكاء
أصبح عادة؛ نمارسها كل يوم.

هذه الريح طفلة تطرق بابَ ملجئٍ من القنابل. دعوها تدخل. دعيني أمسك يديك.
عندما سقطت الدموع، حتى سارة المترجمة بكتْ.
-أضيفيهم إلى البصل،
دعيهم ينضجون حتى يصبح المزيج شبه شفاف،
وتخرج العصارة. نامَ الطفل، القرى تَحلم
تحت بطانياتها الناعمة الغازية ، وتنقسمُ الرمّانات على الشجيرة
مكشرا ت عن ابتسامة دموية الاسنان.

لا، لم أكن أتمنى أن أرحب بك هنا مع المطر يا آيات،
ولا مع هذه الريح العاتية يا ياسمين.
ولكن برغم كل ما قيل، مرحبًا
بكن في بلدي، حيث هناك كثير من الجوعى، لكن ليس للطعام،
مرحبًا بكم في المأوى البارد من الأماكن المسروقة، مرحبًا مع أغاني
الأنهار وأرواح الأسلاف بالقوارب التي جاءت بنا إلى هنا
والقواربُ التي غرقتْ في الرحلة. يومًا ما
أتمنى أن تكون لك حديقة من الأطفال المباركين
وان تجفّ كل دموعك . مرحبا.

شعر: راتشيل روز Rachel Rose
ترجمة: رائد الجشي Raed AL-Jishi

1. «Perhaps the World Ends Here» from *The Woman Who Fell From the Sky* by Joy Harjo. Copyright © 1994 by Joy Harjo.

wild, sacred, good[1]

annie ross

i have walked lifetimes to see you, Salt Woman, pounded wheat
open yellow mums, rose hips, juniper berries, my prayer beads
i count, as you count
a slice of bread in a loaf, a potato in a field, a cup of water in a river
i lay my forehead on the ground every four steps
your face, a mandala
seagulls flock downtown in search of love
loaves of bread, torn, scattered about, as i, as we
Salt Woman cascade like a fall, rest as a lake, dry as a sheet
how many interpreters, chain of translators
do we need for protruding bones
every twelve years, every 28 years, every 3800 years, you pass
you pass, counter-clock to their clock-wise
loaves, potatoes, water

1. Gary Snyder, "Good, Wild, Sacred" in *The Practice of the Wild* (San Francisco: North Point Press, 1990).

annie ross is a teacher/artist working in the Canadian west.

Fish

JOHN PASS

A dozen oysters
count. First

delicacy I devised
for you, fried
lightly in chives
and butter. But more

of your glossology
than mine—lapsed

vegetarian, lips pursed
for the pond's viands,
tiny silver dolphins leaping

on your earlobes, tank-suit
damp over belly, breasts
and behind, a seal

impressed of the water.
I nose about

in aquariums of air, nibbling, fattening,
nearly blind, instinctive. Bright rain
splashes the windows, freshens

your scent. Tang
of April greenery, mint
and fennel. A brush with nettles.

Swim free. Make a meal of me.

This work was previously published in *Forecast, Selected Early Poems 1970 – 1990* (Pender Harbour: Harbour Publishing, 2015).

John Pass is the winner of the 2006 Governor
General's Award for Poetry and the 2012
Dorothy Livesay Poetry Prize.

Kneaded

THOMAS LARSON

You don't wet the bread board. You flour it, generously, as *The Tassajara Bread Book* says. Next, you splat-set the antsy dough onto the wood where it fate-flattens with a shrug. Already, you're speaking up for the lump—to wit, its voice, yours for the taking, such generosity, indeed.

You knead the pile. The pile needs you, so much so that your push meets its fetal mass, serpent-bodied. Its bouldered build yeasts a gathering force, an orneriness that matches your provocation, hail batch, well met.

You put your hands' heels into it and the mass rolls its shoulders and spine back and the water leeches out, and with it the gluten, which sticks to your fingers, gums them up, and gloms onto your intent, hosts this transference, what the psyche of food plots in you, its host-maker.

Eventually, the kneading honeys your hands into stumps, say, palettes or paddles, losing their handedness, and again you plunge one then the other into the Pillsbury bag, releasing the brown-nut-smell, the slightly noxious odor of earthy resolve, flour powering an eternal rotation, a turn for which Nietzsche also had his say, to wit, "When his work opens its mouth, the author has to shut his."

You rub your hands together, warming before a morning fire, and the little curled dough-drops fall like flecks of skin, wormish squibs that re-enter the lot, attach, immerse, melt, and bulk the brainy float, albeit passing, like you, having too brief a parade in which to ever or never know yourself.

Still, you pound the bubbled bulge, the yeast now friction-hot, fermenting, bloated, gaining on you (this'll be over soon), the splay across the board again, an island bulking up and out of the sea, its outer banks folding onto themselves, coves beach, pores tent, cells swell—on and on until the bread is enriched, more single-purposed than when you began, an egoist of the sort you hadn't expected, a psychotherapeutic crossing you wagered would be what was will be what is, to play our minds on and be played, hand to loaf, scent to taste, shaper, shaped.

On your life or not, the dough has had enough: the wheat germ blocked, the oil r-u-n-n-o-f-f, water/flour/salt all rebuffed, the slab rectangled one, two, three in Teflon pans, a last billow, alas, and the oven-bake stays the air within, the hot buns shake down and bound off the board, monument, stone, idle, the loaves cool, a knife bids butter, the toast calls jam, each primal slice betters your rhetorical cast, your metamorphosis lost in the oblivion of language. . .

Whatever you write you've already eaten.

Critic, memoirist, and essayist, Thomas Larson is the author of three books: *The Sanctuary of Illness: A Memoir of Heart Disease, The Saddest Music Ever Written: The Story of Samuel Barber's "Adagio for Strings,"* and *The Memoir and the Memoirist: Reading and Writing Personal Narrative.* He is a twenty-year staff writer for the *San Diego Reader* and the Book Reviews Editor for *River Teeth.* Larson teaches in the MFA Program at Ashland University, Ashland, Ohio. His website is www.thomaslarson.com.

Blackberries

NANCY PAGH

I would like to write you a poem about fat ladies
but you prefer to read of blackberries.

There are eight hundred sixty-four poems about blackberries
published in English; where is the harm
in another?

So let's say that the wildest fat ladies
grow on low runners that snake
unplanted along the driest hillsides
of coastal British Columbia.
The tight knot of their fruit
is smaller than all others, and shaped
like the bud of your own coldest nipple.

I heard a Sixteenth-Century Italian printer
despaired the destruction of cuttlefish
and began making his books with the juice
of fat ladies.

A transplanted Himalayan variety of fat lady
ripens in cow pastures late in the autumn.
It hangs in black clumps
among serrated yellow leaves, tasting
like barbed wire, hatred, and the mineral note
of self abnegation; your tongue thrills
to meet such darkness.

Royalty used to reserve the colour of fat ladies
just for itself, but now
the CEOs all favour a striking red tie.
The American president follows suit.

Fat ladies travel many miles
in the gut of a bear
to colonize the bright waste of clearcuts.
I would like to read the diaries
kept on one of these passages.

Have you ever noticed that the biggest fat ladies
are just beyond your reach?

Fat ladies do not taste
like salmonberries. Salmonberries do not taste
of salmon. Fat ladies taste good
when you are standing near the Nooksack River
watching the salmon
or watching the places you wish there were salmon.

Fat ladies permanently stain everything
except your tongue.

An overripe fat lady drops in your palm
with the slightest touch.
If you try to blow off the roadside dust
you will break its tender skin
and miss the holy communion
of eating the roadside dust.

Oh that first day, that first day you notice
the fat ladies have withered and dried on their vines:
a regret more tart
than the small unripe segments
of the first fat lady
you ate that summer.

Again and again the fat ladies push
in to every unclaimed corner of the neighbourhoods,
reminding the soft palates of children
there really are things in this world
so sweet and so free.

There are so many fat ladies; where is the harm
in sprinkling one with sugar
to watch the materialization
of Homer's wine-dark sea?

This work was previously published in *No Sweeter Fat* (Autumn House Press 2007).

Nancy Pagh has authored three poetry collections (*No Sweeter Fat, After,* and *Once Removed*). Broadview Press published her writer's guide, *Write Moves*, in 2016. Her book on women travelling the Northwest Coast by boat was published by the University of Calgary Press. She was the D. H. Lawrence Fellow at the Taos Summer Writers Conference, received an Artist Trust/Washington State Arts Commission Fellowship, and placed second (of over 4,000) in the 2014 Wergle Flomp humor poetry contest. Nancy lives in Bellingham and teaches at Western Washington University. www.nancypagh.com.

Cooking Class & Marriage Lessons

JANE SILCOTT

A friend invites you to a cooking class. You agree because she's a good friend, a dear friend, but truly, you'd rather do long division in your head. You'd rather do push-ups or side planks or both. You'd rather lie on train tracks and die romantically, a train filled with oversized industrial stoves and sautéed duck breasts rolling over you, then serving you up, still warm with morel sauce on the side. Your husband makes you sit in the front row. Your husband becomes the guy in the class who makes jokes out loud, so the chef starts using his name and you realize you've married the class clown and how have you been married so long and not known that? You're wondering when it can be over and when you can have your wine back. The chef has made everyone put their glasses on the island, an island half the size of your house and almost as far away. He said it was because he didn't want anyone to knock a glass over accidentally but you think he doesn't want twenty inebriated adults playing with knives and fire. After you sit through the lesson about duck with morel sauce and blinis, a lesson that's flown through your head so quickly it might have been quantum physics or gene splicing, you and the woman next to you confess to one another that you hate cooking. You decide this woman might be your new best friend and then wonder if it was destiny or survival that inspired you to marry a man who can turn on the giant fire-breathing stove without pause and pour half of Italy's supply of olive oil in a pan, then watch as it spreads, looking the happiest he's been all day.

"That's too much oil," you tell him. "The duck is going to swim again."

"It's olive oil," he says. "It's good."

You turn away after telling him his love of oil is what's made you fat, and he lies one of his marriage-saving lies, and you mix milk into the bowl for the blinis, which you've learned are just potato pancakes with a nickname.

A moment later, he holds one of the ingredient containers filled with brown liquid above the pan. "Are we supposed to put all this in?"

"Yes," you say, annoyed because hadn't the chef said everything was pre-measured?

"It seems like an awful lot," he adds, and you say, sharply, "Just put it in." The moment after he does, you both look at the ingredient tray where another container of liquid, white and creamy, and much smaller, sits innocent and ignored. You realize you've just made him add the water the morels had been sitting in, with their dirt and wood chips, to the sauce. You experience one of those moments when the possibility that age is affecting your mind hits you full force. Your husband is despondent. "It's okay," you say, "It will simmer and boil away."

The chef arrives at your station when you are slicing the duck. You think you're doing fine, but he says, "How 'bout I do that for you?" and takes the knife from your hand. You suppress a small, but familiar feeling of hurt—you've lived a life of people taking food preparation tasks away from you—and watch as perfect medallions of meat fall from the knife. "Voilà," he says. And you think, again, how clever you were to marry a man who loves you anyway and the two of you go and eat, chewing wood chips with your morels as if they were there on purpose.

Jane Silcott's debut collection of essays, *Everything Rustles* was shortlisted for a BC Book Prize. Her writing has also won a CBC Literary Award, a *Room* Magazine Prize, and been a finalist in both the National and Western Magazine Awards. Jane is a mentor in the Creative Nonfiction MFA Program at King's College in Halifax and in Vancouver Manuscript Intensive.

The Struggle of a Restless Cook

KATARINA BALAZSOVA

My tasting spoon is sharpened
my pan wide and hot—ready to deliver.
The cumin is sizzling in the oil, turmeric
stains the ginger-garlic paste
curry leaves coil.
I have nothing to cook
except the basic spices and my own flesh
which will never turn into gold
without the fucking vegetables.
Bring me the zucchini with cilantro
bring me the madness of poblano peppers
bring me the eggplants and the lotus root!
With wooden spoon and caution in my hand
I wait by the stove's heat.
And when you return from the sunrise
I'll let the plants fuse and stand on their own
without the bloody meat!

Katarina Balazsova, a native Slovakian born into a Hungarian family, moved to Vancouver, Canada in 2004 in search of true identity. She came out of the closet as a poet and now thrives on writing in her second language. Her poetry is published in *Ascent Aspirations Magazine* and *Crap Orgasm*.

My Life in Food

CORI HOWARD

The only thing I learned to cook as a child was *kuffels*
rolling dough on my grandmother's Formica kitchen table,
her soft, wrinkly hands over mine,
cutting paper thin triangles from a perfect circle
slathered in butter and sugar,
flour everywhere.
I remember only the smell
of her cigarettes, yeast and cinnamon
The Price is Right playing in the background,
the apartment window open to the fresh spring air
I would eat the hot tiny rolls as soon as they emerged from the oven,
the raisins burning my tongue

In university, my boyfriend and I would play house,
make soup from beef bones on icy Toronto nights
chopping, laughing, smoking, drinking
enveloped, awash in the briny steam
in our cheap, rental kitchen with the peeling, linoleum floors
lovers unaware the food wasn't enough
to save us

Food, I was taught, was the cure to everything.
Eat, you'll feel better
says every Jewish mother daily.
Are you hungry?
I fought that identity,
still do
but the force of my genetic coding surprises me,
a woman with limited interest in cooking, eating, religion.

As a mother, food became work
Endless rounds of sticky fingers
hands in mouths
food flung on the floor
highchairs and boiling water and
never sitting down to eat
food was no longer a cure, but a chore
So I lost my appetite

Are you hungry?
I ask my teenagers now,
returning reluctantly to the kitchen at midnight
to make noodles
or plates of salami and cheese
I have counted the dinners I've made
now that he is 15 and she is 12
5,475 if you want to know exactly
I've been at this a long time
and still, I struggle to accept my role as cook
as Jewish mother,
flour in the creases of my aging hands,
serving love through food.
realizing, suddenly,
I am so hungry.

Cori Howard has been writing for more than three decades. She is an award-winning journalist and editor of the anthology, *Between Interruptions: Thirty Women Tell the Truth about Motherhood*. She only recently returned to poetry after a long hiatus and she continues to write personal essays, some of which can be found here: www.corihoward.com

Untitled

SILAS HUSSEY and CONNOR FUJITA

Crop failing to grow failing the child with nothing to eat
In the setting sun, the fisherman drives home after a good day's catch
He walked along the cracked earth looking for hope
The farmer walks away from his cattle, many buckets brimming with milk
Flies and vultures keep close watch on the sick and dying
She walks through the dining room, driven by aroma
Final breaths are taken before death
Unwanted food is washed away by those who take more than they need
Farmers drive through the community that's bound to them by agriculture
As help comes in, the dead go out
In the field, crops are growing next to the dam
Meat and bread are sold and traded underneath patched tarps
Stomachs are filled for the first time in three days
Slowly counting the useless money

Connor Fujita is twelve years old, loves to play soccer, jump on the trampoline
and eat sushi.

Silas Hussey is twelve years old and enjoys sushi, baseball, soccer and many
other sports and foods. He lives in Vancouver, BC.

Romanticization

JODY JUNE POLUKOSHKO

When I was a kid, my family lived, pet-free in a regular house, in the midst of farmland and animal husbandry. We were a secular family in a religious town, flower planters and ignorers in an agricultural community.

My parents wanted us to feel connected to food production without being farmers. To that end, my dad brought home live chickens and butchered them with an axe on a stump in our driveway for us to pluck and eat.

We canned pickles made from cucumbers bought from the farm down the road.

Bees swarmed in our summer yard where my dad cleaned fish, bought whole and illegally, arriving in black garbage bags.

We pulled over in the car and pet the heads of dairy cows through electrified fences on country roads.

My sisters and I rode our bicycles to pick raspberries as an incredibly low paying and spider-filled summer job.

But we knew farmers and breeders and ranchers.

My great-granny grew vegetables, poured salt around lettuce to keep slugs away. We ate dirt covered carrots sitting between the rows.

My friend Melanie told stories at sleepovers, confidently using grown-up vocabulary to describe artificial insemination or foals being born.

Kids drove farming vehicles to high school and parked next to the Fieros, dirt under their fingernails in math class.

And there was corn. We knew the names of those families, and whose jubilee we preferred.

I know where food comes from but have rarely eaten things grown by my own hands.

Jody June Polukoshko writes: I am a grade 5/6/7 teacher at Charles Dickens Elementary in East Vancouver. In collaboration with my teaching partners Tami and Karim, we just completed a two-term project about food with our three classes.

Who Takes the Cake?

JUDITH PENNER

I wanted to write about my mother's orange pudding. Or, about the porridge she made so early in the morning that by the time we got out of bed the gruel in the now cold pot had developed a crust. Doesn't the word *gruel* conjure up Dickensian hardship? But it was never like that. My parents—a teacher who survived his years as a University of Saskatchewan science student on a cheap diet of peanut butter, and a nurse whose childhood meals, after their mother died of the Spanish influenza, were cooked by her older sister, then twelve—vowed they would not stint on nutritional food for their children. That didn't mean extravagance. We ate very little cake, no pop or white sliced bread or convenience foods, except for canned green beans and cocoa. It was mostly fresh food, some of it grown in our back gardens.

My father's family had survived the post-revolution famine and chaos in Southern Russia (now Ukraine). My mother's descendants included an Englishman who left his progressive Shropshire family to join the fur trade, Selkirk Settlers exiled from Scotland to make way for sheep, and her poor but well educated father, who emigrated from windblown Caithness. In her story of Depression-era economics her father eventually traded their family home in small town Manitoba, a converted stone schoolhouse, for a car, and a few years later traded that car for a vacuum cleaner. We can imagine—it has happened to others—a further devolution had the vacuum cleaner been traded for a loaf of bread.

My parents sustained their children on a plain but adequate diet of apples, oranges, carrots, tomatoes, cucumbers, green beans, peas, potatoes, tuna fish sandwiches, Sunday roast beef, shepherd's pie, pork chops, chicken, applesauce, Mennonite farmer sausage, dill pickles, etc. My mother made pies and puddings, but not as often as we'd have liked. We thought we suffered from a lack of desserts. I learned to make angel food cake. Sometimes I mixed a paste of cocoa, sugar and water to consume with a spoon in my hiding place behind our oil heater while I read Dickens.

Both my parents grew up on the Prairies and, although not on farms, in a time when milking cows, picking berries, collecting eggs were close-by chores. Both were loving, open minded, curious, knowledgeable, responsible people, interested in Canadian history. They did their best to shape our inclusive world-view, but what they didn't know (I presume) they couldn't teach us.

The Prairies, where my mother grew up and my father came when his family left the chaos and hunger of the place he'd been born in, had been deliberately cleared of the indigenous people who lived there. Sir John A. Macdonald and others made the cynical choice to let First Nations people starve rather than honour the treaties that promised famine relief and medical help. It was politically expedient to empty the prairies of human beings to make way for the railway and the agrarian society intended to sustain this new country called Canada.

This year we're asked to honour the 150th anniversary of Confederation but I find myself spurning the celebratory cake. Now that I know our secret history I cannot un-know it. It changes my story in ways I'm only beginning to perceive.

Born on the Prairies, Judith Penner travelled by train to BC in an apple basket when she was one month old. She has lived and worked as a writer, editor and yoga teacher in London (UK), Nova Scotia, India and NYC, but Vancouver is home.

Learning to Speak

CHLÖE ROWAT

I hadn't been able to recognize
what you had simmering
on the back stove before
I forgot about it, leaving it
long enough that it began
to boil over and overflowed. I used to
eat your words
and the food you served me
whether I was hungry
or not. I forgot
what it tasted like
to know the difference
between cold and hot. I thought
my tongue was getting familiar, but
familiarity isn't a synonym
for sweet, savory, *umami*.
Familiar is remembering
when you'd feed me mushy peas
and carrots as an infant, grazing
your spoon along my chin,
coaxing me to swallow
every syllable. Every mouthful, again
and again. Even when
I refused the meals you
served me, and heard you tsk
through your teeth and told me
to keep chewing, the flavours
of your morals are now indistinguishable
from comfort. You kept
feeding me, no matter
how many times I tried
to spit them out.

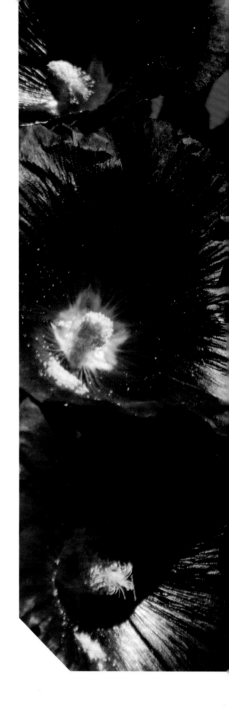

Chlöe Rowat is currently studying Creative Writing at Douglas College and her short story "Invertebrate" will be published in spring 2018. This poem is her very first publication, and she is incredibly honoured for it to be within a collection that not only contains topics she is consumed by, but also items she consumes.

My Trip to Safeway—Food and Gratitude

STEPHEN T BERG

Ours wasn't a 100-mile diet, it was a 100-yard diet, I recalled, while doing my grocery shopping and overhearing a conversation about what constituted local produce. But that conversation triggered another awareness.

Our family ate what sprouted from a large patch of tended soil behind our house. What wasn't eaten straight from the garden was put up in jars and in a root cellar.

And we ate meat. Chickens and pigs mostly, occasionally a young steer or heifer. Sometimes we ate wild meat. Deer or moose—barter with an uncle—as my father didn't hunt. What we raised but didn't sell, we butchered. What we butchered we used.

I didn't mind the taste of chicken-foot soup, it was the thought of the feet that I minded—feet I knew. Feet that'd run through barn-slick mud, feet that scratched up grub-life from beneath the dirt. Feet I snagged with wire and hook, then held skyward while the chicken arched-up, caught my sleeve in its beak and beat my arm and the air with frantic wings. Not effecting its escape, it dropped down in a flurry of feathers, breathless and half limp, while I pulled it across the stained block and chopped the head free of the neck. Blood splattered on the hard-packed dirt, wings flapped then went still.

The chickens were scalded and then plucked as they hung from a length of wire stretched between a stall in the barn. Then they were singed to remove pinfeathers and taken to the kitchen for cleaning and cutting. Up in my room, I caught the smell of chicken entrails as I fell asleep.

When it came time to butcher a pig, a neighbour was called. He placed the gun barrel a few inches away from the hog's forehead and pulled the trigger. The hind legs were strapped to a block and tackle hung from a protruding beam behind the

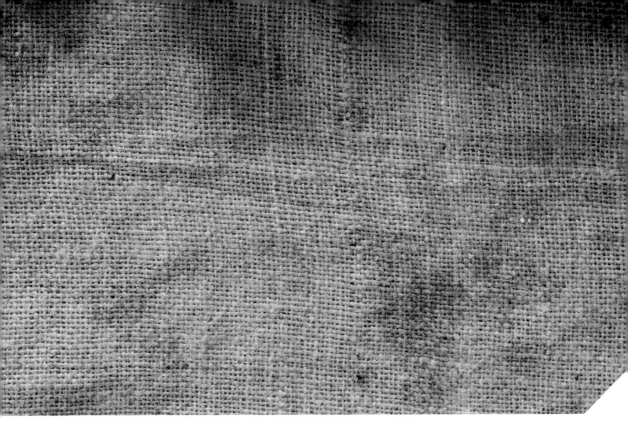

barn, the pig was raised, suspended head-down, front feet grazing the ground. My father then eased a bright blade through the soft skin above the breast bone, sticking the carotid artery.

After the pig was bled it was submerged in a barrel of scalding water, then scraped clean of hair and bristle. Finally it was cut from breast bone to pelvis, and opened up, its offal spilling on the ground. The mound was later shoveled on the manure wagon and taken to the field, but not before the cats and our dog were full-gorged.

The carcass cleaned, my father lowered the pig's bulk onto a makeshift sawhorse table and used a meat saw to cut it into manageable chunks—ribs, ham, bacon.

My trip to Safeway has none of this drama. It has none of the understanding or the connection. As I reach for the well packaged meat, cold and clinical under tight cellophane, I feel none of the strange remorse mixed with reverence that I had for the animals whose lives we took.

Most distressingly, my failure to remember the link I have to the earth, its creatures, and all that sustains me, has glazed me ungrateful.

I walked home under a weight, playing with this thought: that there is no true enjoyment of food without gratitude; perhaps even no genuine nutrition, without thanksgiving.

Stephen T Berg is a poet and writer, with a background in social care—living in Victoria BC. His poetry and prose have appeared in magazines such as *Orion* and *Geez*. His chapbook, *There Are No Small Moments*, was published by The Rasp and The Wine (2014). For more of his work visit: growmercy.org

Elk Heart

TANA RUNYAN

Elk heart, three nights running
captive words in my head
unable to leap the skull's white walls
onto paper

the words throb
a high mountain chant
elk heart, elk heart

each fall, my mother
smothered the wild meat
a gift from the hunter next door

she smothered the meat
for her children's reluctant appetites
simmered it tender
in tomato sauce and green peppers
to disguise the memory of antlers
the bloody velvet
its thick-necked bellow

wapiti   manitou

a seven-point rack
of shining fire

stepped out of the pines
into the yellow kitchen
where our mother hid
its wild heart
safely away
in her own.

Tana Runyan is a poet living and writing in
Vancouver. Her book of poems, *Arithmetic
of Surrender*, was published by Exile Editions.

A Meal from the Past

ANTONETTE REA

Takes me back to a time when I was still in public school and my father would go moose hunting with his hunting partner Ian MacIntosh. Every year they would plan extensively their two week hunting trip to various regions in central and northern BC. A successful hunt meant that we would have a freezer or two filled with the most delicious meat in the world. From a young bull moose. Too much gristle in the old bulls.

Sunday dinner was a moose roast, roasted potatoes, previously frozen pickled carrots and beets from the garden with Grandma's homemade sourdough bread on the side. After the main course Dad would pipe up with "what's daff?" which is the dessert.

My mother was a mom on the go so most meals we were left to make on our own. Her idea of making dinner was to take something out of the freezer to defrost almost by dinner time, which was 6-6:30ish. Mom would be off curling most weeknights.

The one meal my mother prepared well and didn't overcook was the roast on Sunday. My most memorable meals were sitting down at the dining table with the whole family, including both parents for a Sunday dinner of moose roast.

Photograph by Derek von Essen.

Antonette Rea is a writer, poet, and playwright whose most recent work, *Miss Understood*, was nominated for a Jessie award in the category of outstanding original script (2017). She lives in Vancouver and is a member of Thursdays Writing Collective in the Downtown Eastside.

Fed is Best

DANICA LONGAIR

His big, bright eyes stare at me while he lies on my bare chest. Hair still wet, head still oblong. He is so fresh from my womb that his life is counted in minutes. His first task in life was breathing. He needed help. His next task: to latch onto my small nipple. He needs help. We try different positions, the football hold, the cradle hold, both sides. Nurses I have never met before squeeze my breasts. They don't ask permission. It hurts. But he is determined. He works hard for ninety minutes. He is unable to latch. We break. We will try again. Not a drop on either nipple.

Breast is best say the shopkeepers, the nurses, the media, the WHO. Breast is best for your baby, for you, for the world. Moms want what is best for their children. We are programmed to believe the slogan, the propaganda: Breast is Best. We are wicked to choose formula for our innocent newborns. We are told breast-feeding will be difficult but 95% succeed! Women chafe and bleed to succeed. Feed every hour, decimating our sleep. Drops of first milk—colostrum: "liquid gold"—don't arrive until baby is five days old. (For me: seven.) The lactivists expect us to starve our screaming newborns until the drops arrive. Formula will ruin my body's signals to produce. My son's belly is full of Enfamil. Society shames me.

The drops have come. With a flimsy, expensive nipple shield, he has become an expert at latching. We breastfeed for hours at a time. It feels good for both of us. Euphoric. We bond. We love. But there are only drops.

Breastfeed or else. Breastfeed or you will succumb to postpartum depression, obesity, osteoporosis, breast, uterine and ovarian cancer. Breastfeed or your child will succumb to respiratory illnesses, obesity, cancer, infections, eczema, gastro-intestinal problems, type 2 diabetes, a lower IQ, SIDS. Breastfeed or your child will die. And it will be your fault. Because you failed to breastfeed. Formula is equivalent to smoking, unsafe sex, unhealthy eating habits, and other stigma-tized behaviours. Breastfeed or society will pay the cost of formula feeding, yours and your child's medical bills, the cost to the environment. Breastfeeding is your civic duty to humanity and the earth.

My doctor, a breastfeeding specialist, says my milk will never come in. We have tried for two months, breastfeeding, pumping, massaging, taking medica-tion, letting my son cry longer to see if that will stimulate. Only drops. The tears stream. She says I should stop. I was too stressed to succeed. Formula was offered to my child too early. I fed my hungry boy, failing to stimulate my breasts prop-erly with his sustained hunger. I have failed in my first task as a mother. I have failed my child.

Daddy takes turns feeding formula, bonding with his son. Baby's growing well on formula, but is he growing enough? "Smart boy," his doctor says. Bronchiolitis comes and goes quickly. Bed time is 7:30 p.m. Formula digests slowly. Sleeps until 7:00 a.m. Daddy occasionally feeds at 5:30 a.m. I sleep nine hours, uninter-rupted, every night. I can have all the caffeine and anti-depressants I need. Man-ufactured, fake love courses through my son's body. Fake love is still love.

I will try to breastfeed my next baby.

Danica Longair is an emerging writer who lives with her baby son, husband and two cute cats in Vancouver, BC. She is working on a contemporary novel about a three parent family and a memoir about living with depression and anxiety, miscarriage, and caring for family members with cancer and dementia.

I Want to Serve Food to Strangers

BRIAN BRETT

Age gives us odd perspectives.
Suddenly, I am obsessed again.

This time with food.
I want to make a meal out of the planet.

I want to feed you.

I want to feed my friends
grapes and marinated chicken livers
lightly sautéed in butter—
all on dishes of hammered gold.

For you, I will raise
the young calf in a green field,
let it drink the milk of its mother,
eat the best grains.
I will stroke its shoulders,
and treat it kindly
until the day I kill it.

Then I will clean the flesh and cook it
on a spit over maple wood.
This tender, sad calf
stuffed with
a giant pumpkin,
the pumpkin
stuffed with
seven peacocks, an orange sauce,
and a dusting of walnuts.
Each peacock
stuffed with
red bell peppers
stuffed with
a tangerine-coloured tomato
stuffed with
a green and very ripe kiwi fruit
stuffed with
a small okra pod filled with
chocolate and the tiny heart
of a bird that knew

the meaning of song in the morning.

I want to eat everything.
My hunger has grown immense,
and most of all, I want to
serve everything to strangers.

A few potatoes, the yellow kind,
Yukon Golds, organic, washed fresh
from the earth, sliced but not peeled,
dribbled with newly churned butter,
basil, oregano, garlic, and some salt;
then baked in the wood stove.

I will make a sauce
like a river on that stove,
a red sauce,
a white sauce,
a green sauce,
a blue sauce,
yes, even a golden sauce:
sometimes with honey,
sometimes with almonds,
sometimes with curry.

It will flow onto the floor
and out the door and down the field,
breaking into many rivers,
each a different sauce
until they flow together
into the great cauldron of the ocean
having fed every living
plant and animal on the way.

There will also be a salad
of sharp and leaf-serrated endives.
I will garnish it with
the flowers I have loved.
Nasturtium, rose, begonia, violet,
fava bean, borage, day lily...
and on and on and on and on...

A little olive oil,
a squeeze of lemon,

a touch of balsamic vinegar.

Strong cheese and nuts, of course.
Baked, earthy peasant bread
that smells like the good field
ablaze in the bright spring,
the field where they buried
my great-grandfather
and the rest of the clan
in the sun-scorched south of Italy.

Let's forget the world,
and worship it too.
Let's cook up a new world,
so we can all get fat.

I will grow seven varieties of tomatoes
and nine kinds of garlic
just for this meal.

I will candy quinces and plums.
I will sugar flowers in the spring.
I will make jellies from clean fruit.
I will grow chickens and kill them.
I will flee to Costa Rica for coffee beans.
I will chop wood all winter for the fire.

I will make rose scented candles;
then ignite them for mood and shadow,
and play the Brandenburg Concertos
discreetly on the stereo.

I will nurture the greens and the fruits
and the plump vegetables with my stupid
and often over-dramatic tears
like the rest of the mad spaders
who sow the seeds we eat.

The time has come
when I must repay
the many decadent luxuries
I have dined on for free.
And I want to serve
everything to everyone now.

This meal will be made for
my children, each animal,
strangers with strange hair
and odd languages, my family—
aunts and uncles included,
the geriatric cat, all my lovers,
the lost bandits, even the murderers,
sexists of each sex, old friends
who grew tired; cheesy politicians
and ancient, bent-fingered crones;
sure, real estate salesmen too,
a wise farmer going hopeless broke,
hungry children, and birds
thrown too young from nests.

Sit down, sit down
at the great table of our lives.

I will feed you all.

Brian Brett is a poet, fictionist, memoir writer, journalist and former chair of the
Writers' Union of Canada. His thirteen books include *The Colour Of Bones In A Stream*,
Coyote: A Mystery, and the Globe book-of-the year, *Uproar's Your Only Music*. His
best-selling *Trauma Farm*, won numerous prizes, including the Writers' Trust award for
best Canadian non-fiction. *To Your Scattered Bodies Go* won the CBC poetry prize in
2011. A collection of poems, *The Wind River Variations* was released in 2014. The final
book in his trilogy of memoirs, the award-winning *Tuco*, was published in 2015.

Two houses

E. ALEX PIERCE

          one up the road, one down—sand hills in between. River run
salt, at low tide an arm of the sea. Clam flats stretching along the channel—
the Sable River, stopped up by sadness on a perfect June day. Cortège
of cars at the tiny cemetery, mid-way.

The smaller house, whitewashed, old—facing the river—green trim.
We can see it from the rowboat. Sides banked with eelgrass for winter,
windows caulked. Rags of grass and wind. Low roof, ell chamber—

At twelve, and in sorrow unable to speak, outside
the spare white church—waiting for the line of cars
to pass.
          Up at the small house, kids running loose
in the yard—cousins, three to a bed. Grandfather
out by the sawed off August-apple tree. Codfish
hanging up to dry. Everything bitter, salt, vital,
quick. Woodstove roaring hot. A smell of creosote
and tar. Rich taste of beans baked with salt pork and molasses.
Sound of iron on iron—the dinner gong. Oil lamp
on the kitchen table. Kerosene light on the grandmother's face.
White hair, yellowed, pulled up in a knot. Voices
growling—rising and falling, out
into the seamless dark.

E. Alex Pierce is the author of *Vox Humana*, published by Brick Books (2011). Her work has been widely anthologized, notably in *Untying the Apron: Daughters Remember Mothers of the 1950s* (Guernica, Ed. Lorri Neilsen Glenn) and in *Undercurrents: New Voices in Canadian Poetry* (Cormorant, Ed. Robyn Sarah). She holds a Master of Fine Arts in Creative Writing from Warren Wilson College, NC, and has been a participant both in the Writing Studio at the Banff Centre and the Poetry Colloquium at Sage Hill. For ten years she taught creative writing at Cape Breton University, then returned to Sable River to develop E. Alex Pierce Writing & Editing. She is Senior Editor for Boularderie Island Press and conducts manuscript review workshops throughout Canada. www.ealexpierce.com www.brickbooks.ca

Le Temps des Cerises

RHEA TREGEBOV

Massacre in my kitchen, the counter
spatter incarnadine, my hands bloodied
with the juice of cherries splayed, gutted,
for dessert at a friend's; my fingers dyed a red
that keeps in the fine creases, under the nails,
through the next day's breakfast, lunch. I tremble
to sacrifice none of this, even though the cherries, local,
organic, spoke to me, insisting on their innocence, the plump,
burgundy wholeness of them. I didn't think
to spare them, never do; not them, nor the shrimp
I clean for my son's homecoming dinner,
each shrimp life given up, given over
to our celebration. Deeper into that same night
I hear, through my open window, close,
someone else's baby cry—such grief,
and nothing will ease it, not the breast
or rest or warmth or darkness or light;
nothing will ease it forever and ever
or for the long moment till all is well
and silent. We can't help ourselves: who wouldn't trade
their own child's comfort for another's harm,
another child's harm? We can't help ourselves, knowing
it's wrong, knowing there would be a remedy
if we wanted it. Now someone has written a book
I won't be reading, about how the Earth would do without us,
rewriting not the past (airbrushing Trotsky
out of the Stalin snaps), but the future; a projection
sans project-er. It's getting hotter,
we're starting to agree we've fucked it up.
The review says the author has visited fresh
ruins, a city abandoned only decades, and it's easy
to foretell: bougainvillea purpling rooftops,
the small fingers of roots diligently rubbing out
difference. No inside; no out. To some
perhaps it's comforting to think of the Earth
scratching at its ear (*good dog!*) and us no more
than fleas in its coat: a good scrub,
a sprinkling of powder and all

is well again. None mourning our self-
massacre, not the cherries gone wild,
the gleeful shrimp gaining, all
we consumed. He imagines furthermore
humpbacks releasing their arias without contest,
butterflies sculpting air. I don't want to. Useless
though my own life has seemed to me
at times (despite cherries, despite friends), I want
this curious project to continue, our certain hunger,
our subtleties, our complicated contradictions. The arias
less necessary to me than the way a mouth is held,
the look in an eye, that engenders them. Though
my own evaluation of the human
is that, as the song goes, you can't
have one without the other.

"Le Temps des Cerises" reprinted with permission from *All Souls'* with permission of
Véhicule Press, Montreal, 2012.

Rhea Tregebov's seventh collection of poetry, *All Souls'*, was
released in 2012. Her poetry has received the Pat Lowther
Award, the *Malahat Review* Long Poem prize, Honorable
Mention for the National Magazine Awards and the Readers'
Choice Award for Poetry from *Prairie Schooner*. Tregebov's
historical novel, *The Knife-Sharpener's Bell*, won the Segal
Prize in literature and was shortlisted for the 2012 Kobzar
Prize. She is an Associate Professor in the Creative Writing
Program at UBC.

Blueberries, Red Head Cove, Sept. 20th

ANNA SWANSON

Past the radio tower, on through
the quad trails, to where the trees
give way, to where the wind blows
hard up the high cliff and you
bend low, brace, reach toward the edge
for berries. Are batted back, flat
on your berry-picking ass. Berries
hunker better, burrow under wind-lines,
bob in the shallow eddy where life plumps
with sun. You reach again, wanting
in. Grey rain bleeds across the ocean
toward you, gusts picking up,
the light fading, each brief needle of it
through the cloud: to eat this.
To take on your tongue the sum
of all the times the sun came through.
The fierce sweetness of this place
that could kill you any day. All the hours
it hasn't.

Anna Swanson is a writer and librarian from Vancouver, BC. She studied Creative
Writing at the University of Victoria and Memorial University. Her first book of poetry,
The Nights Also (Tightrope Books, 2010), won a Lambda Literary Award and the Gerald
Lampert Award. She currently lives in St. John's, NL.

Union Square

CHRISTOPHER PATTON

slabs of a crumbling white cheese
baskets of onions, & small fragrant leeks
      wild purslane, gold purslane
not all of me will die

          *

gone one whose bones are ground down
grey dust at sift through the scumbled earth
rain on the fruit-spur & light shakes the twig
      mind-ground, root-heart
spring wind blowing wildly, here, now, there
—they thought they had it all but they didn't
—oh, once you have that you don't get rid of it

Pollen floats under the white pines
—Monday she goes, an ontologist,
      that's the specialist
hangs on air, nor pure nor impure
gold fines the lord breaks in through
    Αδοναι
        gold that leavens the tree
        all that was wild, a sweet sauce

                earth-tuft of herb

Christopher Patton is a poet raised in Vancouver who now lives in Bellingham, WA. "Union Square" is from a recently completed poetry manuscript, *Dumuzi*, poems from which have appeared in *Colorado Review*, *New American Writing*, *FIELD*, and elsewhere. Video poems from his current work-in-progress, *SCRO*, have been exhibited at the Whatcom Museum in Bellingham, WA and the Minnesota Center for Book Arts in Minneapolis, MN. His second volume of Old English translations, *Unlikeness Is Us*, will be published by Gaspereau Press in the fall of 2017.

Alchemy

LESLIE TIMMINS

Words chosen for a cake
welcome yazidis!
are too meager to feed
your magnificent hunger.

Carrots shredded for filling, cream cheese
and icing can't say
We honour your courage
to survive.

What can we say with food?
And will you taste the imperfect
freedom of our country?
Free from genocide, but not from rape.

Flour, water, words,
a poor recipe
when you alchemize
our humanity

our heart-broken hunger
to see you among us
one day may your life
taste as sweet.

Leslie Timmins' first collection of poems, *Every Shameless Ray*, will be published by Inanna in 2018. *The Limits of Windows*, her chapbook about the art of Henri Matisse, was published by The Alfred Gustav Press. A writer and editor, Leslie's also a member of the activist group rememberoursisterseverywhere.com.

Food for Thought

INGRID ROSE

My love and I are walking the Cleveland Way on the Yorkshire Wolds. Along a cliff edge, track worn by tread. To our left, the sea six-hundred feet below eats away layers of clay covered by red chalk. In the late Cretaceous period, sixty-five point five million years ago, seawater submerged southern England and two thirds of all life, including dinosaurs, was extinguished as North America and Europe drifted apart.

We walk ten miles a day, thought apace, her orange knapsack beaconing against English green. Words compose in my mind, food for thought, like fuel fodder bread—the staff of life. Knots in back massaged in rhythmic walk as body gentles over grass knolls, sheep bleat and our soles tingle. Cows swipe grass, consume half a day's light ruminating through fourfold stomachs. We human animals sideswiped by language ruminate too through manifold mind. Everything smelled seen heard sensed tasted touched regurgitated, food for thought—our inborn appetite.

When my firstborn clamps to my nipple, his suck quickens me, a cord of desire, moist at both mouths, draws up my gut body. We don't live by bread alone but without earth's generative flesh, who will suckle us?

At Saltburn's Ship Inn, a massive white leg attached to chicken thigh sweats beside soggy chips with a pint of Guinness to wash it down.

Beneath our measured tread, fossils piled in rock strata and black jet are all that remains of the monkey-puzzle tree's ancestors. Need to quicken pace, she's a tiny blue and orange dot ahead in a sea of green blue white.

Kittiwake lofts above, swoops sudden to sea, rises with something white in yellow beak, a small fish mollusk shrimp or worm. Joins shrieking chorus on steep cliff side nest-embedded and streaked with guano—what goes in must come out.

What shit do *we* leave behind for future generations? More than two hundred and forty-four million migrants and twenty million refugees seek a place to belong and a third of the earth's land mass is becoming desert and growing.

We stop to photograph magnificent Angelica, weeds we disdain often medicinal and edible, treats digestion, anaemia, loss of appetite. Cow parsnip, young leaves taste of asparagus, treats migraines. Wild carrot I've hazarded, my love's hawk eyes caution, *Leaves not lacy, don't put it in your mouth! Could be Hemlock!*

No drone or hum, an underlay of uncanny quiet worrisome. We can count bees and butterflies seen on one hand. *Where have all the insects gone, long time passing? Where have all the insects gone, long time ago?* We're going to eat them *everyone*— locusts crickets grasshoppers caterpillars beetles bees ants—our salvation.

Our appetite monstrous—but how can we renounce loveliness in the world? We want it all, down to the very last grub. Eyes nose ears mouth throat heart hands belly cunt cock want.

We've reached the cliff edge, the edge itself has subsided, only a fluorescent orange strip, the English being reserved and ironic, to mark its passing.

Ingrid Rose writes: "I started a lyric prose memoir in The Writers Studio (SFU 2001). Excerpts have been published in *Emerge* and CV2. I teach *writing from the body* in my studio and *essay of desire* in SFU's lifelong learning program."

Swallow

mia susan amir

As a child, my mother collected the rotten cherries discarded by the fruit seller as he passed her house on Bannerman Avenue.

There was polio.

A wreath of garlic around the neck, and cloves of garlic peeled naked on a plate. The flesh of the cloves broken open by teeth. The shock of the slow sour burn of the sap moving over the tongue, filling up all of the air in the mouth, and then the body, until it is the body itself: breathing, total, alive. A charm to ward against all disease, against all dying.

My mother brought a note home from the teacher informing my *Baba* that she should not feed her children garlic on school nights.

Which is to say, water the body down.

Which is to say, that the long carving of the boat across the ocean, that the quiet folding of the cinders of a city with all of its names into the throat, that the abandonment of graves, both those marked with stones and those simply left wide open, that the supplanting of their own names for those more easily pronounced, provided by a seventeen-year-old cousin upon meeting for the very first time, that their survival of all this, that their survival of their survival, was not enough. Wash the body of the defect of leaving and arriving, of remaining the self, of the slow adaptation to one's own foreignness.

There are many kinds of hunger felt in the body.

When they arrived in Winnipeg, my *Baba*, and my *Saba*, and my mother, and my aunt, lived in one small room with a mirror and a brown bureau in the home of my *Saba*'s older brother. My *Baba* was crying all of the time, for Russia. Maybe if her body could make enough water, she thought. At least a return to the ocean would be something closer than this.

There are many kinds of fullness that the body learns to bear.

Children learn to live in the way they are shown. My mother ate like my *Saba*, voracious and without limit, swallowing like quicksand, like too much water in the soil. She drank my *Baba*'s ocean, becoming intertidal, forever in between. Both conditions were not unlike drowning.

My *Baba* boiled a cow tongue. Whole and grey and dead, it sat there between us on the table, the taste buds erect on the meat of the muscle. Some things live beyond their lifespan, and some things are ingested without us even knowing.

Each morning, when I was a child, my mother would set out six garlic pills for me to swallow with orange juice before I left for school. From their exterior, the pills—tiny reflective beige ellipsoids—seemed innocuous. But when the capsules began to dissolve on my tongue, when they evaporated in the acid of the juice, their powdery contents broke open on my esophagus, releasing the smell for everyone to know: this was what was inside of me. I tried to hold my breath forever. I tried to sip the air in through the most miniscule parting of my lips. Despite my effort the stink escaped, and children are cruel, and there are many ways to learn to survive, and to learn to survive our surviving, and to learn to turn the taste of something spoiled into some kind of bearable sweetness.

mia susan amir is a writer, interdisciplinary performer, cultural organizer, and educator who currently resides in Vancouver, on the unceded and occupied territories of the xʷməθkʷəy̓əm, sḵwx̱wú7mesh, and Tsleil-Waututh.

Small Bites

A. L. CARLSON

The women in my family do not eat. We split things in half, then in thirds, then in quarters. *Do you want to share this? I could never finish it by myself. Can we get two plates?*

My grandmother was forever dividing, her portions becoming smaller and smaller until only air was left, and she could gasp it down her throat. As a child I was jealous of friends who would come back from visits to grandparents with sticky-fingers and rotten teeth, tins full of *ice kipferl* and dark, wet gingersnaps. I wanted a grandma who would tell me I was skinny, call me little bird.

My grandma pointed at people on the street (*Look at how fat she is!*), my grandma remarked on second helpings. My grandma rubbed my belly, planted the seed of shame that moved through her hands, to my mother's hands, to my sister's hands to mine.

The women in my family perform fullness to great effect. We are award-winning actors in the role of a lifetime. Puff your cheeks out, hold your stomach, moan: *I am going to explode. I can't believe how much I ate. I will never eat again.*

As my grandma grew older, her small bites grew smaller. Her life grew smaller too; Alzheimer's divided it in half, into thirds, into quarters. *Did I really do that? That didn't happen.* She forgot her friends at normal school, forgot trips she had taken, forgot the rules of baseball and the words of songs. One night on the phone she couldn't remember the name for chicken wings. She said she had eaten bones.

She ate a bowl of ice cream on the day she died. I ate nothing at her funeral. My family gathered at the water's edge in northern BC, and we scattered my grandma for the fish to feast on, flecks of ash that would have been just tiny enough to sit (untouched) on her plate. There was a table in the cabin overflowing with WASPy

Anglican funeral foods: processed cheese, processed ham, butter and white bread. I tried to cut a piece in half and sliced into the meat of my palm, blood welling out slow like syrup.

I did not eat.

I drank—sharp, alkaline sherry from a plastic cup—and I sat alone on the shores of Fraser Lake, hidden by branches bent heavy with blistering Saskatoon berries, the whole world ripe.

I was so hungry, I could have eaten bones.

And I thought then of the great dripping cinnamon bun of my grandma's heart. Butter and sugar and cream cheese icing, turning wax paper clear with sweetness. A heart made of cake and molasses and dark, wet gingersnaps, a heart that sang lullabies about oceans, rocking my bed like the deck of a ship until I grew fat with sleep. A heart that told stories and read poems and played an out-of-tune upright piano, keys ringing like tin beneath her vein-bruised hands.

(This is not acceptance and this is not forgiveness, and I will bite my own fingers off before I pass this seed to someone else.)

But food is not the only thing that nourishes.

And I was full. I couldn't believe how much I ate. I would never eat again.

A. L. Carlson is a mad queer writer, musician and social worker who lives and works on unceded Coast Salish territory in British Columbia. She believes that food, art and kindness can change the world.

The Hale Farm, Whonnock

KYLE McKILLOP

The cows low by the barn, stitched
to their landscape. The glow of dusk
tugs at their stomachs, my uncle
the farmer tossing them bales, the hay
separating like meat off the crockpot bone.

When I was little he slew a favourite elder
cow down by the creek, lovingly, his friend
holding the shotgun steady. After he finished
crying, he buried her remains with a backhoe
and what was left of her lived on in the freezer,
brought out for family gatherings. Some distance,

from the barn to the farmhouse,
one roof's peak visible from the other's.
Not far enough that he'd eat his own
chickens: he knows what he feeds them. The cows
are splattered with the season, the darting
of their calves. The mud sucks at my shoes.
In my hands, a carton of eggs, still warm.

Kyle McKillop is an MFA student in UBC's Creative Writing Program; his poetry
has been published in *CV2* and *English Practice*. He is the president of the Surrey
English Teachers' Association and a past president of Royal City Literary Arts
Society. Find him online at kylemckillop.wordpress.com.

Psych Ward Grub

LUCAS CRAWFORD

I'm the choosy beggar

with a PhD and wet bare feet.
I don't want cold cream of
wheat or sour lukewarm
honeydew.

I want a world of the curly-coiffed trucker
who offered me half of his lunch
because I was new.

I don't want the cornstarch-slurried
puddle of paltry "stew" that would
make a fine papier-mâché

scented with *eau-de-poulet*.
(Are *you* chicken?)

I want the spike of every Louboutin
sidewalk-splashing in Vancouver
to be auctioned off by a nurse

who speaks off-brand-table-syrup-slow
and calls me "dear." Proceeds would
supply psych wards with berries, Twix,
spices, and chips—in perpetuity (which
is to say, year after year after...)

The last time I ate flesh so hard, I was kneeling
for communion, a young gun dreaming

of Funyons just to Pavlov's-dogs
that dry wafer down.
Now is the revival:

imagining pink Jolly Ranchers
just to psych up my saliva.

So please don't balk when I say

I WANT SOME FUCKING SALT.
Sodium chloride? NaCl? *Sel de mer*? Yes,
freshly cracked, crunchy, and coarse…
Mrs. Dash? MRS. DASH?
The word that comes
to mind, Madame, is *divorce*.

Due to irreconcilable similarities
to the colour of human waste,

I don't want to choose between
this pabulum or this one or that.
I wish my tablemate would stop

calling me fat, but when I'd been crying
and then offered him Sun Chips, he said,

"I've got your back, brother. I've got your back."

       Did you know there are professors who proclaim
       that tough men know no tender feelings?

At teatime, we bleed Red Rose, but where's
the Chai, the Earl Grey, the Darjeeling?

From the "ketchup is a vegetable" file, one might ask:

is an "Appetizer" of cranberry cocktail known to promote healing?

No. So, we need a psych ward 500+ item buffet:

      "ALL YOU CAN EAT IF YOU LIVE ONE MORE DAY"

          (Now With Sundae Bar)

I want every *Acadienne* to spread

into the thick bliss of buttered rappie pie.
The old-timer who has never left her zombie
town might not die if she had sushi to try,
pad thai wok-fried, or Montreal bagels.
(Hush, New York, take it in stride.) What
else? I don't know…Nanaimo bars made
in a dive bar in Nanaimo?

In lieu of a menu, there'll be a petition to
sign to be sent to the Gastronomati.

It will demand that the word "forage"
be proprietary to those who
niff out hospital storage

in order to (with plastic spoon,
crackers, and sludge) scavenge
their way to a passable porridge.
It's semi-homemade *and* lean!
Call it 'Sandra Lee meets Rene Redzepi' cuisine.

No disrespect to the meat loaf
machine, that surgical-steel beef-
guillotine,

the aloof silver tooth that pre-
portions us from on high.

Far be it from I
not to give my atheist
thanks to the underpaid
ranks who shepherd *any*
grub here.

I worship thee,
sacrificial spam
on prodigal bun.

But my fruit cocktail came
back up ipecac-quick and
now I can only eat these
words for fun.

> My cohorts on the ward are mostly poor
> and all white and might not be well-versed
> in appropriation debates.

Who would deny
a schizo a schnitzel
if it extended her
own expiration date?
Who would refuse

a California roll to
my electroshocked
friend with the
shakes?

(Yes, the rice would be gummy
and the crab would be fake.)
Could you call my friends
lucky? Would you let them eat
cake?

It hurts here.

Bruised clingstone brain.
It hurts here. We eat swill
then try not to shit
shame. We are very different,
but our farts all smell
the same.   Excuse me –

Until the utopian buffet opens
I'll be here rocking in my bed
Cradling a plastic ladle

Remembering chili, chowder, and daal.
Repeating one thing over
and over until I'm free of
good-stew withdrawal.

No, I'll say it 'til it's
fucking foodie folklore:

the food in the psych ward
must be ~~to die~~ to live for.

"Psych Ward Grub" was first published in *Room Magazine.*

Lucas Crawford is a poet and assistant professor of English at the University of
New Brunswick. Until July 2016, Lucas taught gender studies at SFU, including a
seminar in food writing that shared some sessions with the Thursdays Writing
Collective. Lucas' poetry book is *Sideshow Concessions* (Invisible Publishing 2015).

Act I: Basic Ingredients

JAN TSE

Zero hunger, domestic hunger
protect
contradiction
intolerable
emotional
biological
feed hungry people
vulnerable people
symptoms
valve and
attention of state
corporatization,
guarantee

Act II: Amendment Article: Spirit of the Law

Zero in hunger, concentrate on domestic hunger;
protect the big corporation and create massive contradiction.
Make living condition intolerable: both emotional and biological.
Never feed hungry people, and don't you dare to teach
the vulnerable people. Treat the symptoms, and don't forget
about the cause. We never value the human.
You must pay attention to state spin doctors' jargon,
corporatization and glorification of the feeding the poor
program, with gibberish voodoo chants.
Within 40 years, my Lord, Ladies and Gentlemen,
before long, success is guaranteed.
The Act is enacted on this date AD 1066
and shall be carried out by the power invested to us by God.
Amen

Jan Tse is a poet who has published in two Thursdays Writing Collective anthologies. She has the same profession as David Bowie's mom: An Usher. She loves singing, cooking and reading. This poem scavenges and repurposes words from the Food Donor Encouragement Act of Canada.

Preserving

SHASHI BHAT

You once asked if I could write a poem
about some pickles. But I couldn't muster
up emotion for fresh produce thrust
into a jar, then soaked acidic, prone
to warts, profane as frogs, in drowning bloat
like thumbs. I wonder how they keep their crunch,
how long they last pressed peel-to-peel, not much
in store but fermentation's sour wait.

On our first date, flushed pink with sulphur salts,
we kissed, so indiscrete our waiter left,
our teeth and glasses clinking. We can't brew
in cellars, sodium benzoate, or malt
slow under seals of paraffin, in theft
of staleness, praying to preserve us, too.

Shashi Bhat is the editor of *EVENT*, and teaches creative writing at Douglas College. Her novel, *The Family Took Shape,* was shortlisted for the Thomas Raddall Atlantic Fiction Award. Her writing has appeared in *The Journey Prize Stories, PRISM, EVENT, The New Quarterly, Grain,* and other journals.

A Baker's Dozen:
13 Vancouver Food (In)Securities

BILLEH NICKERSON

1.
Every summer the fig trees
look like they just walked home
from the salon,
but it's only old Italians
using mesh nets
to keep out the birds.

2.
My favourite blackberry bushes
were torn down
to stop homeless people
from living there.
Now it's a condo complex
I can't live in either.

3.
At my local café
a customer explains
he's never considered
food security before,
and now he might need
to get a lock
for his refrigerator.
I continue to sip my coffee,
burn my tongue.

4.
Sometimes I purchase ginger snaps
from Uprising Breads Bakery
where my friend was a manager
before his untimely passing.
Each morsel is a small memorial,
a sweetness against the salt
in my wounds.

5.
There's a store in Kitsilano
with organic jelly beans
that retail for $25 a kilogram.
This makes me think
of *Jack and the Beanstalk*.
The beans are not magic though,
just expensive.
There are no golden eggs.

6.
Inside the cheap pizza place
customers debate
the merits of pineapple

while outside someone tries
to scrape enough together
for a single slice.

7.
Gelato stores are the cockroaches
of the hospitality world.
No matter how much
or how often rent increases,
they somehow survive.

8.
Small bones litter the ground
under the bald eagles' nest
in the park
with the advisory
to watch out
for poisoned sausages.

9.
My friend stipulates
she wants a birthday party
where everyone shares
the restaurant dishes,
none of this ordering
for yourself crap.

10.
Crow-proof.
Rat-proof.
Raccoon-proof.
Dog-proof.
Bear-proof.
Human-proof.
The ultimate
dumpster.

11.
Minimum wage,
maximum rage.

12.
The restaurant offering
a delicious lentil dish
with a pay-what-you-can option
closed down.

13.
At the First Nations Restaurant
at the Folklife pavilion
during Expo 86
I overheard a tourist
ask a busser
what did your people drink?

Um, probably just water,
the young man answers,
which disappoints the tourist,
and makes me think.

Billeh Nickerson is the author of five books
including the 2014 City of Vancouver Book
Award nominated *Artificial Cherry*. He is also a
founding member of the performance troupe
Haiku Night in Canada, and a silver medalist at
the Canadian Gay Curling Championships. He
lives—and loves—in Vancouver.

No-cook woman

MARN NORWICH

I don't cook. My mother didn't cook. My daughter doesn't cook.
— Erica Jong

I read this playful quote by Erica Jong with a sense of relief. If it is true, then I am not the only woman artist lacking skill or interest in the culinary. The sweet kitchen area of my loft is all but wasted on me. I'll prepare food there, but only out of dire necessity. And lately, being obsessed with a new project, what little cooking I do is a sore distraction to me at best. I don't even own a kitchen table; I prefer to eat sitting at my pretty wooden desk by the window, all the better to keep on creating.

When I was a child, my mother told me that she consciously refused to learn to type in high school. This was so she could never be forced to work as a secretary, one of the few jobs for women at the time. I respected my mom's small act of rebellion. It had worked: she became a teacher. In my opinion, however, the plan hadn't been entirely successful: she also became a wife. In the observation of a young girl, this seemed to be a worse fate.

I am always intrigued by how we daughters continue where our mothers left off.

I grew up in a traditional Jewish household of eastern European heritage, and I watched my mother, grandmothers, sisters, aunts and female cousins prepare, serve and clean up hundreds upon hundreds of meals for their menfolk. I colluded in this activity, too. I had no choice, it seemed.

To my great pain, my mother gave up her art for eighteen years while she raised her family. For eighteen years, she stubbornly refused to squeeze her Muse time into the spare moments between meal prep, grocery shopping, laundry and child care. If I didn't understand it then, I sure do, now. The pain of having life, pre-

dictably and perennially, cut off one's creative process would be too much for me, too. When she did return to her art in her final years, it was to create veritable masterpieces during long hours at her studio. Seeing the galleries-worth of fine pottery that survived her, prompts the question: if she had lived her life differently, what would my mother have created in those intervening years?

Twenty-five years after leaving my family home, I live a life of sharp contrast to the one I was born to. Like my mother, I refused the metaphorical typing course, with it all the attendant paraphernalia. As a woman, as an artist and as myself, I nurture—but not in the manner to which I was raised. I've shirked the thorny crown.

Great *bubbes*—creators of Sabbath *challah* and *rugalach*, *kishka* and *schnitzel*, *purim hamantaschen* and *rosh hashanah* honey cake—I have not forgotten you. I carry the complexity of your histories and recipes in my bloodline, like DNA. And if this great-granddaughter lives a life of singledom and childlessness, of quietude and focus, it is not a life without love, or even transcendence. After all these generations of privation, the wide and coveted vistas of the inner plains are open to me, and I ride them in freedom.

Marn Norwich is a writer and writing instructor with her businesses, Vancouver Writing Courses (vancouverwritingcourses.com) and Writing for Recovery (writing4recovery.com). She's also a poet (Wildflowers At My Doorstep, Karma Press).

Mama's Garden

JULIA PALAHICKY

Spring

Matted fleece tucked into rubber boots, checked flannel buttoned to her neck, she walks to the garden, unfolds worn paper from her pocket, finger tracing each straight line her husband drew. Furrowed eyes squint into misted sunlight, find her shovel propped against a greening apple tree. Yesterday, she turned the earth for the peas, today, she will turn it for the beans, tomorrow the carrots, until soft earth buries the withered remains of last year's crops. String pulled across the rows mirrors her paper.

Summer

Bent hands drive a crowbar deep into the ground, spear a long pole into the hole beside shoots of green. She stomps it firm, finishes the row she started the day before, rests on the rusted garden-bench under a lop-sided cedar where he used to sit, watch her work.

The beans wind up the poles, dwarf her, shelter hummingbirds that fight for the nectar in red flowers, squawk, whizz by her head. She laughs, lets them chase her to weed the carrots and kohlrabi hidden behind the dahlias.

Fall

She fills jars with hot peppers, green tomatoes and chopped cauliflower; others with pears. Red-knuckled hands peel apples, steam them in cinnamon and sugar. She watches *Dancing with the Stars* while stiff fingers shuck beans into the large bowl on her lap. Her husband used to help, but he's in a wooden box behind the couch.

Winter

Her raincoat covers checked flannel and matted fleece, mud sucks her boots, cold rain throbs into her hands. Shriveled stalks cling to the poles she pulls from the ground. Naked trees guard fallen dahlias, empty flower pots and a single row of green that lasts all winter. She chops the carrots into sticks for the great-grandchildren, tells them they can pull string to mark rows in the spring.

Julia Palahicky grew up in Vancouver, born to Hungarian immigrant parents who grew many of their own vegetables. She has a BA in Creative Writing from Kwantlen Polytechnic University and resides on five acres in Maple Ridge where her mother still tends a vegetable and flower garden.

The Farming Way of Life

MANDEEP WIRK

I remember the shock when my parents told me that we were going to Canada to live on a farm. Periodically, Dad would burst into song with some lines about being a *Jat Sikh* and his great yearning for the farming way of life. My sisters and I would roll our eyes and laugh; my Mum would just smile.

"Live on a farm?!" I blurted.

"Yes. When you were a baby, you lived on a sugar cane and pineapple farm in Kenya and loved it," replied my father.

"I don't remember, Papa. I like England now and I want to stay here," I retorted.

At any rate, I was under age and had no choice but to migrate with my family to Canada in 1972. We settled on a raspberry farm in Abbotsford, British Columbia. Luckily, we arrived in August and the harvest was done. However, the next Summer my father put us to work on the farm. My sisters and I picked berries every summer after school was out. Our reward was a trip to the Pacific National Exhibition where we would buy a ticket hoping to win the PNE house, just like our family friends had done. During those early years, we lived in a "shack." Eventually, my folks paid off the mortgage and moved into a better home.

Dad went on to lease a hundred acres in the fertile Fraser Valley and provide jobs to many of the South Asian newcomers whom the white farmers would not employ, thus making it possible for them to stay on. Canada had just opened the doors of immigration to people of colour like ourselves—thanks to the visionary leadership of former PM Pierre Elliott Trudeau who had brought in the policy of Canadian multiculturalism. However, at that time many white Canadians resented our presence here out of prejudice. Although we were Sikhs, the white Canadians called us "Hindoos."

"Hindoos cannot grow Brussels sprouts. Only Dutch can!" a Dutch-Canadian farmer told my Dad.

Well, my father's Brussels sprouts grew taller than this Dutchman's on the adjacent farm.

One day, the Dutchman came over to ask my father his "secret" in growing such robust plants. Dad just had a good laugh and told him he showered his sprouts with love. From that day on, the two men became friends.

I remember how hard my sisters and I worked on that farm every summer right through university. Father grew everything well because he has a green thumb: cabbages, cauliflower, peas, broccoli, strawberry, and rhubarb.

In my twenties, I tried my hand at making jam and found out how much better home-made jam tastes than store bought. I made all kinds of jam: raspberry, strawberry, peach, apricot, and blueberry jams.

My mother was a wonderful cook and we always enjoyed hearty Punjabi fare like chicken curries, lentil curries, and samosas. I learnt how to cook Indian food well from watching my own mother in her kitchen. I learnt how to make pizza from scratch and Chinese stir-fries from cookbooks. I am an ESL teacher now and when my students ask me what is Canadian food, I tell them that it is all the delicious food in the whole world, because Canada is a welcoming multicultural country.

Mandeep Wirk was born in Kenya and as a little girl immigrated to England with her family. Then in 1972, the year that multiculturalism became official policy in Canada and the doors of immigration opened up to people of colour, she immigrated again with her family settling in British Columbia.

Smoke Signals

KIM DAVIDS MANDAR

We sent annual smoke signals from our kitchen to conjure and collect community.

Every spring, Dad did a religious fast. Money Mom squirrelled away was produced to buy ingredients for a collaborative cook-fest that stockpiled our fridge with Cape Malay cuisine. Samosa pastry became a beacon, initiating a sizzling flare, filling first the oven, seeping into the hallway, then surging into the street.

"Xhosa, open the windows!" Dad called to Mom.

And so it began.

In Canada, Dad pined for his family's curry and *roti*, *biryani*, his sister's homemade samosas (with Mrs. Ball's Mango Chutney), *koeksisters* (doughnuts spiced with cinnamon, cardamom and anise seed, glazed with coconut). Pined not for the calories, but for the community. Far from his native land, there was something primal, healing, connecting about a taste of home.

Take saffron, for example.

Carpels collected from the *Crocus sativus,* or "saffron crocus," have been traded and used for over four millennia as dye, spice, and medicine; for centuries, worshipped worldwide as a panacea of life-giving bounty. By 1730, in the Philadelphia commodities exchange, saffron was trading at the price of gold. Saffron: the taste of nourishment and care.

Back home, vivid stigmas from the life-giving centre of this vibrant flower were a staple in my aunts' Cape Malay, South African cooking. The aromatic crimson threads bled orange into *biryani* made in a pot over an open fire that was big enough to be mistaken for a Jacuzzi. Feeding guests at weddings and funerals, the resulting colour brightened every plate. It mirrored the sunsets over the ocean on the peninsula near Cape Town. It resonated with the citrus exports from Constantia—a valley of paradise and prestige fifteen kilometres south. Mom regularly made *biryani* to bear dad home, collaborating with the gods of spice in our tiny kitchen, South African *Soca* music making the frame of our little house dance—the soundtrack of my childhood.

We didn't always bond with our neighbours, but food helped a lot. Mom learned recipes from Dad's culinary traditions: samosas, curry and *roti*, *koeksisters*, *biryani*, milk tart, *pakora*, pumpkin fritters, *boeber*, tomato rice with roast lamb.

Samosas were my favourite. My brother and I used to sneak into the kitchen and swipe dough clippings, sit under the kitchen table, dip them in butter and stuff them into our salivating mouths, until Mom caught us, made us peel the leftovers apart and fry them into crispy chips for everyone to enjoy.

Dad could only stomach homemade samosa pastry, from dough Mom crafted a day before. Thin, light and crunchy, it gained a reputation for delectability in our ever-expanding circle. Round pizza trays suspended the seven layer pastry in the oven, edges dripping butter as it baked, yielding smoke that grew, sneaked into the kitchen, the hallway, finally escaping like a cloud of obedient messenger pigeons through the windows.

"We saw the smoke—can we come in?" It was Jeff and Dave from across the street. "Sure!"

I put them to work peeling apart dough clippings—round edges from the rectangular strips cut to vault mom's spicy filling. Chris and Lynn were next, then John, Jennifer. Our family's motto: more is better, anytime is a good time. Just follow the smoke, dance, play, eat and enjoy the flavour of community.

As a student in the Creative Writing Certificate Program at the University of Guelph, Kim Davids Mandar pursues creative non-fiction as her genre of choice. Kim writes and serves as Content Coordinator for *Neighbours of South End Guelph* magazine and instructs at The Conestoga Language Institute at Conestoga College in Kitchener, ON.

Bio(me)/Us: An Experiment in Friendship-Poetics Between a Geographer-Poet and Agriculturalist

SARAH de LEEUW and RENEE PRASAD

1

She. Is bees. She is rutabaga carrot cranberry crop kale. Soil. And sons. Two sons. She refuses her mother. Works in fields. Speaks with farmers, hands sticky with dirt knowing the politics of planting in the Fraser River Delta, the Sumas flats, and insect larva pupa wings pollination. She gifts me lamb meat from her students: they grow and slaughter sheep on their own farms. Her father taught her if bugs can eat it so can we. She taught me how to make *roti*, to be generous with turmeric, to watch for the "R" that begins all her siblings' names. Sometimes I love her hands more than anything else in the world, long nails ending long fingers, the way everything is a gesture, moving.

2

Sustenance. To me, food is first about safety. It is how I nurtured myself when my family did not. If it weren't for toast, I would not be here now. Food is about well-being. When food is grown well it can nourish the earth and nourish our bodies and nourish human relationships within society especially the producer and consumer relationship. As an instructor and researcher, I care about the production of food. I want to help farmers protect crops. I want to help them continue farming. I want to inspire, support new farmers. I made food for my son. I want my son to have memories of his mom and food that nourishes his soul. I want to give him a different relationship to food. Food sustains me emotionally. Food sustains me financially. Food sustains me spiritually. I show my love by cooking for people.

3

Sustenance. To me, food is a mystery but not unknown. I have skinned deer and eaten freshly fried moose-heart. I have picked chanterelles and gathered mussels crab crayfish, clubbed salmon with rocks and milked goats. I have eaten so much. Through it all, I still love the grocery store. I fell in love with both poetry and geography because, in some ways, they make me feel as good as a delicious meal, prepared by someone I love. I have yet to understand how food can be so emotional. My father died when he was sixty-seven years old. This means he died at a young age, compared to many in Canada. Often when I think of him, I think of food. He cooked most of the meals in our house when I grew up. I show my love by cooking for people.

4

She. Is loud north wild maps. I think of her shoes, irreverent, a yellow Volvo, she is busy with words, ideas. Sometimes we are feasting together, we are talking, she is swearing, we are feasting on sushi (I introduced her to that, to city to suburb to farming and insects). I spoke with her father about those insects. She has so many words. I know she is loving, generous. Sometimes I think of meeting her, in Victoria. It was windy and rainy. And that time we went skinny dipping in Duncan—the boyfriend gone, but she is still with me. And sushi in Prince Rupert, with other friends who are again gone, but she is still with me.

We are two friends who have known each other for more than two decades. One of us, Renee Prasad, is an agriculturalist broadly interested in sustainable food systems, and grew up in the suburbs of Vancouver where her family migrated to en masse from Fiji. The other, Sarah de Leeuw, is a human geographer and poet who, while born on Vancouver Island, has spent most of her life in Northern British Columbia, landscapes where she works on social justice issues and about which she both produces creative and academic writings. This "experimental poetic project" is divided into four blocks the way a field experiment in agriculture would be set up in a section of a grower's field to measure things like insect control or to compare various crop-species. We are interested in a reading process that 'cross-pollinates' across grids of meaning, illuminating new meanings of sustenance and food and land in British Columbia and beyond.

Axel

REBECCA NICHOLLS

On the first day I met him there was homemade banana bread, and coffee, and Axel taught me how to eat fire.

When touched, jumbled, we had juice and frozen grapes.

Later, there was meat breads hot dogs with everything green cake and peanuts and candy fried tomatoes horse whale salt chicken wings and beer.

This is a love story in breakfasts. This strange animal in the kitchen; zebra-print underwear, blue hair, only owns one pan. He's got extra long chopsticks.

Bacon was always first, and every day it was measured against yesterday. Are these pieces thicker? Are we missing out on length. On fat.

He let me tend to the bacon sometimes while he made side salads (red onion/strawberries/what else) and I am a nervous apprentice. In one of his robes I always felt small and I was timid with the slices—this matters.

Everything chars, and tastes the same, and the fat binds to something in me that needs it.

One night you come home to us caramelizing bacon in the microwave.

There is the time we buy a deep fryer, staying up late playing games. I think this night was the least beautiful I have ever looked next to him, too large shirt, flour in my hair, cold sore. It made him shy.

There is the time we invite strangers for dinner and they never show. We lose track of things to talk about, and stare at a candle flame. Spaced out in our fires. When we notice awkwardly that we often don't talk, he takes my hand and pulls me up into a dance. Lifting me into his arms like we are in water. Like we are water. Like if we don't keep moving I will turn into ice. I don't remember talking. I don't remember dessert.

Later, Axel visited my home in Vancouver. Unfamiliar, he settled in at the 7-11, and made me a dinner of rice with bananas, sriracha, and whipped cream. It tasted like an adventure, but it didn't taste good.

Rebecca Nicholls studies writing and visual art at Emily Carr University. She is the author of the self-published chapbook *Other People*. Rebecca lives on Coast Salish territories (Vancouver).

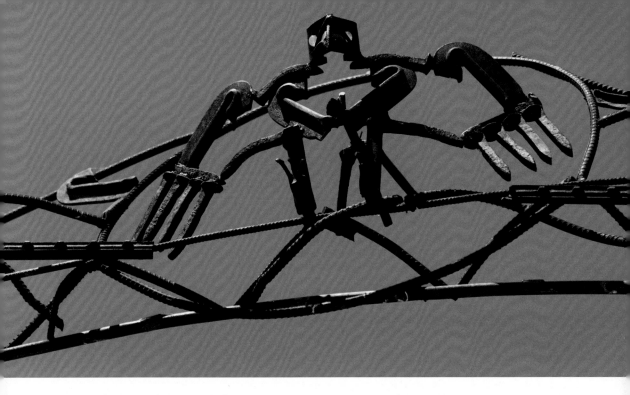

Snapdragon

SYLVIA SYMONS

No great shame that no one
showed me when I was small
the trick of unlocking the jawbone
of a flower
to make it talk—I never thought
to pinch the hinges of a snapdragon
or make a puppet
from its ruffled petals but

the road from Prince George to Hixon
was hilly
it had dips and when my stepdad
gassed it!
my stomach flipped
it was fun
we went fast
past
Stoner! Redrock! Woodpecker! Hixon!
Supper was Aunt Kathy's newlywed spaghetti
dessert was
tapioca—fat as
bath beads in a bowl

fish eyes! my brother
chimed then mushed them with his tongue.

I kept my mouth shut.
My stepdad said for chrissake,
prodded my jaw till it popped open
and shoveled fish eyes heap by heap

I gagged
and splashed it back
with bile in my bowl.
He opened my face again,
the way you squeeze a change purse
with a slit in the middle he
spooned me the same food twice
I was quiet by then
I knew enough
to keep it down.

The road from Prince George to Chetwynd
has ruts and puddles. At a Greyhound break
in Windy Point I buy ripple chips
from an older girl, her sundress
went nice with her smile
a jar of flowers by her till

she pinched a snapdragon,
coaxed a floral *hello* from its lips—it
wasn't just
that I loved her,
I wanted to be her
and not someone who knows the hills
between Prince George and Hixon
and how they make
your stomach flip.

———————————

Sylvia Symons lives with her husband and sons in a 1970s low-rise apartment in East
Vancouver. She has her name on a waiting list at a nearby community garden in hopes
of growing carrots and snapdragons. Her poems appear in *Geist, Room, EVENT, and
Best Canadian Poetry 2016.*

Untitled

MEGHAN TRAN

A lot of people don't buy misshapen food because they look weird and they think it doesn't look as good as it should but it really tastes the same way. Think about it! The farmers buy the seeds to grow the fruits which means that you need to use money to buy the seeds. After days of waiting for the fruits to grow, some don't look like what they should be. They get thrown away and if they're lucky, get shipped to market. But when the fruits are at the market, not many people would buy them just because they don't look the way people think they should. Then at the end, the fruit could go bad and rotten and they get thrown out or composted. Some don't go into the compost which means that you're generating garbage. Garbage goes into the dump. The dump is basically a huge pile of garbage and it expands every day. When it gets bigger and bigger, we'll have less space to build things and grow things. That is not only wasting food but it's also wasting fuel, labour, money, water and time that goes into shipping and growing all the food. Do you really want that to happen, and is eating misshapen, perfectly good-tasting food that bad?

Megan Tran writes: "My name is Meghan Tran. I am thirteen years old and I love basketball. Basketball is my everything. I play it almost every day. It's really fun."

Blackberry Fever

KAREN BARNABY

I first savoured blackberries not from a bush, but out of a book. My home province of Ontario is not wild blackberry country and Tom Robbins' novel *Still Life with Woodpecker* painted a utopian, Pacific Northwest blackberry vision for me.
   He writes:

> *And in late summer when the brambles were proliferating madly, growing faster than the human eye could see, the energy of their furious growth could be hooked up to generators that, spinning with blackberry power, could supply electrical current for the entire metropolis. A vegetative utopia, that's what it would be. Seattle, Berry Town, encapsulated, self-sufficient, thriving under a living ceiling, blossoms in its hair, juice on its chin, more blackberries—and more!—in its future.*

Upon settling in Vancouver, I was disappointed to discover how despised they were. Reviled by the locals, no crack in the sidewalk, no parched, dime-sized piece of earth was safe. Anywhere a seed landed was fair game for taking root. I admired their tenacity, and would occasionally eat one from a bush I was passing, hoping to catch a glimmer of that utopian vision.

Enthusiastic when asked by a friend to come and pick blackberries at another friend's home in Langley, we were greeted by miles of brazen, and merciless blackberry bushes. Trembling like novitiates, we gingerly picked for a while, then froze the berries when we returned to Vancouver. My friend made ice cream with hers, and mine sat in my freezer, smirking at me, for longer than I care to admit.

The next year and with resolve, we went out to pick again. This time, something happened to me while I picked. The prickly bushes inoculated me with blackberry fever and I became obsessed with blackberries. My vision filled with tides of berries rolling gleefully onto grassy shores and into my waiting bucket.

On the weekend after, I was fortunate to be with friends who dragged me out of the brambles because I couldn't stop picking. We shrieked when leaving, noticing the bigger, riper blackberries on the bushes along the driveway. We stopped to pick those beauties because they too had succumbed to blackberry fever. Every conversation we had during that week centred on blackberries.

I loved picking, being lightly scratched by the thorns as I probed deeper into the bushes, searching for the blackberry mother lode. I liked the repetitive motion and watching my bucket fill. I liked feeling complete when I opened the freezer and saw the Ziploc bags of berries pile up. I felt good when I gave them away to friends who had no revenue in the blackberry bank. Most of all, I loved the scent: feral, alluring, mysterious, and fruity. Blackberries are the wild boar of the berry world.

It was becoming apparent that I was heading into dangerous territory. What would happen in the off-season with no blackberries to pick? I found something else to do for the next few weekends and my withdrawal was mercifully short.

Can frozen blackberries warm your spirit? Yes, yes they can. No matter how cold, wet and dreary it is, outside, I can take a bag of the deep purple berries, inhale their musky aroma, and watch the curtain rise on a story about a beautiful, sunny day in a blackberry utopia.

Photograph by Derek von Essen.

Karen Barnaby is a Vancouver chef who spins local fleece & flax, carves spoons from fallen trees & spoils her cats & dog. Cookbook author, *Vancouver Sun* columnist, product developer & recipient of a Minerva Award for Community Leadership, she sits on the board of EarthHand Gleaners Society, offering the skills to be a producer, without first being a consumer.

Horizons of the Pedon

TRACY BIRD-MOTUT

Late spring, press seeds into black soil
imagining them bursting to life in the soil.

Before cooking dinner wash hands in
hot water to scrub off the soil.

An earthworm twists, ingesting leaf debris
and creating new soil.

Seedlings wiggle up, fresh green,
shedding grains of soil.

After three hours of weeding throw the jeans
in the washer. Setting: heavy soil.

Pick off the first lettuce leaves and swirl
in cold water to wash off the soil.

Photo of gnarled hands holding purple carrots
freshly pulled from the soil.

Five second rule, no worries,
it's good to eat a little soil.

Hens pick over the compost,
in three days there's soil.

Dried cornstalks left twelve inches tall to
protect the precious soil.

A mole tunnels fifteen feet eating earthworms
and grubs under the soil.

A basket laden with chives, oregano,
onions and beans, fruit of the soil.

Walking though the backyard, step in dog shit
and wish it was soil.

The rhubarb leaves are inedible,
send them back to the soil.

Prairie grass roots reach down fourteen
feet deep into the soil.

Three sisters; beans, maize and squash,
as they grow they amend the soil.

Beefsteak tomatoes are ripe, a few
fall and rot into the soil.

Yukon gold potatoes with dill in the pot,
dug straight from the soil.

Too lazy to rake all the leaves
but they'll only turn back into soil.

Geography 103: I inspect the pedon and
identify six horizons, an infinity of soil.

Tracy Bird-Motut writes: "I live in the Fraser Valley and am working on a BA degree at
University of the Fraser Valley and have taken several writing courses there to hone my
skills and feed my passion for writing. My backyard garden is a source of nourishment
for my family and an inspiration for my poetry."

hungry in Tofino

kjmunro

3-day camping long weekend
with a celibate vegetarian
& all I can think of
is barbecued steak…
almost all I can think of
is barbecued steak

Originally from Vancouver, BC, kjmunro now lives in Whitehorse, Yukon Territory. She
is Membership Secretary for Haiku Canada, & is an Associate Member of the League of
Canadian Poets. She has a leaflet with Leaf Press, & her work has appeared recently in
Vallum: Contemporary Poetry.

Inside the Garden: Bees

WENDY MORTON

Outside the garden, the newspaper lands
on the driveway each morning, bringing terrible words.
Inside the garden,
we speak another language.
We say esmeralda, brunia, arugula, cylindra;
we say bordeaux, bolero, fiesta.
We speak in flowers:
we say alstromeria;
we say sweet juliet, wildeve.
We say tango.
Bees hear us,
dance.

Wendy Morton has been a teacher, a printer, an insurance investigator and always a poet. She has seven books in the world. She has grown an organic garden in Otter Point, BC for forty-four years and is well acquainted with bees. She has received many awards, the latest of which is the Meritorious Service Medal from the Governor General of Canada.

Photo Credit: Wendy Morton

Scottish Shortbread

RENÉE ALEXANDER

My mother was a terrible cook. Whether this was from a genuine lack of talent or a rejection of anything that reeked of women's work, I will never know for sure.

On the other hand Nana, my father's mother, prided herself on being an excellent housekeeper and a good cook. Nothing fancy, but a repertoire of solid *stick to your ribs* recipes: oatcakes, soda bread and stew with dumplings.

Mother's casual approach to cooking involved reading the paper while preparing a meal with a home-rolled cigarette stuck in the corner of her mouth. I was always amazed at how long the ash could get without falling into the saucepan. This well established contempt towards cooking made it surprising when she took an interest in my Nana's Scottish Shortbread recipe.

Now Nana, a Scots/Irish from Belfast found my mother an irritating woman and not worthy of her son let alone one of her recipes. She did eventually give my mother her recipe probably because she thought there was no risk to her being outdone, BUT before giving it over she extracted a promise that my mother was never to give it to another living soul.

Little did Nana know that my mother possessed the most important ingredient for making shortbread—ANGER. In order to work all that flour into the butter and form it into wee fingers one had to bash away at it for quite a long time and mother had a lot of anger to work into that dough, so, much to everyone's surprise, she made excellent shortbread, even better than Nana's.

One December afternoon, while preparing the Christmas shortbread, mother was visited by her neighbour Donald. Donald was a kind and gentle vegetarian who made up for the absence of meat by treating himself to sweet wine, desserts and candy. He took an immediate interest in the shortbread production and sat down to watch. Now technically mother had not broken her promise to Nana, but by being caught in the act of making it she inadvertently gave another person the sacred recipe. Donald went home immediately and tried his hand at it. The next time he met up with my mother she asked him how his shortbread had turned out.

"Well it wasn't the same as yours," was his response, "we didn't have any berry sugar so I used Demerara, and there was no refined, white flour so I used whole wheat and I didn't think that the rice flour would be missed since only a tiny amount was needed."

Donald didn't have to add the presence of margarine to his litany of substitutions. It was a given that there would be none of that dreaded animal fat in his baking! He was also far too passive in nature to make a good shortbread.

During Christmas dinner Nana caught wind that Donald had HER recipe. Around the table conversation halted as Nana narrowed her eyes and thinned her lips at my mother. To placate her, my father related Donald's failed attempt. With each muddle listed, Nana's sour mood slowly evaporated leaving her very smug.

Over the years my mother's sources of anger disappeared: her husband and mother-in-law died, her children all moved on. She also lost the ability to make good shortbread.

Renée Alexander is a professional Vancouver calligrapher and illustrator. Her work is published internationally and has been called upon for many film projects including the Netflix Series "A Series of Unfortunate Events." She is a Continuing Studies faculty member at ECUAD. Her précis submission won the CBC Vancouver stories contest.

Nutritional Torture

MONICA MENEGHETTI

Before my taste buds gauged the taste of tripe, I was living inside you, innocent of such Italian delicacies.

Before my nose knew aroma from stench; before I had teeth to gnaw the rubbery, gilled surface; before my throat could gag on the worm-like flesh; before I knew it was "cow's stomach" or even what "cow" or "stomach" meant, I had no need for pulling faces and you, no need to admonish me for it. *Non fare la smorfia*, you'd say while serving up those hideous strips stewed in tomato sauce.

Trippa. More reviled than liver or tongue, more dreaded than *baccalà*—that ram-rod salt cod standing on its tail in a water bucket near the washing machine, stinking for days as it softened.

Long before you locked me in the bathroom with *trippa* and shoved another plateful through the door when you heard the toilet flush, I was lounging in uterine brine, my face relaxed and smooth as a marinated mushroom, my guts naïvely willing to digest whatever you fed me.

Beyond the umbilical lies tripe. Had I known, I would have spelunked to your fallopians and bribed some other ovum forth to take my place. To save my face.

Monica Meneghetti is the author of the memoir *What the Mouth Wants: A Memoir of Food, Love and Belonging* (Dagger Editions, 2017*)*. Her work has been anthologized in *Absent Mothers* (Demeter Press, 2017). Her first work of literary translation *The Call of the Ice* (Mountaineer's Books, 2014) was a finalist in the 2015 Banff Mountain Book Competition. She lives on the unceded First Nations territory of the Musqueam, Squamish and Tsleil-Waututh (Vancouver, Canada).

New Plot

SARAH TURNER

In the spring of the year I think my marriage is ending, my name comes up on the waitlist for a plot at a large community garden in Coquitlam. I've been waiting for three years. I send my confirmation immediately. A project. Maybe this is what we need.

Two weeks later I head out on a sunny morning clutching a map of available plots. I traipse the muddy seven acres, a novice wearing the wrong shoes. An incredible variety of gardens butt up against each other—some well-manicured, full of spring blooms and garlic shoots, others flat expanses of weeds and mud. There are fences and lattices, teepees and complex greenhouse systems.

I choose a plot tucked away at the back, near the tool shed and the river. Behind its rotting fence an old plastic lawn chair sits upended between two neglected raised beds, barely visible under thick grass. We pay our dues and it's ours.

Every day I drop the kids at school and make the fifteen-minute drive to the garden. Suburban streets give way to highway, and the highway leads to a narrow country road, potholed and overgrown. I roll down the windows and turn up Tim McGraw.

The garden demands immediate physical work, and I dive in gratefully. I love the way my shovel resists the hard earth, the way I have to throw my whole body against it and find my strength. I pull up clumps of grass the size of dinner plates and shake the heavy soil from their roots. I dig and dig, my back straining under the hot spring sun. I rediscover muscles. Dirt lines the creases in my skin, blackens my nails.

I go home hungry and happy and filthy and tired.

Some days I take the kids after school, bribing them with Slurpees. Together we push impossibly full wheelbarrow loads of manure and compost and mulch. They work for a bit and then lose interest, disappearing into the long grass to explore.

On Sundays we go as a family. I watch in quiet awe as my partner cobbles together a fence with a swinging gate, urging the boys to take turns with the hammer. It's a joy to see him shed his office clothes and work with his hands. To watch him pretend to be handy. At the garden we can be who we want to be. On that 10 x 25 foot plot of land, our family works.

At home in the evenings, though, the confines of our daily lives push against us. After the boys are in bed we fight quietly in the kitchen, choosing opposite counters to lean against, arms folded tight.

I sleep restlessly and dream of earth.

Next morning I'm out there again. Working.

By the end of the summer the boys bolt from the car as soon as we park, excited to see what's grown. My oldest crouches by the strawberry bed, confidently pushing aside leaves to find ripe berries. My youngest pulls a purple carrot and whips it by its top like a lasso.

I wrap my arms around my partner and try to freeze this moment. The four of us in the golden light of late afternoon. Our harvest of zucchini and cucumbers, tomatoes and beans. It might not be enough to get us through the winter. But maybe, just maybe, it will.

Sarah Turner was the 2007 winner of *EVENT* magazine's Creative Non-Fiction contest and her writing has been shortlisted for the *PRISM* Non-Fiction contest. She lives in Port Moody and gardens when she gets the chance.

Life Support

VANESSA SHANTI FERNANDO

I stopped at the grocery store before going to the hospital to watch my brother die. I bought small round cheeses wrapped in red wax, the skin-like kind that peels off slowly. Mandarin oranges mottled green and orange; pita bread wrapped in plastic; a squat, oval container of mayonnaise-drenched spinach dip. I looked at my phone, refreshed my emails over and over, cycled through Facebook then Instagram, opened the string of text messages from my father—the ones that said *You probably heard* and *Please call me when you get this.* I switched my phone off.

Six months ago, my stepfather made a pot of Moroccan couscous (his usual recipe, with thick *merguez* sausages and juicy carrots), brought a portion to his neighbour, and then took his bike out along the seawall. On his way home, he braked suddenly to avoid a car reversing, fell forward over the handlebars, cracked his neck, and died. After the hospital, and the meeting with the social worker, and the decision to donate his eyes-heart-liver, and his family of origin arriving, my mother and his sisters found the pot there, still, on the stove where he'd left it. They couldn't get rid of it. They ate what he left behind.

Before (because now there would only be Before and After), we had a constant stream of family dinners. My brother's signature dish was potato salad. My stepfather made the world's best scalloped potatoes. My dad has a monopoly on vegetarian lasagna, with a signature recipe he's calibrated carefully over the years by identifying the ideal ratio between tofu, spinach, and feta. We could all eat his first wife's egg curry and string hoppers for days. Dinners had a simple formula. All we had to do was show up.

I'd shown up then. I didn't want to show up now. Didn't want to drive back to the hospital, back to the intensive care unit, back to the cardiac unit with its red

doors that swung out towards us as we approached, like a mouth opening. I put more food in my basket. A bag of chips (baked, flaky). Cookies shaped like maple leaves with soft sugar in each centre. A bunch of kale; a brick of pressed tofu. The crowd at the store was thinning. I turned my phone on again. One new message. My sister. *If you want to see him before the ventilator is pulled, come before 8 pm. No idea if he will survive a few hours or a week.*

I felt my heart working fast and alive. Pictured the familiar passage. Long hallways with gurneys on one side, and locked doors on the other. Inside those doors: more doors. Codes; telephones mounted to the wall; waiting rooms with broken televisions; hand sanitizer every second step. And finally, the inner sanctum. Four beds. Four broken bodies. My brother's body, kept alive by buzzing machines and thick tubes. Two days ago he'd been digesting the meal replacement drinks they poured into his feeding tube and we were all ecstatic. Two days ago the CT scans were coming back clear. A lot can happen in two days, or two hours.

I took my basket to the checkout. Texted *I'm on my way. Just getting us all something to eat.*

Vanessa Shanti Fernando started writing when she was five years old and never stopped. A queer mixie femme, she is also a social worker who works primarily with survivors of trauma. She lives in Vancouver with her incredible family, biological and chosen. This piece is for Rémi Barrette and Suresh Fernando.

Picnic

ALISA GORDANEER

Bring the bottles of wine from the cellar, reds
and whites forgotten under dust. Bring the
glasses, too, rubbed clean with linen. Bring love.
Bring the olives, slick with salt and oil,
the taste of hot days far away. Bring the
artichokes, asparagus, avocados, everything from the beginning
and bring the creamy brie, the creamy blue, the creamy skinned
camembert knowing it will stick on my face.
Bring the beginnings of conversations, bring
the cloth we've carried since the first
day of marriage, the gift meant to be spread
on grass, sand unfurled like a flag. Bring it
because we haven't used it in years, bring the wrinkled
fibre and the faded roses
and the fraying edges.
Bring these small things, and bring the intent to lie
on this green hill and tell me again, with water and wine that you will
bring bread, too—
and yams, and zucchini.
And if you can't bring food,
bring love.

"Picnic" was first published in her collection *Still Hungry* (Signature Editions, 2015).

Alisa Gordaneer is a poet, teacher and communications professional in Victoria, BC.
www.alisagordaneer.com/

Afterglow, Early September

KIRSTEN PENDREIGH

The sun x-rays veined chard. Scarlet capillary silhouettes
course and throb through shocking green,
lipstick red stalks are limned with light.

Is this how I appear when the probe goes down
through discordant chords
and burnt tracheal walls?

Is the camera light the only glow?
Or is there another energy, pulsing
through bruised bronchioles and frail pleura?

Outside my bedroom window,
green tomatoes hang on for dear life. Summer's fading,
and they're too late. I've lost the will to mother them,

to cover and uncover them, dust the powdery mildew
from the pumpkin leaves,
while tired cucumbers curl and brown.

Oh, the summer feasts I wanted:
charred oysters on an alder fire,
licking briny fingers, our damp hair framing lambent faces.

Flash-fried prawns our strong, tanned arms hauled up,
and sliced tomatoes,
their blood red bellies sucking up salt.

But I cherished the strawberries of June,
each one a warm morning offering
of hope.

And peppery arugula in its lemony coat,
lotus blooms of romaine, kale by the pail,
tangy, tangled scallions.

I'll stay inside now, eat potato chips
and cheap chocolate, by the TV's flickering blue light.
Like a McGarrigle sister, when the hunger's gone.

Kirsten Pendreigh writes: "I'm a former CBC and NPR journalist, now writing in the medical research field. I have won a couple of municipal poetry competitions and was a finalist in last year's *Canscaip Writing for Children* competition."

A Taste of Home

ESMERALDA CABRAL

To be an immigrant is to be restless. At least it is for me. My heart is forever in two places. For Portuguese people, there is a word that describes this feeling succinctly—*saudade*. There have been numerous attempts to translate this term but there is no one word in English that captures it all. *Saudade* is about nostalgia, longing, 'missing you,' yearning, and so much more. It's a deep feeling within your soul of love and loss combined.

Portuguese immigrants have long been dealing with *saudade*. How do we best do that? With food, of course. Food is part of our psyche. And in the Azores, where I'm from, our traditional foods are an integral part of our identity, and differentiate us from our mainland cousins. We are island people.

Azoreans eat a lot of fish and seafood but also meat, including delicacies like sausage, black pudding, and pig's ears. We have special foods to celebrate different seasons and *festas*—there's *malaçadas* (fried dough sprinkled with sugar) for *Carnaval, massa sovada* (sweet bread) for Easter, sardines in the summer, and *bacalhau* (salt cod), for Christmas Eve and well, anytime. Birthdays and anniversaries, christenings and weddings, every occasion is an excuse to gather the entire extended family for a multi-course meal that can last for hours.

When we are sick, we have *canja*, a healing version of chicken soup with rice and a hint of lemon, and when we are homesick, there's *caldo verde*, Portuguese kale soup, which can transport us to our homeland, even if only in our imagination.

This traditional soup is made with potatoes and onion, garlic and kale. But, back home, the greens used are more like collard greens, not kale. And the purists will tell you that a specific variety is required. And so, Portuguese Vancouverites

will plant and grow *couve*, harvest it with care and meticulously collect the seeds to plant next year's crop.

The traditional soup also has a few rings of sausage. And yes, it matters where you get the sausage. You know someone who makes their own? That's even better!

It's important to capture the flavour of our foods but the ingredients are not always easy to find. Luckily, there's a very effective Portuguese network in Vancouver. It's not a TV show or a blog or a website—it's word of mouth. Information gets around on where to buy the best salt cod, the fattest sardines, the richest olive oil, the most authentic pepper paste, or the freshest corn bread.

Over the years, I have occasionally grown my own *couve*. Most of the time, though, I get it from my sister's garden. In a pinch, I buy curly kale at the market and use that. Sometimes I use store-bought chorizo from my local grocer. Other times, I skip the sausage altogether and produce a vegetarian version of the soup. "What?" I can almost hear purists exclaiming in disbelief. "Sacrilege!"

Maybe. But it's my Vancouver version of the traditional soup of my homeland. It may not be pure or authentic but it's mine. And sometimes I think I might even like it better than the real thing.

Esmeralda Cabral was born in the Azores, Portugal and now lives, writes and cooks in Vancouver. She teaches English at an international school in downtown Vancouver and she writes creative nonfiction. Her work has been published in various anthologies, *The Globe and Mail*, and aired on CBC Radio.

The Soup

JEN CURRIN

I finally started to warm with thick soup.
I lay on my back as she ladled it: soup.

The perfect bookmark for a soiled holy book.
I wanted to pray but instead licked up soup.

The room was listless, the wine stale.
We unpacked the candle, lit the wick to heat soup.

Out the window snow falters as if forgetting.
Your aunt calls, but it's a trick—no soup

The revolutionary poet, coal-less in deep winter.
His window shattered by a brick as he sips cold soup.

The headachey poet writing *ghazals* while dying.
Ginger for all cancers: kick them with soup.

Bears, foxes, woods, mountains. Dusk and deer.
Friends said, "Give up the nature poetry. Stick with soup."

On the stovetop bubbling, white as schoolroom glue.
For the mourners you had only this sick soup.

You want someone to miss you, a snowflake to pray?
Then get on your knees, poet. Quick! The soup!

Jen Currin lives on unceded Coast Salish Territories (Vancouver, Canada), where she teaches creative writing and English at Kwantlen University. Jen has published four books of poetry, including *The Inquisition Yours*, which won the Audre Lorde Award for Lesbian Poetry in 2011; and *School*, which was a finalist for three awards. Jen's first collection of stories, *Hider/Seeker*, will be out from Anvil Press in 2018.

Pectin

LEEF EVANS

I'm not so generous some times and do not miss the things that look like you. But the cannibal world reckons for hostile selfish thoughts, and when I chew on my self I miss the hard-scrabble tangle of your hair; the hypnotic negative space between strand and strand and strand. Hints of skin I miss. The smell of cold water and drizzled apple juice. I miss the tickle, too, on my neck the first time we smooched (you ducked below my arm and laughed and ran. & I ran, also, too, after you, and cornered you in that ghoulish, rough-spackle tenement portico and moved in and finished the space between us and you didn't duck or laugh).

I remember it was the sandstone-rain before winter in Winnipeg. It was rain-ing—a Dr. Seuss kinda rain, full of happy portent and poster paint.

The pickups on Portage flitted dirty roadstuff smut up from the blacktop and the sky grumbled some gravel-thunder when we brushed the grit from our pants. The rain rolled off your lip when you smiled. The wet tyres wet tyres wet tyres sang a looping song, & I said, "this this this," as everything seemed to sound in threes.

This is what I miss when I don't miss you: sugar and grit, instants and specifics distilled; you, jarred like jam with all your aspic finery and the jammed hologram of *you* in the fickle sparkle of dirty sugar, Sugar.

I crack white wax seals, rub dust from rubber rings and dip in to congealed Winnipeg preserves or Peterborough jellies, the mad quince of Quito even and I just spread you on my hot bread and taste you only (roadmap) all over, and some-times rub that wax and sometimes smell that jar and sometimes grind that dirt between finger and thumb and think of things that taste like you.

Leef Evans writes: "My name is Leef Evans. I am with the Thursdays Writing Collective at Carnegie."

Oroboros[1]

YOSEF WOSK

The universe is a single cannibalistic organism, a self-sustaining unbroken circle; autonomous, terrifying and utterly unstoppable. Herbivore, carnivore, omnivore, orovore—the serpent consuming its own tail in an eternal vortex of renewal, its own creation and self-destruction, the endless knot, eternal return, historic re-currence.

Food culture is a pilgrimage to discover the universal elixir. The Greeks spoke of *ambrosia* and the Hindus of *soma* or *amrita* that ensured anyone who ingested it their immortality. *Milk* is accorded related prestige: there are almost as many milk myths nursing ancient cultures as there are stars that pave the Milky Way. The universe is draped in a shimmering gown of lactic lace from which creation emerged and continues to be sustained. Hoary streams of moon milk gush from nursing mothers, each one a goddess concealed beneath the masks of *maya*, sur-vivor of love's last labour. Mother Moon bathed in blood of birth, ablution of honeyed milk, spilling her first food into insistent mouths of ravenous newborns, forever to be fed. The Philosopher's Stone metamorphoses into Virgin's Milk, the tincture of transformation: whoever drinks it is renewed; whoever encounters it *in veritas* achieves immortality. Consider, also, semen, male milk poured as viscid broth flush with propagating seed in search of receptive ovum. And the milky sap of the Sacred Fig, the *ficus religiosa* that sheltered the Buddha and en-couraged his enlightenment. The fig leaf covered our first nakedness, a gift from the Omnipotent Creator turned modest tailor who taught us how to clothe em-barrassment, assuage poverty and to give before being asked. The Promised Land flows with fattened milk and immortal honey,[ii] a noble substance that, like gold, does not spoil and whose sweetness bears learning upon the tongue. It has powers of healing and skill in seduction, an aphrodisiac in metaphor and fact. It is also associated with the sun for both are golden and givers of life. Mead, fermented honey, was drunk for a moon month—honeymoon—after marriage to ensure fertility. For the Celts it was the favoured drink of the immortal gods; the Norse identified it as the Mead of Inspiration and Poetry; and in Africa it was considered a sacred Liquid of Knowledge. These elixirs—*ambrosia, soma, amrita, lapis philosophorum,* milk and mead—are material equivalents of *Tat tvam asi,* Thou art That of the Vedas: from that imperceptible essence all things manifest. I wonder if one day the gods and their priests will be satisfied; if one day hunger will be sated—no more ceremonial cooking in cauldrons of flesh to celebrate symbolic holidays; if one day there will be no need for this endless sacrifice of life for the sake of life, no fodder because no hunger. I wonder if one day all will re-turn to its origin or arrive at its destination—the death of birth and its incessant struggle to exist—to a place where there is no space, to a time beyond counting, to reconciliation with the Cosmic Wars of Creation.

Meanwhile, existence persists as a feeding frenzy like the old Earth Lady who swallowed a spider to catch the fly, perhaps she'll die. These interconnected food chains—Gaia's elegant bio-necklace recumbent upon *Oroboros*'s endless neck—

with their related trophic levels are woven into larger mutually dependent webs. Plants and algae absorb nutrients from their environment and produce their own food; herbivores—primary consumers—eat plants; predators hunt and eat them; carnivores that eat other carnivores occupy the fourth level. Apex predators—lions and humans—are at the top of the chain. Decomposers, like fungi, feast on dead matter, converting it back into nutrients for primary producers. The process continues under various disguises in every particle of existence from the air we breathe to massive galactic cannibals that have been digesting their last celestial meal for a billion years. Some even say there is a restaurant at the end of the universe.[iii]

It took thousands of generations of experimentation and accidental discovery to determine what was edible: some things could be eaten raw while others had to be cooked; some were avoided as poison while others became daily staples or occasional luxuries. Some products—red Afghani flower, cactus, cannabis, shroom, jungle brew and the vine of Bacchus[iv]—were regarded as magical, medicinal, sacred or forbidden. Some nourished the body, others the mind, a soul source to spirit dreams and prophetic visions, mythic manna, shaman's wings, the addict's prison. Injected, ingested, smoked or drunk, they were purveyors of synaesthetic perceptions, psychedelic tickets to the Heart of Heaven, a meal in the presence of the Sapphire Throne, face to face with Divine Madness. While some of these substances were tolerated, then prohibited and finally permitted-under-advisory for recreational use, others were deemed destructive to societies and death sentences to individual users. They became controlled substances, banned as illicit stimulants, forbidden fruit craved by the human mind. The sapiens species has two mouths to feed: its corporeal body and its conscious spirit that has evolved—according to our conceits—in the Image of the Gods. We belong to Heaven as much as Earth and have appetite for one as much as the other. We yearn to escape the chains of unbearable limitations, to dance at the Gates of Infinity just beyond the portal to the Valley of Ten Thousand Winds. Yet we remain fragile creatures and sometimes, like Icarus, fall from enchanted heights to mundane realities below.

The house—whether in dream or actuality—corresponds to the body: windows are eyes, door is mouth, electricity is nervous system, plumbing digestive system, and basement the unconscious. Each room and how we perceive it, holds a message. The kitchen represents heart and hearth, nutrition and caregiving. It is scene of shared meals, social gatherings, intimate conversations, secret cabinets, well-worn memories, quiet reading, inherited recipes, and cutting/combining/cooking ingredients to patiently nourish body and soul. The table can be austere—broken furniture veiled by tattered stained cloth—or king's royal cookery; any shape; private or public, invited or not, set according to function, and seated according to protocol. Human consciousness turns us into meaning machines: the ritual table takes a simple meal and dresses it up so that ceremonial meals attain cult status. Appreciated in such a light, the eating board becomes hierophant, mediating altar between Heaven and Earth. It stands in the embrace of gravity—love incarnate—attracted to all and all drawn to it. Upon this altar some commemorate redemption of the First Meal and celebration of the Last

Supper, the Eucharist sharing of a common meal, ingesting the ritual wine blood and body bread, the union of male and female principles,[v] drunk from the unifying cup, the shared chalice. As an act of gratitude and in recognition of its ethereal provenance, some bless every item on their plate before and then after eating. We declare holidays with incantations like *ha lah ma'anyah*—"this is the bread of affliction, the stale scraps of slaves now freed." Foods become our teachers; they remind us that freedom is a daily struggle and that most of us—politically or psychologically—are still enslaved. Open now to welcome the afflicted. Quickly, before death do us part as always it will. The Earth itself is a Round Table suspended in space, host to every meal, scene of feast and famine alike, caterer to the stars. It is the stage of diets, rituals, etiquette, festival fares and beggars banquets. Even tragic starving martyrs—too weak to rise from grave-like ground as they feebly chew on old leather in a desperate attempt to extract another moment's sustenance—find timid place at her vacant lot.

Diets are many, let me count the ways: some eat when hungry, others when nervous; some suffer pathological eating disorders, others fast to enhance spiritual attributes. There are those who follow the Doctrine of Signatures, homeopathic and medical diets, personal, ideological, ethnic, religious, and athletic diets. There are fussy eaters, gourmands and epicures, vegans, health food aficionados, consumers of genetically modified Frankenfoods and junk foods laden with tens of artificial chemical ingredients, five kinds of sugar and petroleum-derived products. Cuisine is enhanced with sensual stirrings: we are seduced by *sight*—colours, shapes, and plating presentations; *smell* of fragrant aromas; *feel* for firm and fresh, along with fingered tongue determining variegated textures; and the diverse indications of *taste*—sweet, sour, salty, bitter, and umami. Taoists refer to varying degrees of the Life Force in everything: they know what edibles to choose and what to avoid, and strive to ultimately not even require victuals at all because one can be nurtured by absorbing cosmic *qi*, akin to Bergson's *élan vital*. The Koran describes that which is *halal* (permissible) and *haram* (forbidden). The Bible introduces laws of hygiene and *kashrut:* quadrupeds must have cloven hoofs and chew their cud; *kosher* fish also have two signs—fins and scales; permitted birds cannot be raptors; one must be sensitive to animals' comfort and pain; there are directives to provide for the poor and hungry as well as to feed your domesticated animals before eating yourself; rest the land and acknowledge the Creator for we are only hired hands on the rotating Sky Farm below.

Mouth is the primary instrument of eating. As in lovemaking, it is a sensual devouring of the other, the swollen red rung lips miming genitalia, passionate mistress to love's arousal, feeding desperate hunger in search of pleasured release. The woman's Lower Mouth—through which life enters and departs—is impregnated by the Rising Sun in which she is initiated as both Holy Whore and Matron of Life, as Temple of Birth itself. She is ground and being, one who suffers so that life may emerge. The mouth is a many-mastered thing: it can laugh, gargle, whistle and eat; speak in every language and sing in every song. It can also remain silent and closed, a sentry between inside and out, rejecter of censored words and forbidden foods. Garlanded by elastic lips, equipped with ivory clad teeth, bordered by hard and soft palates, and featuring agile tongue, it is

Mile Zero of the Alimentary Highway. From mouth to anus, desire to dust, the mouth contributes to digestion—teeth masticate; salivary glands dispense secretions; tongue adds taste buds, licks, and assists swallowing; lips grasp, suction, slurp and smack. The mouth is mother of language, treasury of logos, carrier of breath, and cave of creation as when Yahweh spoke the world into existence or when the toddler Krishna mischievously ate clay and his mother Yashoda pried open his mouth where she saw the entire universe within.

World Tree is *axis mundi*, navel, and *omphalos*, the universal spine that extends through all realms. Occasionally depicted as inverted with roots in Heaven and branches brushing the Earth below, a variant is the Philosophical Tree of the *Opus Magnum* whose offshoots support dissolving and binding powers,[vi] topped by the tripartite crowns of the three realms—vegetable, animal and mineral. The Tree encourages diversity—the multi-patina-ed coat of survival—and then unifies it just the same. It is transcendent and immanent, one whose fruit nurtures all and whose canopy shelters everything. It is graced with supernal dew and roots of eternity, with divine messages communicated through the rustled leaves of Spirit Breath *Ruah* that stirs creation from its dream into awakened quintessence. The earth is a forest of Cosmic Trees—the birch, fig, plum and almond, the oak and the olive, the Linden, *Yggdrasil*, Bodhi, the Cross—each nation recognizes its arbour, each climate knows its soul. Not only do these trees provide symbolic spiritual values but also sustenance, light, medicine, fuel and building material. They partake of fecund female and potent male characteristics, incarnations of Mother Earth and Father Sky, Triple Goddess and Father Phallus, Wizened Witch and her Old Man. *Yang* and its *yin* are omnipresent partners in *pas de deux*: hard and soft, delicate and gnarled, yielding and resisting, the one because of the other and the other because of the One. Other great trees that were pleasing to the eye and good for food were planted in the east of Eden in the paradigmatic Garden of Earthly Delights. All were permitted to those first humans except for the berried branches of two trees in the midst of the enigmatic garden—the Flower of Life and the Tree of the Knowledge of Good and Evil—for, they were told, "When you eat from it you will surely die." And die they did, transformed from one state of consciousness to be reborn into another. We insist on recapitulating this etiological narrative, for just as they were driven out of primeval Paradise, our present world has begun to vomit[vii] us out of its injured habitat as a consequence of our noxious actions. We, too, now retreat into an exile where we eat bread by the sweat of our brow, into a world where we have smeared every tree with the blood of victims, where virgin hearts are eviscerated in imagined appeasement to harvest gods.

Cosmic Egg. The seed and the egg are symbols of eternal resurrection. Humbly swaddled in terra's incubating cradle—within Mother of All Life's dedicated womb or beneath the nested body of patient parents—they grow into nascent life. They also tell the story of that which must be broken in order to be whole. The seed cannot fully germinate unless it breaks its jacket, pushes up as it sprouts, breaches the soil ceiling to leave the underworld and emerge into an alternate sphere of light. Similarly, the fertilized egg—ovarian vault—is nursery to bird/reptile/platypus until it, too, must be shattered in the service of life. And then there is the broken heart that opens in pain and deepens to character. The Orphic Poems—the mysteries of ancient lore—tell of Night as she who was in the beginning a black-winged oracular bird. Inseminated by the Wind, she laid a silver egg in the Ocean of Darkness from which Eros, the golden god of love, was born. These are the stories that may never have happened and yet are eternally recurring as the Drama of the Cosmic Egg described in ancient world mythologies. Contemporary physicists speculate that fourteen billion years ago the universe was compressed into a gravitational singularity—a world egg—from which it explosively hatched and is still expanding. One day, it, too, will collapse upon itself as it has so many times before in the circuit of universal respiration. What interests me, however, is what preceded the First Breath and what will follow the Last. All issues of sustenance dwell within the parentheses of those vast questions.

Destination. We end where we began in the grip of serpent circle, eating—and being eaten—our way through the universe. There is no judgment in the Archetypal Kingdom of *Uroboros* from which I've emerged just long enough to tell you this strange story. *Es, es, mein kynd,* for the journey is long and littered with obstacles.[viii] On the day you arrive you will no longer recognize yourself[ix] for if you did it would be a sign that you had not yet reached your true destination.

[i] Commonly spelled *ouroboros* or *uroboros;* from Greek, a compound of *ourá,* "tail" and *bóros,* "-devouring", "-swallowing." It is "a circular symbol depicting a snake, or less commonly a dragon, swallowing its tail, as an emblem of wholeness or infinity" (*Oxford Dictionary*). An ancient archetype, Jung referred to it as "a dramatic symbol for the integration and assimilation of the opposite, i.e. of the shadow" (*Mysterium Coniunctionis*).
[ii] *Ex.* 3:8; *Nu.* 14:8; *Deut.* 31:20; *Ez.* 20:15. Cf. *Ketuvot* 11b, "milk flows from the goats' (udders), and honey drips from the figs (and dates)".
[iii] Douglas Adams, *The Restaurant at the End of the Universe* (1980), second volume in *The Hitchhiker's Guide to the Galaxy* comedy science fiction trilogy.
[iv] *Nikhnas ya'yin yo'tsai sod*—"Wine enters, secrets emerge"; *In vino veritas*—"In wine there is truth."
[v] Wine—an intoxicating, heady and impregnating liquid—represents the male principle; bread—associated more with nurturing, the body and the earth—is symbolic of the female principle.
[vi] "Earth thickens and attracts, water breaks down and purifies, air makes fluid and dries, fire divides and completes" (Johann J. Becher [1635-1682], *Opuscula chymica*).
[vii] In addition to modern science, a number of traditional sources caution consequences including *Lev.* 18:25-28; *Lev.* 20:22; *Is.* 24:5; *Jer.* 12:4.
[viii] See Franz Kafka, "My Destination", from *Parables and Paradoxes.*
[ix] See *Conference of the Birds* by Farid ud-Din Attar, twelfth century Persian mystic poet.

Yosef Wosk, Ph.D., OBC, is an Adjunct Professor and Shadbolt Fellow at Simon Fraser University where he developed *The Philosophers' Café* and *The Canadian Academy of Independent Scholars.* A recipient of numerous awards, he has founded hundreds of libraries worldwide and is a community activist in the areas of education, libraries, museums, the arts, social services, heritage conservation, gardens, philanthropy and religion.

My Fridge is Full of Endings

LYNN EASTON

You recoil at the sight of the half-eaten avocado,
Brown and cracked.

Ask why I can't let go
Of fermenting fruit
Wrapped in yesterday's tinfoil.

Catch the eyes of two shriveled spuds
Staring out from under wilted onions.

Watch slimy slivers of peppers slide
Into stale heels of cheese
Too thin to grate.

You tell me my collection of dead ends
Is proof I lack a certain hunger for hope.
I lack wholeness.
I lack taste.

I lack class.

I Lack.

But I remember the thin slips of butter
Mined and measured like melted-down gold
By my mother,
Put aside for safekeeping to make batter once a week.
A delicate mix of alchemy
Miracle-whipped into reality.

I remember butt ends of bread
Warmed soft in the oven
Or smothered in milk and sugar
For a mid-week main meal.

She peeled each carrot
In swift, smooth strokes
Gave the cleanest shavings to me.
Saved each inedible last bite
To soak for second-hand soup.

In my leftover memories
Her fridge is always full of ripe endings,
Bursting with the promise of abundance,
A raw trust in
enough.

Even now,
They lack nothing but salt.

Lynn Easton is a former journalist who graduated from SFU's Writer's Studio in 2015. She was the 2016 recipient of *The Malahat Review's* Constance Rooke Prize for her essay "The Equation." Her story "Nine" was included in the Caitlin Press *Boobs* anthology. She lives in Maple Ridge, BC.

Hyperphagia

YVONNE BLOMER

Hyperphagia (abnormally increased appetite for food) is a central feature of inherited disorders (e.g., Prader–Willi Syndrome) in which obesity is a primary phenotypic component.

Food's Child will always, always
be hungry. Vegetarian, as he grows
he will eat his mother's fingers, her face.

Can he feed the fish, the ducks or dog or will he eat their food?
His limbs are getting long, soon nothing out of reach.

At the library, Food's Child wears yellow ear defenders,
a woman stares at him, her eyes long with no loosening
smile. Food's Child is unaware, his every sense overwrought
and something maybe edible, in the carpet, caught.

Food's Child does not talk, his tongue fears
heat, he gasps always, always when he means "help."

His father, half-eaten by grief, never cries.
Food's Child's finger noodles dad's hair,
chopsticks his beard.

"No harm can come from food,"
someone once said. "Let the child decide how much."
"This too shall pass." On a walk his mother's thoughts
consume her thoughts
this her daily (milk, salt) bread.

Yvonne Blomer is Victoria, BC's Poet Laureate. Her most recent collection of poems is *As if a Raven* (Palimpsest Press, 2014). Her first collection, *a broken mirror, fallen leaf* was short listed for the Gerald Lampert Memorial Award for best first book by a Canadian writer. Her travel memoir *Sugar Ride: Cycling from Hanoi to Kuala Lumpur* is forthcoming in the spring of 2017.

Fava Bean Stew

SOPHIA KARASOULI-MILOBAR

I am making fava bean stew. The fava beans are from Egypt, the olive oil from Italy, the onions Canadian, but the oregano is from Chios, the Greek island where I was born. Aunt Foteini picked it fresh from the hillside, dried it in the sun and left it for me in a small bag on the table of the old family home, a gift to welcome me back when I visited last summer. The only way our loved ones know how to welcome us home: with a carnation and jasmine blossoms from the garden, with a jar of honey, with oregano and wild sage.

My father sits at the kitchen table and remembers his mother, my grandmother Sophia, how she survived so many hardships, sickness and poverty, wars and famine. My father says that in the years of want she cooked fava beans almost every day. "What shall we eat today, Dimitri?" she used to ask my grandfather. "Fava beans," was always the answer. "Again..." my grandma mumbled and filled the pot with water, putting it on the wooden stove to boil. Sometimes, there were no fava beans left in the pantry. Then, she would go to the old grocer's and buy some on credit, yet another debt added to the long list under the family name in the grocer's ledger.

The stew is cooking and my father's monologue goes on: "In September of 1941, the grocer had no fava beans left to sell, nothing. We were waiting eagerly for the first rain to bring out the snails on the nearby hills. But the rain wasn't coming and your grandma, already frail, began to swell from hunger. Father took her earrings to one of the shepherds at Fyrolakas. He gave them to the shepherd and in return he got milk every day for the next ten days. That's what saved her. Later on, in December, just the week before Christmas, we heard a rumour that they were rationing fish downtown. My father sent me to find out whether it was true. It was! Down at the fish market, they were giving away one hundred drams of fish per family. I remember the line up, several blocks long, and the freezing cold. The hours went by, I was getting closer. Suddenly, someone behind me collapsed. People gathered around him, but soon they said he had died, and got back in line. Finally, I was only five people away from the fish when the fish monger announced there was no more fish, and shut the roll-up door in a hurry."

Now the house smells of Chian oregano and fava beans. I ladle out the fava bean stew in a bowl and put it in front of my father with a piece of bread. "Do you know what saved us in the end that horrible first winter of the war? Fava beans! Fava beans and potatoes. We worked all day at the estate the Germans had commandeered and that's all we got for our labour." My father crosses himself, kisses the bread, and picks up the spoon.

Sophia Karasouli-Milobar writes: "I was born in Chios, Greece and lived there until my early twenties. I studied Classics as well as Library and Information Science. I have been working as a reference librarian for VPL since 1994 and have published a book on the folklore of Chios."

Breaking Bread: The Quest for Human Connection
KELLY DOUGLAS

For as long as I can remember, food has been a powerful catalyst for human connection in my life—whether while serving Sunday dinner to my family or as a volunteer preparing a meal I've found that sharing food can ignite conversations, translating into ideas, and often leading to innovative city projects for marginalized residents.

As a volunteer, I've cooked spaghetti, and sat down to dinner with incarcerated youth in a stark, institutional kitchen. It was impossible to avert my gaze and not notice that so many of these foster-home ravaged children were of Indigenous heritage. Later, while working within a maximum-security correctional institution, I witnessed male inmates, many charged with violent crimes, combining their bland prison food with other inmates' meals. The inmates would add their own spices, purchased with modest canteen money, to recreate their own cuisine within the prison unit walls. Aside from their red prison uniforms, they looked like any other group of men quietly breaking bread together while on a resolute journey to maintain a little grace within their own trauma-filled lives.

Just over a decade ago, while volunteering at a Lower Mainland agency that served lunches to people living with HIV/AIDS, I noticed that the salad dressing bottles were labelled to distinguish between staff and clients. Unfortunately, it wasn't the staff salad dressing bottles left in the refrigerator for private use that were labelled—it was the clients' bottles that were prominently displayed on the community dining tables. On the clients' bottles, a bright white label was emboldened with large, black letters "HIV Only."

Although I was very conscious of my low status as a new volunteer, I approached the staff to politely request we remove these salad dressing bottle labels since it only served to further stigmatize the clients—many of whom were already very ill, homeless and just trying to survive while engaging in street-level sex trade work. The staff was somewhat taken aback by my request, but readily agreed. I don't believe the act of labelling was done out of maliciousness—instead, due to fear and momentary lack of proper judgment.

However, fear can often propagate greater fear and isolation. In the sharing of food —regardless if it's family, friend or stranger—I passionately believe that kindness, trust and redemption alchemize during the making of the broth, derived from our deepest desire to fully engage at the most basic human level. For it's within the marrow itself, symbolic of the very heart of our conversations at a communal table, where the sustenance lies.

Eleven years later, I hope that the labelling of identity thru illness has sharply declined and that we have learnt from our shared painful lessons of perpetuating greater isolation. However, I urge us to *never* become complacent. To always remember that sharing food remains one of the most powerfully intimate primal acts that collectively binds us together evoking social change in renewed collective hope for a better future.

Kelly Douglas writes: "I'm a freelance writer with a strong interest in social justice issues. I have published in a few local newspapers and an art gallery anniversary booklet. I believe that housing and food security are basic human rights."

Halfers Make A Whole
(Before Fire Took Kam Gok Yuen)
LEANNE DUNIC

Chinatown is dying, I say.
How to prepare?

A spray of oolong—you laugh.
I like your instinct.

The wallpaper, a photograph,
a garden faded to pastel.

Succulent *siu yuk* and *siu kai*
hang in the window.

From torn plastic menus, two
char sui rice noodles in soup.

The waitress mutters dialect
as she walks away.

Cantonese: my mother's muddled
yours never spoke a word.

Two tables away, an elderly couple
rinses chopsticks in tea.

Is that normal? you ask.
I shake my head.

Will we do the same
when we're old?

I click sticks between my fingers.
I don't even hold them properly.

Soup noodles arrive. We don't clean our chopsticks.
You shoo a fly from your bowl.

A morsel of pork slips from my grasp.
You lift it with your fingers
ply the fatty meat between my lips.

Leanne Dunic is the author of *To Love the Coming End* (BookThug),
and is the singer/guitarist of *The Deep Cove.*

The Corporation's Prayer

DAVID ESO

O Safeway Canada head offices,
who art in Alberta,
branded be thy name.
Give us this day our day-old bread—now
and in the hour of your closing.
May your waste be delivered to dumps
as it is to dumpsters. Hallowed are you
among corporations and sterile
the fruit of your produce section.
Forgive us our petty larcenies
as we forgive the Muzak played against us.
In the name of the C,E.O, the C.A.O
and the Head of H.R., Amen.

David Eso writes poetry, cultural history, and literary criticism. He helps edit *The Malahat Review* and, with Jeanette Lynes, prepared *Where the Nights are Twice as Long: Love Letters of Canadian Poets, 1883 – 2014* for Goose Lane Editions.

21. *Shih Ho*, Biting Through

CORNELIA HOOGLAND

I resented the visiting cousin served the choice cut at meals,
depended on my expert tongue to guide gristle from my mouth
to my plate, politely. The meat in this hexagram is dry-lean, old-dry,

and tough. I know this poem is pathetic, but its refusal to suppress
the drudgery of *getting through* is kind of majestic. At ninety,
even your applesauce is pureed. That too will take humor.

"Biting Through" is part of a collaboration with the visual artist Ted Goodden, whose ceramic sculptures together with Hoogland's poems illustrate each of the 64 hexagrams of the *I Ching*.

Cornelia Hoogland's seventh book, *Trailer Park Elegy*, is forthcoming from Harbour Publishing in 2017. She has served on international and national literary boards, was the founder and artistic director of Poetry London, and most recently, of Poetry Hornby Island, the BC Gulf island where she lives. www.corneliahoogland.com

Eggs

TERRIE HAMAZAKI

In 1968, when I was seven, a typical Friday night for our family was a dinner of grilled salted salmon, gifted to us from other Japanese-Canadian families whose fathers were fishermen, steamed white rice and stewed vegetables, such as carrots and green beans from our backyard garden. There was a richness of *umami* (savoury) flavour from the dried bonito flakes, soy sauce and *kombu* (kelp) used in many of the dishes. We ate very little red meat or chicken and my mother canned fruit and pickled *daikon* (white radish), which were a delicious mix of sweet, tarty bitterness. I became well versed in stealing a piece from each of the dozens of tightly sealed mason jars stored in the basement. Then, after dinner, we'd drive to the grocery store for staples such as sugar, toilet paper and white bread. Much to the dismay of my immigrant parents, who were reluctant to spend their hard-earned wages on processed foods, I insisted on tuna sandwiches, instead of leftovers, for school lunches after my classmates' comments about my "stinky" food. We'd come home, unpack the groceries, and take individual baths using the same tub of water to save money: first my dad, then my two younger brothers and me, and finally, my mom. The reward after a busy week was a slice of homemade pie eaten in front of the second-hand black and white television set.

On such a Friday night, I was sprawled on the living room floor, concentrating on my spelling homework. My dad chuckled at the physical humour of a sitcom, not understanding the English; mom was clearing away dishes and my brothers played with their toy cars underneath the kitchen table, their childish mock crashing sounds a soothing undertone. I yelped when my dad jumped up from the couch and stepped on my toes.

"Go to your mom," he half-whispered.

I could hear muffled voices and then clattering noises outside the living room window. Someone was running down the stairs. I stood behind him as he pulled back the floral patterned drapes and we stared into the darkness. The pale grinning faces of three brothers who lived on the block, gleamed underneath the streetlight, their cowlick topped heads and lanky bodies jerking to the rhythm of their baleful psalm.

"Chink, chink, go home, chinks!"

My father closed the drapes and, pushing me aside, went to open the door. I noticed a slight trembling in his hands. Raw eggs dripped down the metal screen door and pooled on the shell-littered porch. An empty cardboard carton lay strewn to one side. Without a word, he shut and locked the door. Nothing more was said then or the next day when he cleaned up the sticky mess. I don't recall if the boys' parents knew. But it frightened and hardened me in equal measure. Over time, as more immigrant families moved in from the Philippines, Fiji, and India to the formerly white working-class neighborhood, my brothers played street hockey with the boys and my mom took over an apple pie when their father died of a heart attack. Fifty years later, I'd like to believe that in my dad's mind, the most shameful part of the incident was that a dozen eggs, valuable protein, were wasted in such a careless manner.

Terrie Hamazaki has performed her plays at the Vancouver Fringe and Women in View Performing Arts Festivals. Her writing has appeared in *Beyond the Pale: Dramatic Writing from First Nations Writers and Writers of Colour*, *The Fed Anthology*, and the *Hot & Bothered* series. She works in the anti-violence sector.

History in a Jar

CHRISTINA MYERS

I hold the glass jar up to the light and squint my eyes. Is that a bubble? I think it's a bubble. I turn the jar, inspecting it from every angle. Definitely a bubble. And there's another. And another. The recipe I've been following all week tells me to check the smell, so I remove the lid and inhale. A ripe, warm odour tickles my nose. It's my first time so I don't know if it's exactly right, but it sure seems like it is. It's working. It's really working. I want to squeal, jump up and down, call my husband at work, and tell him the good news: we've got bubbles—you're going to be a sourdough daddy.

For most of human history, yeast didn't come in small packets with instructions printed on the back, but from the air around us—a magic, invisible ingredient that no one could see, but whose existence was evident in the creation of a soupy, bubbly paste that could, with a little effort, be turned into fluffy loaves of bread. I'm baffled when I try to imagine how we figured this out. Like most great leaps in human history, leavened breads were no doubt born from a combination of accident, ingenuity, resourcefulness and curiosity—refined and perfected, with trial and error, over a great period of time. The specifics are lost to history.

It's the fermentation that drew me to sourdough as a project. My daughter had been hospitalized with pneumonia and a blood infection, and then came home with a nasty intestinal infection that got a foot-hold thanks to scorched-earth intravenous antibiotics. I started reading about gut flora and became obsessed with "good" bacteria: I made lists of which vegetables are the best prebiotics, hid powdered probiotics in her milk, and stocked the fridge with fermented foods like kimchi and kefir. Sourdough, my sister told me, is fermented, too. She recommended a documentary about the history of bread and I watched it, twice, hypnotized by the notion that quick yeasts have cost us something valuable in our diet—and, by extension, in our bodies.

Of all the things we eat, a true sourdough bread is perhaps the simplest: flour, water, a sprinkling of salt, and wild yeast for an engine. Sounds straight forward, but it's a finicky process. Tap water has too much chlorination and will kill your fledgling starter—the base by which you'll make your dough—and a cool draft or too much heat will do the same. You have to "feed" your starter every day by removing a portion of the paste and adding more water and flour in specific quantities, the ratios and frequency of which can change based on elevation or season. What works for a baker in Montreal will not work the same way for a baker in Vancouver.

But the basic process—the fundamental steps of what I'm doing here—have been the same for thousands of years. Growing these bubbles is a small and simple thing but it feels like looking down into a dark cave and seeing images drawn on the wall. I am equal parts cook and archaeologist as I hold up my starter and inspect the bubbles: the history of humankind, in a jar.

Christina Myers is an award-winning former journalist and a freelance writer in the Metro Vancouver area. Her work has appeared in the anthology *Boobs*, on CBC Radio, *Skirt Quarterly*, *Voices of Motherhood*, *Room* Magazine online and others. She is a graduate of the Writer's Studio in Vancouver and a UBC alumnus.

Fragments

CLAIRE SICHERMAN

My family loves bread. Most kinds. Even the squishy white bread that has no substance or nutritional value. When I go to Vancouver's Granville Island market with my son, instead of whining for a cookie, he asks for a baguette and then walks around gnawing on the end. No butter. Nothing. Just plain.

My freezer is full of bread. The bottom is so stuffed with bread there's no room for anything else. These aren't whole loaves either. These are fragments. Bits and pieces, odds and ends from last January. Seriously. I usually end up composting some, although my mother would be horrified to hear this. She'd take those pieces and eat them herself, lest anything go to waste.

My mother has bread in the freezer. My sister has a freezer full of bread too. I don't know what happens with her bread. I don't ask.

My grandmother loved bread.

In my family, a meal isn't complete without a good piece of rye, with butter spread an inch thick.

In Auschwitz bread was like gold. The stale piece a prisoner was sometimes given was often gobbled up. A few times when my grandfather hid his piece of bread beneath his thin mattress at *Schwarzheide* concentration camp, it disappeared during the night and he'd have nothing for breakfast to go along with the chicory coffee, or black mud as he called it. Other times it was carefully saved and used as a bargaining tool, a way of trading. As my grandmother stood in line for her prison serial number, she used this piece of bread as leverage to ensure her tattoo looked nice, that the numbers were straight, that the ink didn't bleed. The bread that was supposed to go into her starving belly went into someone else's stomach instead.

*

I watch my mother as she finishes an apple. She doesn't eat it like your typical North American mother. She tears into it like it's the best thing she's ever tasted. She devours the entire thing. Her teeth bite through skin, to the flesh, and when she's done that, she finishes the core. She even swallows the seeds. When I was young I used to worry she would die from arsenic poisoning.

I carry snacks with me wherever I go. I avoid ever feeling hungry. Hunger scares me. I grow shaky and unstable. There is fear in not having enough, of running out, of not knowing when the next meal will be.

I come from a family that knows starvation. Whose bellies weren't distended from eating too much, but whose bodies were so deprived, I imagine it felt like a bunch of knives were cutting up their insides.

My family never throws out food. Leftovers become second and third leftovers. Furry bits of mold lovingly and carefully scraped off.

Now I use my compost. But only when my mother isn't looking.

Claire Sicherman writes: "I am a writer who is exploring intergenerational trauma. I have recently earned a certificate from the Creative Writing Program at Humber. I live with my family on Salt Spring Island, BC. This essay, "Fragments," is part of a larger project, which will be published in my book, *Imprint*, forthcoming from Caitlin Press in January, 2018."

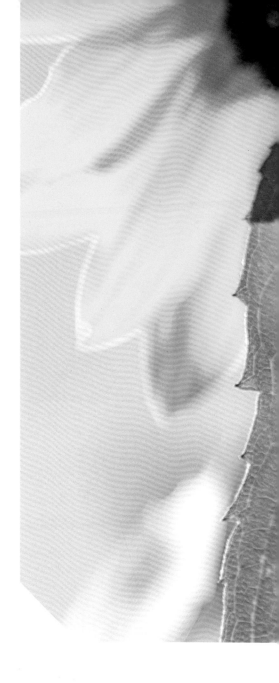

Like the Sky

ABBY WENER HERLIN

Clouds, cumulous
        out the window I see bits of sky
between pumping milk
while David kicks
staccato
at the air.

He reaches for the grey bunny
with a missing white ear
biting down,
gnawing.

All this milk, I focus on
his toothless grin,
the drool anticipates a tooth.

All this milk, pump
has a rhythm, a lullaby.
I have to force my eyes to open,
focus on the fullness of clouds
and David's kick
               kick
                  kick
his rolling over,
hitting the bunny
watching it fling back and forth,
into giggles.

My milk, the slight blue hue
like the sky.

Abby Wener Herlin's poetry has been published by Leaf Press and Motif Press. She has been published in numerous literary journals including *The Antigonish Review*, *Bitterzoet*, and *Room*. She is an academic, creative writing facilitator, and instructor in the Department of Language and Literacy at UBC. She is a proud mother of David who is two and a half.

Bread

ELEN GHULAM

My hyphenated identity comes with three dashes, each one annotated with an asterisk or two. Let me give you a taste. In my kitchen cupboard, the soya sauce resides next to *zaatar* (a divine herb from Palestine). I have been told that I make the best Russian salad there ever was—this at the same potluck dinner to which I brought my famous hummus. In my stew, the cardamom makes love to pomegranate juice as naturally as it does to mole sauce.

Over-immigration leads to cultural diarrhea.

Acrobatically, I have eaten languages, danced to the rhythm of perspective and cultivated attitudes in a rainbow of colors. Yet no matter how earnest my effort, I could never quite satisfy my lust—the desire to belong. It molests me ceaselessly. When I am here, I want to be there. When I am there, I am missing here. But the delicate aromas of the poetic East don't mix with the bright glare of the seductive West. This kind of gluttony can only be soothed with a seven-layer dip of beans, guacamole, salsa and who knows what else is in that thing. Perhaps cheese?

No. I will replace sour cream with mashed sesame seeds. That orange layer, whatever it is, with diced tofu, roasted bell peppers and add extra virgin olive oil. Mmmmmmm! It tastes good. Even better than …

I must discover the recipe where forever the twain shall meet. It is my quest. One day it will be my gift to the world. MY LEGACY.

How I envy all of you who speak just one language. You intuit a flavor I shall never taste. You eat bread and cheese and innocently say: "It's bread and cheese."

In Iraq, we called it *Iranian bread* because it was immigrants wearing tattered thread from Iran who made it. In Israel, the same bread, same taste, is called *Iraqi bread* because it's made by Jewish immigrants from Iraq. In Vancouver, the Iranian baker calls the same exact bread, the same smell even, *barbari bread* because in Iran it was immigrants from Khorsan who brought it. Do you realize how terrifying bread is to me?

Khobos, pan, chleb, lachem, eish, nri, nan, pain. Repetition, in all the languages of the world, soothes me.

One morning after a weary sleep, I woke up declaring to the Universe: "I give up!"

Twenty years of this tasteless, useless quest: be good, be authentic, find a place to belong, to have my life mean something. All have led only to spoilage. I accept my lot: rotten. Gillian has vanquished herself in a mustard storm. Zaev taunts my imagination with his razor sharp looks. Healing alludes me. I can neither satisfy this lust, nor make it go away. Defeat!

The ocean doesn't care if fish believe in water or disbelieve. All get caressed by currents just the same.

All the landscapes belong to me. The Alps. Euphrates. The heartbeat you skipped. All mine. I don't need to learn your cuisine. Shhhhhhhhhh! Listen with a whisper.

Mix flour and water.

Apply heat.

Elen Ghulam is the author of *Spoonful Chronicles*—the story of a woman on a mission to discover the purpose of her life, she accomplishes this by recounting everything she has ever eaten. An Iraqi-Canadian living in Vancouver BC, she worked as a computer programmer for eighteen years before turning to writing fiction. www.ihath.com

fried onions

PARDIS PAHLAVANLU

sizzling onions dancing
in turmeric yellow
passing through the material barrier
and making their way to eternity.

who would have thought paradise was the smell in one's hair?

Pardis Pahlavanlu is an exiled Iranian artist living on Coast Salish territories. Her work focuses on loss, diaspora and the intersection of mental health. She aims to rediscover home in each piece she creates.

Sei Turni (6 spells for #CanLit)

AMBER DAWN

1. *Stregaghi una Mela* (Bewitch an Apple)

Hold a winesap apple to your brow and think of the worst possible outcome.
Or has the worst already happened? How do you define cataclysm?

Cut the cursed fruit in half, with a black-handled knife, if you own one. Eat the half
that falls to your right. A winesap will honey your nose and sop your tongue.
Bury the left in your garden.

2. *Proteggi i Tuoi Libri* (Protect Your Books)

Gather rosemary.

(If you live near Italians, we nurse the woody bush in our yards. We're big on protection.
We don't mind if you pick some.)

Use the sprigs as bookmarks. Mark the books that allowed you to stand
humiliated and willing to root your feet into this immeasurable earth.

A sprig for *Disappearing Moon Café*. A sprig for *Bleus de mine*. A spring for *Blood Sports*.
A sprig for *Land to Light On*. A spring for *Lullabies for Little Criminals*. A sprig for *Runaway*.
A sprig for *Desert of the Heart*. A sprig for *The Predicament of or*. A sprig for *The Kappa Child*.
A sprig for *This Place Called Absence*. A sprig for *Rabbit Ears*.
A rosemary sprig for *I Am Woman*. Infinitum

3. *Accendi un Piccolo Strenuo Fuoco* (Set a Small Brave Fire)

A lit candle. A wooden match. A pinch of salt. A shot of bourbon.

Sprinkle the bourbon with salt and pour a spoon's worth into your cupped left palm.
Take up the match with your right hand and light it off the candle's flame.
Your nervous system will say "no," though you've set fire to yourself before,
haven't you? Kiss the firewater you hold
with the match head. The flame knows
what to do. You will see the spirit leap blue before you feel heat.
Clap your hands before you burn.

Notice how, this time, fear was not followed by consequence.
Notice how, this time, fear only asked to be respected, to be seen.

4. *Versi Nord* (Face North)

Flip your bed so that your feet point south.
Pray the magnetic north pulls your bad dreams away.

5. *Vaffanculo! Luna* (Fuck! Moon)

Direct your anger at the waning moon. She's the oldest woman around and she knows
how to take a punch. (Do women learn how to take punches from the moon? Our traumas
are as recurrent as the lunar cycle, true, though far less visible than a halo.)

You have about thirteen and a half nights to tell the waxing moon, fuck you fuck this
fuck me fuck him fuck her fuck pain fuck poor decisions fuck indecision fuck power
fuck powerlessness fuck anger fuck pretending not to be angry fuck silence fuck this noise

When the moon disappears take a deep breath. Reset. The waxing moon
is a time for wishes. Consider this carefully—what will you wish for.
What will you call into being?

6. *Bevi Lo* (Drink It)

Maybe your cinnamon sticks have slept too long in a glass jar?
Your canned Serrano peppers, too. Your bay leaves. Your black pepper.
Turmeric and ginger powder. Whole cloves. Salty plum. Rose buds.

Maybe your dried sage has hung too long beside the kitchen window?
Your garlic braid veiled in dust. Cobwebs lace the willow wreath you spun last winter.

Maybe you've forgotten the smell of strong herbs until they are boiling together
in a iron pot on your stovetop. Maybe you forgot the words of your mother,
or grandmother, saying, drink it, I know it tastes bad, but it will make you feel better.

Maybe you have forgotten. But I promise you, dear ones,
magic and medicine have not forgotten you.

Drink the brew as you re-read that poem. You know the poem I'm referring to.

Amber Dawn is a writer living on unceded territory of the Musqueam, Squamish and Tsleil-Waututh
First Nations (Vancouver, Canada). Her memoir *How Poetry Saved My Life: A Hustler's Memoir* won
the 2013 Vancouver Book Award. She is the author of the Lambda Award-winning novel *Sub Rosa*.
Her newest book, *Where the words end and my body begins,* is a collection of glosa form poems.
She currently teaches creative writing at Douglas College, the University of British Columbia and
Simon Fraser University's The Writers Studio. She is also the director and creative mentor of
the Thursdays Writing Collective: a drop-in, community-driven space in the Downtown Eastside.

Source: A Triptych

MELISSA SAWATSKY

i. Safeway, Fall 1985

I'm sorry sweetie, we have to go.
Mom abandons the grocery cart,
pulls me past a row of cashiers where
packaged dinners and Granny Smiths
advance across rubber ribbons. We dash
through the sliding doors, take refuge

in a mustard-yellow station wagon.
Beneath my plastic jelly shoes,
I read a faded grocery receipt. A deal on
Tylenol and Tums—items to ease human suffering.

In the driver's seat beside me, Mom
presses her right hand to her chest. Takes deep breaths.

I interlace my fingers and squeeze—glimpse
her left hand, white-knuckled on the wheel,
fingers swollen around her wedding ring.
I push the faded receipt in circles
beneath the passenger seat,
calculating the cost.

At home, she musters
energy for bland broccoli and chicken.
I push the soggy trees around the plate,
calculating how many I can stomach.

ii. Shepherd's Pie, Winter 2007

Mom blows up a Shepherd's Pie.
Sets it atop the stove to cool with an element left on—
a pile of dinner-gone-wrong on the kitchen floor
to be lapped up by the dog.

But Mom is a master gardener—
allows winter to do what it will,
grinds dead leaves to mulch for
a new year. A bed for seeds.

I live in a subterranean icebox without a stove,
thinking of my grandmother's kitchen.
She handwrote her recipes in a spiral notebook
for Christmas 1993. I inherit words:

zwieback, vereniki, paska, perishki.
Her cursive hand instructs me to
cut dough into ½ moon-shaped perogies,
moisten the edges and close securely.

I try my hand at kitchen choreography
one step at a time with pre-made pie shells,
frozen perogies from the European bakery.

iii. Farmer's Market, Spring 2016

Think fast HIPPIE!
The bumper sticker pierces my eye line
like a prolonged assault
at the farmer's market. Incongruous:

a snowmobile in the bed of a pickup
in early spring. A dragon's mouth
prepared to swallow hippies
who fail to think fast enough, catch
what's coming at them—a grenade
decaled on the side of the dragon.

The gardeners are still planting.
For now, there are preserves,
fresh bread from a wood fired oven,
homemade fudge, frozen free-range chicken.

The gardens will grow.
Think *slow,* think *perennial.*

Think of Mom—how she grows
back into the garden, stirs the compost.
Think of my grandmother in the hop fields,
pulling at the bines—tendril-like growths
reaching out to be selected,
dried, fermented.

I fill my soiled bag with market goods—
taste the dirt,
taste the fruit.

Melissa Sawatsky is a writer currently living on unceded *Witsuwit'en* territory in Smithers, BC where she serves on the Board of the Bulkley Valley Community Arts Council and works at Smithers Public Library. Her work has appeared in *Room Magazine, Northword, The Maynard, Poetry is Dead, OCW Magazine, Sad Mag,* and *Rhubarb,* among other publications. She has an MFA in Creative Writing from The University of British Columbia.

Grandmother Preserves

CARLA STEIN

I told myself I'd write it down—
would keep a record of
the way she decided
blackberries balanced sugar

whether crabapples, raspberries or
pears would be a good addition.
how long to boil them together, the
trick to knowing jars were sealed.

methods crafted by mother,
aunts, etched in her visual
guide. no wordy details.
intoned instructions: *Just watch*

Did her mother whisper: *Watch*
as fathers, uncles, chose shovels,
picks, and rakes to counter hard-eyed hatred

Did her aunt admonish: *Watch*
whether jars of jam, bushels of wheat,
sacks of flour would trick or
seal a Cossack's bloodlust

Who did she watch sailing toward
streets paved with gold; city districts
located by whether gooseberries or green
grapes graced a peddler's cart

Who looked on as she calibrated
English consonants to Yiddish vowels,
marched with unionists, dodged nightsticks,

sold peppermints, fed depression-hungry
sons and daughters; lost everyone
who had not sailed.

Blue and black berries slowly
simmer in my kitchen, sugar added—
just enough to set the fruit. Jars clean,
ready to fill, soft cloth handy to wipe lids.

between stirs I observe roil and
thickening, notice dark syrup, skim
lighter foam; monitor temperature.

notebook and pen at hand
I begin writing it all down,
imagine she is watching.

Poet and visual artist, Carla Stein began writing word pictures about the same
time as she discovered crayons and tempera. This love affair with language
morphed into a career in both broadcast and freelance journalism, which
included stories aired on CBS and CBC radio. Her artwork has been featured
in *Ascent Aspirations, Island Arts,* and the *Stonecoast Review.* Her artwork can
be viewed at: www.roaeriestudio.com

Salt and Ashes

ADRIENNE DROBNIES

A fine sea salt sifts through my hands with the feel of ashes in the *cloisonné*
        vase on my desk—its cold metal waiting to be kissed
when loneliness hacks through my chest and stuffs it with pepper and smashed garlic sorrow.
        The aromas of rosemary and thyme burble up through the wound like the scent of
a garden on a Greek Island abundant in grapes
        where I make wine that has aged for fourteen years and will continue to age
to place on the table to drink whenever the full moon slides into Virgo.
On the white cloth, I'll cut open cherry tomatoes, drizzle the most virgin olive oil,
        and beside them rest slices of crusty and yeast-aerated bread, while I alternately roast
and cool my hide in the summer sun and water outside a hotel
                lost on the Finger Lakes near Aurora on this Gloomy Sunday.

Adrienne Drobnies lives in Vancouver and graduated from the SFU Writer's Studio.
Her work has appeared recently in *The Antigonish Review, EVENT,* and *Riddle Fence.*
Her long poem "Randonnées," was a finalist for the CBC literary award and selections
from it are in an artist's book with Julie Baugnet.

Milky Way

ELIZABETH ROSS

I'd put off the decision all winter.

My belly tightening
around the baby's kicks,
death drum.

                    *

Dead moons
followed my dog.
His back legs collapsed

on walks; he staggered
to his water bowl, drizzling piss.

                    *

When my first daughter came home
and cried, he barked.

When this baby came home, he was quiet.
He knew before I did.

                    *

Her tied tongue
bringing in my milk
carved away the flesh

between nipple and areola,
crescents sucked clean.

                    *

Each time her mouth
            eclipsed the wound,

                        diamonds pierced my toes.

The paediatrician had cut her stubborn
            frenulum twice; twice
                        it had re-webbed—
    evolutionary

                reversal—her tongue
                        into the tell-tale heart.

                    *

From his
bed he rose,
shaking, caked
in shit. I
told my
husband
to make
the call.

*

As he booked
the appointment
I nursed her.

Dead stars howled.

*

I explored
the pain, listening
for a quiet space

between tongue and skin. I latched
the baby forwards
and backwards, sideways,

clockwise, counter clockwise
we spun. Then numb,
the ring

of nerves
                    swallowed. I decomposed,

          wanted
what I remembered

          from my first baby—how good

                    it could be—feeding
her from my body,

          sleep tingling, lush

with each other.

*

My dog loved the vet. He loved her
even when she shaved above his paw
and inserted the catheter.

*

My baby spat up
curds of milk
and blood.

*

The catheter wagged.

*

I would need to nurse
her soon. All I could think

was the store next to the vet's
sold nipple shields.

*

From an old baby food container
I fed the dog death

carrots on the stainless examining table.

    *

I trusted the sleep
of my baby, tucked into the stroller parked

next to him. The place she had just come
from, cell by cell.

    *

The vet said *take your time*.

    *

He crunched his carrots.

    *

The vet
injected the
catheter with
creamy
liquid.

    *

He breathed
        jerkily. I waited

for a reflex—groan,
        whimper—

but

        he lay

still, gross

        plush.

    *

The wet circle
of my baby's mouth

opened –

    *

My face dry,
ribs dripping.

Elizabeth Ross is the author of *Kingdom* (Palimpsest 2015). Her work has been published in a number of literary magazines, selected for inclusion in *Best Canadian Poetry (2013)*, and longlisted for the CBC poetry prize. She lives in Toronto, where she's at work on a series of personal essays and a book of poetry.

Backyard Brewing

TOM HARDING

For thirty years, I have experimented with beer-making. What began as a curiosity as an undergraduate Science student, transformed into a deep fascination with how to create nuanced combinations of water, yeast, barley, and hops. Scores of friends and family from ages five to eighty, have joined me over the years to collect local mountain spring water, to grind grain, to culture yeast, to build hops trellises, and to brew, bottle, and name beer. Birthday gifts have come in the form of cast iron burners, eighty-litre cauldrons, and Gandolf-style driftwood mixing paddles. On brewing days (often rainy Vancouver days mid-winter), we have gathered two or three under tarps, with buckets, siphon tubes, thermometers, and great food to make beer and to share tales of recent adventures.

Beer-making has its notable rhythms and seasons. Winter is the time for brewing. After brewing day, carboys wrapped in towels take over the living room, and house temperatures are adjusted not for people's comfort but for the optimal fermentation process. Some weeks later, the beer goes into bottles, bottles are capped, and the yeast moves into carbonation duty. Spring involves the cultivation of hops plants. It was once the season for the annual high school chemistry lesson (now banned) that inspired one of my students to become an award-winning local brew master. Late summer is time for the hops harvest.

Humulus lupulus, or hops, grows in our backyard in Vancouver from March to September. From an emerging purple shoot, the perennial vines grow Jack-in-the-Beanstalk style to over five metres in height. The hop's female cone gives beer the bitter resins and aromatic oils that contrast with the sweetness of the barley. Each harvest season, we clip thousands of cones that look like dainty, light-green, papery flowers. The hops connect us with people across time and

place. I have farmed three varieties of hops for a decade, and discovered some years in, that my great-grandfather had grown hops for Labatt's Brewery in London, Ontario for sixty years. Hops cultivation and beer-making find traces in communities in Egypt, Mesopotamia, and China going back 6000 years. Hops figured centrally as one of the four key beer ingredients in the Bavarian Purity Law of 1516. It also preserved the quality of beer for multi-month, sea-faring journeys from England to India. India Pale Ale, a type of beer famous now in the Pacific Northwest, gets its name from the role hops played in sustaining the quality and taste of beer on those transcontinental journeys.

Most importantly for me, hops harvesting, and the beer-making process overall, cultivates and sustains relationships much like a quilting bee. Returning each September to our sunny back deck, people of all ages gather with scissors in one hand and a pint of ale in another, to clip thousands of light green cones from the hops vines. As our fingers get sticky with yellow dust from the cones, we share stories about travel, books, the joys and vulnerabilities of living, and we get still with one another. At every stage of the process, we dream up names for beer batches that savour little truths, treasured moments, and good living.

Tom Harding is a dad, son, friend and partner, outdoor and beer enthusiast, and science educator. He has taught Biology, Physics, general Sciences, and Leadership, at the high school level for twenty-five years. He is keenly interested in the generative spaces where teenagers and science meet.

Fare Trade

PENN KEMP

I would eat local food only were it not for temptation.
A green invitation of open avocado in emerald halves.
An alluring variety of mango hot to eye, cool to tongue.

The seduction of dark chocolate.
The slurped fulfillment in oyster.
The simple necessity of rice.

Otherwise, I would be content with my yard's fall produce.
But having tasted the world's fare, how to return un-jaded
to simple pleasures that this ground offers? Beans.

Corn. Squash. Corn. Beans. The three sisters thrive.

Yes, I will eat local food mostly. Except for. Except for…
Accept.

When The Bare Naked Ladies sing "Snack Time," not one of the stars
they record choose celery sticks. No one claims carrots for their own.

O banana. O chocolate. Chicory can never compare to *café au lait*.

On to political rant: our food too cheap, our farmers ruined.

Our eyes closed, we rest easy, spoiled ripe fruit in the docks,
turning sleepy to sun-rotten. Given so much, we reach for more

even when over full. And poems break off as the lunch bell rings.

Penn Kemp's book of poetry, *Local Heroes*, will be published by Insomniac Press in Spring, 2018. Her latest works are two plays celebrating local hero and explorer, Teresa Harris, produced in 2017 and published by Playwrights Guild of Canada.

Still Life at Family Dinner

a collaborative *shiritori** poem by

STEPHEN BERG, CARA WATERFALL, EMILY OLSEN, VIOLA PRINZ and LIAM MCFEE

"Even casseroles can scream…"
—Pablo Picasso

Scream green beans and cheddar cheese,
slender emeralds of health in tawny arterial muck,
muckrakers besieged in a crockery coffin
on a table angled to twist and tilt—
tilt like a merry-go-round without reprieve
as our stomachs churn with unease—uneasy
careening of brush on cold canvas as still life
distills life into chaos—pathos breeds
like a stampede of rats as "Art is never chaste"—
chased with cool milk, the earthy undertones
an alkaline lustre—fluster, fuming dysfunction
ruling the mangled table, each insignificant
magnificent grievance or grudge ready to roil—
bring to boil and let simmer, uncovered

*Based on the *shiritori* word game in Japanese, and its "word chain" game counterpart in English. Poets from Australia, England and Canada joined forces to mine Picasso's famous quote.

Authored by a mysterious international consortium of Poets.

Oregano

DIANE TUCKER

Oregano has overrun everything.
Let your vision puddle and spread and you'll see
the little mistresses, the honeybees, waving
their arrogant tails on dozens of the oregano stalks
hung with armloads of tiny purple flowers
like miniscule ropes of garlic.

Oregano has overrun, its nectar's wiles drawing
six-legged love in crowds, every sweet soldier
shoving her face straight into each cup for a slurp.

And there is a little mountain of these
foxglove-purple wee cups, a thousand stacked
shot glasses strung over the parsley and chives,
a hundred legs hooked on these sweet brims.

The oregano, as long as it flowers, is allowed
to overrun everything. It brings all these cheeky
round-bottomed drunken ladies, their humming
bodies lifting and shifting millimeters over
to get at the next drink, their hen-party
flower-bed debauch, their quilt of leaves
and furry abdomens and shiny pinhead eyes.

Two square feet of the garden is a thatch-stemmed,
shadow-cooled, mauve-peppered feast, summer game
of hovering musical chairs, a persistent up-and-down
hum, a velvet-thrum, green and purple drinking song.

Vancouver native Diane Tucker has published three poetry books and a YA novel. Her poems have appeared in numerous anthologies and in dozens of literary journals. Currently she is sending out her poetry manuscript *The Five Seasons.* She serves as one of the organizers of Vancouver's Dead Poets Reading Series.

Lunch with My Father

DANNY PEART

We worked a half-day on Saturdays,
locked the shop at noon and drove in his truck to market.
That truck was a red International pickup, his right hand working
the H pattern shift on the steering column.
We needed tomatoes, cheddar cheese and a loaf of brown bread, sliced.
Then home.

My father would toast the bread for two sandwiches.
I'd find the jar of gherkin pickles in the fridge
and use a fork to catch three for each of us.
His three pickles always on the lid to save a plate.

He'd slice the tomato, butter the toast and build the sandwiches.
A hunk of cheese beside for each of us, and two glasses of milk.

So ended our working week.
Both of us tired.
Both of us content.

Danny Peart currently resides in Vancouver, BC. He is supported by his wife, Janette
Lindley, two sons, Max and Nick, and a Yellow Lab, Mila. In 2012, he published a slim
volume of poems, cheerfully titled *Ruined By Love* and guided by Aislinn Hunter
(Milagro Press). In 2016, he published a collection of stories and poems titled *Stark
Naked in a Laundromat*, edited by Zsuzsi Gartner (Milagro Press).

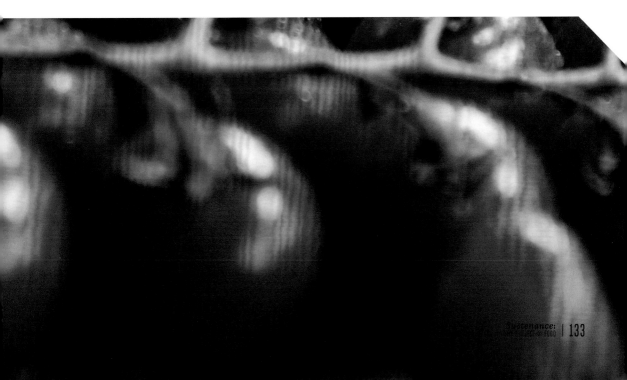

Your Stomach and the Lives of the Saints

JULIE EMERSON

eat like Hildegarde: chickpeas, fennel, no eel
eat like Nicholas: bread dipped in water, no meat,
the chicken on his plate flew out the window
                    your kind of saints or not, eat

eat like Antoine: honey-tongued and saint of bees
eat like Bishop Honorė: saint of bakers,
a blackberry bush grew from his bread paddle
                        kind of saints or not, eat

eat like Macarius. raw, nothing cooked
eat like Mary of Egypt: grass, nothing more,
a bird grabbed poisoned food for Benedict, the luck
                        of saints or not, eat

eat like Paschal, with angels' help: cabbage broth
eat like Drogo: holy wine, bread, and barley,
a multi-tasking monk, the saint of coffee
                        saints or not, eat

eat like a skier: icicles, fir, hoar frost
eat like a cyclist: breezes, bugs, pollen, pitch,
theobromine with a side of pigeon wings
                        or not, eat
eat like a princess: tulips, gold, placenta
eat like a politician: hot dogs, applause,
babies, interns, fresh young men in uniforms
                        not, eat

eat like an artist: ultramarine pixels
eat like a writer: fingernails, commas, pulp,
drumbeats, darkness, absent fathers, adverbs, crumbs
                eat

Julie Emerson, writer and artist, lives in Vancouver and on Mayne Island near her vegetable garden. She helped found Slow Food Vancouver and GEFree BC. Her five books include *Twenty-Seven Stings* (New Star) and *The Herons of Stanley Park* (with photographer Martin Passchier) and *A Hundred Days: A Botanical Novel*.

Luanda Street Children

PAMELA PORTER

Night in the shadow of the cathedral
gutted back in the seventies, the week
the Portuguese left Angola.
We ride in the bed of the truck
with a pot of porridge so weighty,
it took two to raise it there. There's Rob
and me, and Rowan the Irishman
who knows all the kids, and Abell,
a local, driving. When we turn a corner, still
a block from the cathedral, children chase us;
Rowan calls, *Cuídate, cuídate,* waves
off those trying to climb into the truck.

They speak a kind of Spanish
with *sshhh* added, have come
out of nowhere, everywhere. No one
wants them; they keep quiet, invisible,
sleep curled in the spaces between high-rises,
dodge falling bags of feces, hunt trash heaps
for empty tins of coffee
or baby formula, or cardboard
they can roll into a cone.

Standing in the bed of the truck, I burn
my skin with porridge, dip a cup,
pour it fast toward hands reaching out
with cardboard or tin. Rowan
keeps them in order. Sometimes I pour twice
into one cardboard cone—two are sharing.
Rob hands bread to hands, pours water,
often straight into their mouths.
Then we slam the lid on the pot
and rock in the bed of the truck to another station.
Seven times a night we do this.

Since the international presence arrived,
the girls don't line up much. They make money
standing under any working streetlight.

Next night we're back in the truck.
In the shadow of the burned-out cathedral,
the children's eyes shine, a hundred little moons.
Sshhh, they say. I stoop and pour,
stoop and pour for all
who have been thrown away
in the world.

Pamela Porter's work has won more than a dozen awards, including the Governor
General's Award and the *PRISM International* grand prize in poetry. Her ninth volume
of verse, *Defending Darkness,* was released in 2016 by Ronsdale Press. Pamela lives near
Sidney, BC with her family and a menagerie of rescued horses, dogs, and cats.

all this

DANIELA ELZA

if you get up before the bees
     you can see where the day is going.

in the low buzz and hum of the hive—
thick clusters   clumps   and fists

of bees.   entranced I ask:
               when will they dance?
my soul already leaping ahead   rolling

in a meadow of   white sweet clover.
in a couple of hours   you said.

a morning dance
      blossoms into purple coneflowers
               fireweed   butter cups.

and the words grow   leaves and petals
again shed pollen   on my page.

in winter they dust and knit themselves
eat honey to make heat. the centre rotates

slowly from   within   to without.
as far as the eye can see   gentle hills

open fields   valleys filled with
endless sky   echinacea   alfalfa

golden buckwheat   and
what the farmers choose to grow each year.

we announce our arrival   with smoke.
you pick a frame   examine it carefully

more activity on sunny days   less on rainy.
you are not afraid of stings

see the queen?   and words   again
begin to dance their thirst.
               regain their sensitivities.

it's market day today   but first
I bend down to the dying
                pray they will never leave.

       *

what is a poem to do? amidst honeycomb
propolis   mouth open in wonder
nectar on the tongue   mind abuzz.

the meniscus of my attention—
                      an altar.

*am I living a life worthy of dreams
every day here anchored with the bees?*

yes you said.   *the spirit of this place
hums*   *through my days.*

in the morning a jar of echinacea honey
captures the sun on the windowsill.

viscous unpasteurized spoonfuls of
amber light on my tongue.

        I taste a whole field
a view to spell the day with.

      watch the poem run up *dirt hill*
past the blue bee house

    the grove of apple trees
        the row of hives

drenched in dew and August dawn bliss
   it rolls in the meadow   naked

hides in the sunflowers
   refuses to get in the car
      refuses to leave
wants to be
    all this.

Daniela Elza's poetry collections are *the weight of dew* (2012), *the book of It* (2011), and *milk tooth bane bone* (2013). Her latest manuscript, *the ruined pages,* will be published in 2017. Daniela's chapbook *slow erosions* (collaborated poems with poet Arlene Ang) is also forthcoming. *all this* is dedicated to Cat Majors, a small offering on the altar of her bright, playful spirit, her love for life and laughter, for honey, bees, and poetry.

How Does a Warm Animal Come to Her Death?

DC REID

I have punctured my finger nails / to fill one thimble / with blood
· Phyllis Webb

And love is a cord woven out of life,
And dyed in the red of the living heart;
And time is the hunter's rusty knife,
That cannot cut the red strands apart:
· Isabella Valancy Crawford

The elk lies in its body of ribs, fallen
together as hands in prayer. I see
xylophone bones and meat's white growth

of fly. The skull has no one to look at me, but
a pink toe becomes a blood eye left to find my own.
Half an ungulate jaw, the other not found

in second-growth bush, or century of sweat
down my black hair shirt. Could she,
if she she be, have mewed her own

small ending? A jaw of long white fids
un-spliced her arteries: adventitia, media,
intima, to snuff the life of eyes.

I consider teeth-shortened bones,
not lungs around which they
breathed and returned. Hamstrings

on my calves, I finger hide too
worthless to be eaten. Where are mouths
that ripped warm life to feed their own?

I might stagger among alder haze pursued
by green fly. But I know no fear. No wolf,
no cougar. I am short-sighted bear

and shamble wilderness, as though I own it,
the chocolate lily on the grading that bore
a railroad a hundred years ago, taking

skeletons of cedar to men. All the men
with sweat from their mouths. Plank holes
chopped in trunks, and double-ended

blades with teeth many inches deep.
Now, the bones of elk starve perfectly,
fed on by mosses taking them to calcium.

The white hair, the white bone, the white owl
become a winter. What else is there to know?
Ah, the maple tree, grown from shore,

topples a century into river. So many
questions. Such indifferent curiosity.
No one eats a carnivore.

Photography by Derek von Essen.

DC Reid is a past president of the Federation of BC Writers and the League of Canadian Poets. DC Reid writes: "This poem is from my 8th manuscript of poems: *These Elegies*. My most recent award is the 2016 national Roderick Haig-Brown Award for sustained environmental writing. My current book of poems is: *The Spirit of the Thing and the Thing Itself*, a formalist book of glosas."

Food: A Fairy Tale

TERENCE YOUNG

The parents grew the usual things in their backyard—not a victory
garden because this was after the war—mostly carrots and peas, which

the children they'd always dreamed of having liked very much, and
chard and spinach, which the children hated, and reams of raspberries

that the mother boiled into jars of jam for the winter, along with
pears for dessert and apple sauce made from the Kings on their tree,

filling the preserve cupboard in the basement, until one day
the parents stopped gardening and sowed the beds with easy grass

and bought food from the new supermarket, which the children liked
equally well, or even better, and the years passed and the children

grew into hippies and took a stab at growing their own lettuce and
tomatoes in the middle of forests where the soil was piss poor

and so deficient in nutrients that the lettuce shot up broad and
pale green and the tomatoes bore no fruit at all, and the children

gave up and moved into the city where they had their own children
who grew up far too quickly and turned their backs on dairy and meat

and eggs and forced their parents to shun all processed food and to
tear up the lawn for potatoes and broccoli and kale and onions and

beans and beets, advising them on appropriate methods of pruning and
fertilizing and rotation, so that in the end their parents found

something about their lives they had forgotten and got their hands
dirty with manure and compost, instead, and sat at the dining room

table with their children and grandchildren filling their faces with salad
after salad and teriyaki beans and roasted fennel root, raising their

glasses of homemade beer and toasting their labours, the wisdom
of the young, and the boundless patience of the good earth.

Terence Young lives in Victoria, BC, where he teaches English and creative writing at St. Michaels University School.

The First Vegans

PATRICIA YOUNG

> *Heart attacks—God's revenge for eating his little animal friends.*
> —Anonymous

In the beginning Adam and Eve spent their days gaping.
Their eyes bulged and their jaws hung slack.
Look at this. What's that? Who made that hooting sound? Did you?

They gaped at the persimmon-streaked sky,
a dewdrop balanced on the tip of a leaf.
The moon! Dangling white orb.
They gaped at water, the way it trickled
over rocks and through their fingers.
Gaped at each other, their wondrous beauty,
and also their own twiddling thumbs.

They wandered the garden, plucking breakfast
straight off the trees. Pulled lunch out of the ground.
Munched and grazed through dinner.
Like the other herbivores, their intestinal tracts
were long and convoluted, their molars flat.
Even the dirt tasted good enough eat.

In time they grew bored of Eden's cornucopia.
Life had become a succession of peeling rinds, grinding nuts,
spitting out husks. One morning Eve woke with strange
hankerings. She set to work inventing things:
knife, spoon, pot, recipe. Experimented
with roasting and broiling, sauces and marinades.

You're a genius, babe, Adam said, nuzzling her neck
after a hard day of naming the animals.
Puleease, she said, *it's the least a helpmeet can do.*

Evening meals were now elaborate feasts,
after which they'd make buoyant love, then gape
at each other until they fell into a deep and heavenly sleep.

The first baby arrived. Then another and another.
Every nine months a baby popped out.
Eve was fond of them, sure, but they were so helpless
and needed her, body and soul.
                                        Soul?
She furrowed her brow. *Adam, honey, what's a soul?*

No time now for chopping or dicing, mashing or mincing.
Who had the patience for de-seeding a pomegranate
just to garnish a yam and chickpea tajine?
Vegetables were more demanding than babies.

And then the night in bed when she moaned,
Can't do it anymore. Grate another carrot. Hack up another cabbage.
Besides, the kids hate cabbage, hate turnip, hate eggplant.

Adam grunted. *Want me to speak to Yahweh?*
Eve stroked her husband's belly, her fingers like the tendrils
of young pea shoots. *Oh no,* she whispered, *don't bother Him.*
You're a smart guy. You'll think of something . . .

Patricia Young has published thirteen collections of poetry, one collection of fiction
and five chapbooks. Her work has been widely anthologized. Baseline Press will publish
Consider the Paragliders in the fall of 2017 and Gooselane Editions will publish
Amateurs at Love in 2018. "The First Vegans," was first published in *The Antigonish
Review* and then in *Short Takes on the Apocalypse*, published with Biblioasis.

Supply and Demand

ADRIENNE GRUBER

Jan 30th

D goes back to work. I lactate. The midwife listens
to the tiny heart. Massages my belly. Jots down weight
before and after feeds. Mom makes virgin cocktails.
Dismantles the birth pool. Moves the table back into place.
We eat dinner. Nursling sleeps in the bassinet. The first and
only time.

Jan 31st

Suckle and snooze. Spine fused and barbed against
pillows piled into a throne. Udders leak and mix with drool.
Cat sleeps on her face again. People visit with gifts.
Flowers, balloons. Lasagna. We trance in stupor
of the newly dead. I wet the bed with my tits.

Feb 1st

No one wakes with us at night. Exhaustion
is nebulous. It asphyxiates. My brain ossifies
by the flush of bedside lamp. My breasts are
sacks of rubble. Inamorata widens her heavy
navy eyes. She knows everything.

Feb 2nd

D sings her to sleep in the crook of his arm.
I wrench her, a clammy question mark. Feed her
after midnight (it's okay, she isn't a gremlin).
My bedroom is a back alley. Used diapers, take out
containers, breast pump. Granola bars. Lonely texts. Netflix.

Feb 3rd

Postpartum—the sewage system of a shrunken world.
She splays my chest. Starfish. Milk wastes under her weight.
My stomach is a flaccid blueprint of her past life.
Vacancy sings. It was a good harvest.
You pat my belly, the old stomping grounds.

Adrienne Gruber is the author of two full-length poetry collections, *Buoyancy Control*
(BookThug) and *This is the Nightmare* (Thistledown Press), and three chapbooks, *Mimic*
(Leaf Press), *Everything Water* (Cactus Press) and *Intertidal Zones* (Jack Pine Press).

The Chocolatier's Place

RUTH DANIELL

Purdys Chocolate Factory, Vancouver, BC
    for Rachel McKinley

During the factory tour a candymaker asks you a question
and you walk away, gesturing towards a giant tray
where an apprentice is smoothing down clouds
of marshmallow in rhythmic motions with a flat knife—

Why don't you watch while you wait, you say,
and I am wide-eyed. There is something mythic
about this place. An exaggerated scale of
sweetness in the world. One thousand kilograms

of sugar is suspended in a bag on the ceiling.
And here marshmallow is poured in a tray
the length of the kind of silver-rimmed slide
that delights children in city parks.

The apprentice presses the soft candy flat,
he is methodical and sincere. Asks me
where I'm from. I say, Here. He tells me
about India. India has the same moon

as we do here, the same sun, and clouds
like marshmallow poured warm across
a long cool silver tray. You return
to hear me say, I especially like marshmallows.

You smile at my declaration. I know that.
Of course. I used to come to your little shop
for hot chocolate and handmade marshmallows
every week. And now you are here

in this factory that reaches into so many other
places. Hundreds of chocolates will travel
in gold-papered packages so much farther
then the orange crème you hand me off the line.

*

Place is important. You've found yours.
In your test kitchen we chat about your wedding
as you invent a chocolate marshmallow lemon tart.
Last summer you were married in an afternoon

after you attended a funereal in the morning.
This is why we do this thing, you affirm,
We have this ceremony so that years later
we have this other ceremony. It was sad

but it was also celebratory. In happiness
the man had lived with his wife until he died.
That's kind of the point. You grate lemon curd
into a bowl of cloudy chocolate. I want to

redeem a cliché, you explain. Phenyl ethyl alanine
is an adapted amino acid present in chocolate
and also generated in our neurological system
when we are physically close to someone.

Infants have the highest level because they are
are always being held. We all want to be held.
Eating chocolate is like eating a hug, eating the act
of kissing, of being in a place where we are loved.

*

Food tastes differently depending on whom
you are with and where you are. You recount
a kitchen party in Manitoba. You do not like coffee.
But after eleven courses your host offers you

a tiny cup of espresso with sugar. Thick as motor oil,
it is sweet and delicious and non-repeatable.
It becomes a narrative. A cumulative experience.
These are the stories that you want to tell.

Imagine, you ask me. Imagine you are canoeing
on the west coast on a hot summer day
and you stop at one of the small islands
and from out of your canoe you pull out a basket

and from the basket you pull a fresh Okanagan peach
and you eat it. You smell the salt of the ocean air
and you taste the sweet juice of the peach.
It will be the best thing you have ever tasted.

I nod. In a place like this it is easy to believe
that life is a series of best things. It is easy
to accept a slice of chocolate marshmallow lemon tart,
still warm, fresh from your imagination.

About our collaboration:
Ruth: I first met Rachel when I was a regular customer of her shop, CocoaNymph, which used to be near the corner of Alma and 10th. While I was still a grad student at UBC, I would go to CocoaNymph for hot chocolate and marshmallows and sit down with drafts of my poems and sip. There, in the cozy, pillow-laden nook by the window, I came up with the idea for Swoon, the reading series on love, sex, and chocolate that I founded in spring 2013. Before Rachel had to close CocoaNymph's doors, CocoaNymph was Swoon's home. Cocoa-Nymph, and Rachel, were integral parts of my community as a writer and as a person seeking comfort in the big city. I brought several friends to CocoaNymph with me, too, for long conversations about writing and love and sex and the weather (so much rain! Such a perfect reason to drink hot chocolate!). Some of my favourite conversations, however, while I sat there sipping my hot chocolate, were those with the person whose delicious creations I was enjoying so completely. Rachel indulged me in questions about the creative process and chocolate. We stayed in touch even after her shop closed. I've followed her adventures and was thrilled when she became the newest chocolatier for Purdys Chocolates at their Vancouver factory. When I first saw the call for Sweet Verse submissions, I knew immediately that I had to ask Rachel to talk to me about chocolate again.

Rachel: It usually took a few visits before a customer became a regular, and a few visits more before they became a friend, but when Ruth walked into my store the first time, her smile lit up the room and her humour brightened an otherwise challenging day. I felt connected from the start. She continued to visit with her friend and colleague Jeffery Ricker, and their antics always delighted me. Her love of chocolate and her ability to take the commonplace and spin it into fairy gold was evident in everything she did—her manner of dress, her calm yet vibrant mannerisms. I was so pleased when she humoured me with some reading of my own work at Swoon, and am always pleased when I get to hug her and hang out. It was a true pleasure to share my love of chocolate with her.

Sad Smiles

ANWER GHANI

The Iraqis can't live without war or *kebab* and can't smell morning breeze without their red voices. I'm an Iraqi man; my soul has been kneaded with war's tales and *kebab's* lure. Our streets have been immersed in its perfume and the dry desert of our sad sumac has coloured its lips. Look at their eyes; our girls always dream on days without fire. The *kebab*, which we inherited from our Babylonian ancestors, can't be made without our tears and you always need the sad smiles of Iraqis to experience its glory.

Anwer Ghani is an Iraqi poet and writer born in Alhilla. His work has appeared in *Adelaide, Zarf, Peacock, Otoliths, Algebra of Owls,* and others. He is the founder of "Expressive Narratives Group" and the chief editor of *Arcs* an expressive narratives magazine. He has, in Arabic, forty books of poetry, literature, and religious sciences.

Clean

KATE BRAID

> With thanks to Seamus Heaney for "Markings"
> For my aunties, Kelly and Kathleen

You loved the shine of clean pots,
round hosts of your kitchen where
(hot water steaming), reflections off glass
sang clean. Each utensil and dish was baptized
daily into the holiness of soap and water.
The wet lines of your mop marked the spot
beyond which dirt dared not go,
all swept with the Christian rod
of elbow grease, hot water and will.

You entered your cleaning with a full heart,
as if it was you being cleansed by water and soap.
Crusade. Your vacuum parted red seas of shag,
polisher spun floors into bright shining halos.
Your own arms lifted you closer
to the purity of white so that you seemed to give off light,
to rise above the dark shadows in your bucket,
never looked down
into the halo of its dangerous dark water
reflecting back at you.

Kate Braid has written, co-written and co-edited fourteen books of non-fiction and prize-winning poetry. See www.katebraid.com

Simple Foods

SONYA LITTLEJOHN

My father's culinary past is:
Mostly simple foods
Eat it all.
Ration the best things.
Don't live on milk.
And a sense of humour
will get you through anything.
Even war.
Creamy potato leek soup is creamier with coconut.
If you haven't got much
use the old wilting spinach and the drying kale.
It's all good, until it's bad.
Don't use the green potato, as is.
Peel it down to the white flesh.
The green is toxic.
An old banana can replace an egg in your baking.
Cook the black-eyed peas in three cups of water, boiling for five minutes.
Let sit off the heat in the hot water for one hour.
Drain and cook in three times the volume of water or stock,
for forty minutes to one hour.
Make sure these are fully cooked as well.
They can also be toxic.
You could probably make a meatloaf
with a couple cans of corned beef hash
or ground spam
and some old bread.
I've never tried it, but I bet you could.
There is risk in everything.
Everything can be simplified.
Even simplicity can be delicious.
Delicious doesn't have to cost an arm and a leg.
But it can, and some prefer it that way,
but that's anything but simple.

Sonya Littlejohn is a British Columbia based poet and language arts facilitator. Sonya's second poem, "Grey: a Biracial Poem" was published in *Other Tongues: Mixed Race Women Speak Out* an anthology of poetry about cultural identity, by Inanna Press in 2010.

Check the Ingredients!

AYLA MAXWELL

Allergies are one of the most confusing things that can ever happen to you. When I was little I got upset about everything. I could not put my socks on without crying. When I was five my mom got diagnosed with celiac disease which means she was badly allergic to wheat. I still was getting upset a lot so my mom said that maybe I was allergic too. She said that one of the most effective ways to know was to get a blood test. I'm the kind of kid who gets scared about everything so if you ask me "hey want a blood test?" the answer is definitely going to be NO but I agreed to at least try to go off gluten. So until I was around eight, I did not eat wheat. One day I said that I did not want to just guess that I was allergic any more so my mom took me to a kind of doctor that does that sort of thing and don't even get me started on how much that hurt (I have very small veins, apparently). When the test results came back it said that I was allergic to whey, gluten and a bunch of other stuff. So then I was off gluten and dairy which for an eight year old does not leave much. After I turned nine I decided I wanted to be a pescatarian (basically a vegetarian that eats fish) but that really did not leave me much to eat. Now I'm eleven and I can eat whatever I want. Don't ask, I don't even know. It's still hard to know what is good for me and what is bad. If you know someone who is allergic to something especially gluten, my advice is take some time to find out what it is, be supportive and DON'T eat the food they can't eat in front of them!

Ayla Maxwell is a grade six student at Charles Dickens elementary and she loves animals, especially sloths!

Green Gun Garden

MURRAY REISS

I'm filling my virtual shopping cart at the *Guns 'n' Gardens* website —
       Is your *Food Security State*
under seige? — It is, oh yes, it is; and I've just clicked on

the remote-controlled predator drone and joy-stick combo to blast
       the next few dozen quail try to bury
my tender transplants in mountains of scratched-up mulch.

Throw in the spy-eye module with built-in buzzer alarm,
       I can fry them
from the comfort of my bed. *Are* you *fghting a losing battle against*

Mother Nature's minions? I am, oh yes, I am
       pondering the Seven-Setting Tase-a-Slug,
with Adjust-A-Jolt for every size from tiny pearly-greys

that munch kale leaves to a lacy flutter to monstrous
       banana slugs that swallow
baby broccolis in a single slimy gulp, but a starred review

warns the stench can make you gag,
       but a 90-day money-back guarantee …
Go retro on your rabbits! blares a banner ad. I toss in

the shotgun with organic biodegradable soy-based
       fish meal buckshot—
Feed your soil while you save your carrots! — a combo hard

to resist. When I was a Buddhist I vowed to train myself to refrain
          from harming life.
As an anarcho-pacifist I tried to overthrow the state

by peaceful means. But now I'm a man of the soil, gone
          back to Old Testament roots.
An eye for an eye — do they have eyes? — those pillbugs

who colonize my greenhouse? No sooner do spindly seedlings
          poke through the cedar box soil
than they're gone. Like the pillbugs, once I've deployed

my crustacean-seeking NanoDestroyBots —
          a battle-hardened battle-ready
battalion you can barely see for fifty bucks!

To keep from getting too carried away I'm tabbing back and forth
          between Guns 'n' Gardens
and costpercarrot.com, a cool conversion site that tells you —

once you plug in square footage, crop, expected yield, soil
          amendments, likely weather,
planting dates, and growing zone — just how much you've spent

per carrot, cucumber, pod of peas, and I'm inching
          into the red zone,
the-ten-dollar-a-carrot-and-up zone, so I figure I'll scale back

the bots from battalion to squad, agility over firepower,
          nimbleness over numbers,
and spend the rest to crush invading tent caterpillar hordes

in their cocoons. But do I opt for the laser's surgical strike,
          or the broadband
blast of the blowtorch — or go for broke, buy them both, decapitate

and incinerate — *Can* you *destroy your orchard*
          to save it?
Can *I* remember when I gardened out of love?

Murray Reiss lives on Salt Spring Island. His first book, *The Survival Rate of Butterflies in the Wild* won the League of Canadian Poets' 2014 Gerald Lampert Memorial Award for the best first book of poetry. His second book, *Cemetery Compost*, came out in 2016. Reiss brings his poetry to life on the stage as well as the page as a Climate Action Performance Poet and founding member of the Only Planet Cabaret.

Muffin Shop

FERNANDO RAGUERO

I want to open up a muffin shop
call it Damn Muffins
I want people to come in and say
I'll have a damn muffin
I would get a kick out of
this every time they did
an in joke taken to elaborate extremes
I'll be the only one who
thinks it's funny
but that's nothing new
it'll be a one man operation to keep overhead low
I'll live in the room at the back
furnished with a futon and a radio
a hot plate and all the great books
I've always wanted to
read but never had time to
between damn muffin
sales I'll pull out
Moby Dick or *A Tale of Two Cities*
I'll wake up at five every morning to
bake the damn muffins
I'll be dedicated like a farmer
but instead of

milking the damn cows I'll
be sprinkling blueberries and walnuts
on damn muffin dough
this will be my life and it will be good
it will be a one man operation to keep overhead low
my muffins will be the
best damn muffins around because of all the love
and care I'll put into them
it'll be the only thing I do besides read
my life will be muffins and books
books and muffins
I won't sell anything else
no damn biscotti
no damn sausage rolls
no damn soup
if someone asks for a fucking coffee
I'll tell them to go next door to my brother's
people will come from
miles around by word of mouth
to eat my damn muffins
because I'll have cool flavors
with hippie names like
sunshine and barefoot flower
it'll become popular
it'll get hectic
I'll think about expanding
maybe hire someone to help out
but I won't
it'll remain like sex with myself
a one man operation to keep overhead low
I'll get franchise offers but I'll refuse them
I don't ever want to get big and evil
like Starbucks
I'll stay a mom and pop outfit
without the mom
without the pop
just me in my
small corner of the world
happy doing what I love to do
selling my damn muffins
reading my damn books
and laughing at my own
jokes

Fernando Raguero is a Vancouver based poet. He has his moments.

My Mixed Up Past

PHOENIX WINTER

I am a berry compote, consisting of a mish-mash of flavours. No *pure* for me, no bleached blonde advertising white, white milk. Call it lactose intolerant, call it colour-loving, call it fresh from the cow pasteurized and not organic. We want our mixtures, our fruit smoothies, our hemp hearts.

I was born *masala* and chai tea, curry and turmeric with its health benefits, and *dahi,* which is yogurt, sitting on the counter, fermenting milk in the kitchen sunlight placed there by my father. Plates of mince, known here as ground beef, on a large bed of jasmine rice, clashing with my mother's *kartoffel kuchen*—potato pancakes and sauerkraut, red boiled cabbage and hearty lentil soup.

The tastes clashed, caused indigestion and left us sitting at the table, unsure where our loyalties lay. I loved boiled beef tongue, crispy on the outside, the way my mother made it. It was exuberant, unlike the silence that descended at the supper table, where children should be seen and not heard. My growling stomach disagrees, betraying me, because I am a berry compote, and still slightly sweet.

From *The Menu,* Otter Press, 2016.

Phoenix Winter is getting old, but isn't over the hill yet. She has done a homeless tour across Canada and is grateful to have landed on the West Coast by virtue of a bus ticket that got stolen, keeping her here. She is grateful for the company and people that are like family in the DTES. She has one son, Hunter, of whom she is very proud. Being a mother was one of the best things she ever did.

Ricey Dancing

FRED WAH

I finally realized I had to find out how to cook rice. My craving for the food I was raised on demanded an action more immediate than catching a bus on 10th just outside the UBC gates and hoofing it down Hastings to Chinatown. There was, of course, the Varsity Grill next to the Varsity Theatre where I'd sometimes take my girlfriend and we'd order a "two-for-one" for two; something like chicken *chop suey* and egg *foo yung* with some steamed rice with two plates, around $2.40. But the Varsity closed early in the evening and I'd get this incredible craving for rice around 10:30 p.m. when I was studying late or I'd just got home from a night in the library.

So when I was home that summer I started to watch my dad when he cooked supper for us. The rice, it turned out, was easy: water just a finger thickness over the rice. The stir-fry was a little more challenging. After he'd done all that chopping (green peppers, celery, onion, broccoli, carrots, Chinese mushrooms, chicken or beef), I needed to perfect a perfect slap with the flat of a butcher knife on a chunk of garlic on the wood chopping board. My garlic just splattered over the counter in little pieces; Dad's was as flat as a dime, and in one piece, that he then chopped into slivers. How much soy sauce? Oh, about two of these spoonfuls; he held up the worn-out wooden spoon he used for stirring the dish. Ginger? The end of your thumb. And the corn starch to thicken? Just enough to make a little paste in the bottom of the dish.

It really wasn't too difficult. I made some notes so when I went back to UBC in the fall I'd know what to buy and roughly how to put it together.

But what he didn't talk about when he was cooking was, for me, one of the most important things I learned from him: rhythm. Cooking needs rhythm.

And when it comes to a stir-fry, the rhythm is fast and with the same feeling of purpose as kicking that solid kitchen door in the cafe. I just picked it up somehow, I guess, from simply being there, in tune with him moving over the counter and stove in a dance of hands, shoulders and feet, flip, shovel, stir, slice, scrape, mix, all improvised in a rush alongside the sounds of the grease crackling and the frying pan (we didn't own a wok) scraping over the stove. I don't think I consciously watched him do his cookery dance when I was just a kid, sitting at the kitchen table, but it's there, in some corner of my body, and I can feel it when I cook. Some taste of urgency moves me over the ingredients and pots and utensils in a rhythm of intention and speed. That rhythm is as natural and expected as the rice simmering on the back burner, though my precipitous movements around the kitchen are an irritant to my wife's more relaxed approach to making a meal. But I can hardly cook without that rush; some genetic pocket of appetite spurs me into combinations of necessity—locate, chop, brown, crush—and I move with gusto between the counters, sink, and stove— a little salt in the rice water, don't forget to soak the mushrooms, just a pinch of pepper, shot of whiskey on the meat —until it all comes together lightly touched with heat, steamed, fried, and tossed and then, "you mucka high," there, garnish with chopped onions, some cilantro, maybe some Thai hot sauce, a pot of steamed rice, that's it, done! Then settle down into the savour, the tongue, slow and quiet in its tasting and its memories.

First published in *Apples Under the Bed*, ed. Joan Caldwell, Hedgerow Press, 2007.

Vancouver poet Fred Wah is the essayist of *Faking It: Poetics and Hybridity*. Some of his recent poetry can be seen at highmuckamuck.ca and in recent collections: *Is a Door*, *Sentenced to Light*, and *Scree: The Collected Earlier Poems, 1962-1991*.

Everything Makes Broth

EUFEMIA FANTETTI

My father calls me every evening and asks, "Have you eaten?"

He buys triple the produce he needs and pressures me to take the extras home. After a meal where I've already stuffed my face with two, possibly three servings of greens, carbs and chicken, he suggests a slice of Swiss cheese. Or a piece of cantaloupe. Or a plate of roasted chestnuts. I tense up wondering why I never have a big enough appetite to suffice, to stop his endless offerings.

I take deep breaths and remind myself my father frequently went hungry during his childhood—he turned two only a few weeks after Mussolini aligned with Nazi Germany. Sometimes he ate *pasta fagioli* (pasta with kidney beans), *rapini* (a bitter, leafier Italian broccoli), green beans and on a few special occasions, rabbit or chicken. Growing up in Toronto, I stuffed my face with rippled chips, Cheezies, licorice, sour keys, Fudgsicles, and Creamsicles as frequently as possible. On my birthday, we feasted on a *torta*—an Italian sponge cake (three layers) flavoured with rum syrup (sugary goodness) that also contained a layer of vanilla custard, a layer of chocolate custard and was covered in buttercream. His diet was basic and mine was luxurious.

I was badgered daily to eat and considered wasteful or ungrateful when I wasn't hungry. My father didn't starve but experienced intense lack of needed protein with barely any eggs to eat and scarcely enough meat. He was rejected by Italy's mandatory army duty due to being underweight; a young man of six feet, one hundred and twenty pounds—he was considered too skinny, too scrawny to serve.

I hardly had room in my full stomach for my father's carefully prepared prosciutto. I was laid back about the spiced Italian sausages, lean with little fat. I would shrug my shoulders, indifferent to the barbecued filet mignon wrapped in bacon.

At twenty-two, my father learned a trade so he would never be out of work and would always be able to feed his family. He was trained in Switzerland and then worked as a butcher for forty-six years.

I laboured for eight months at a McDonald's when I was 16-years-old. My supervisor taught me the motto *time to lean, time to clean.*

My dad's boss immediately noticed his mathematical ability, attention to painstaking detail, and strong (Catholic) work ethic.

I was a waitress for a year in a sushi restaurant when I was twenty-four, scrambling to make rent and grocery money on paltry tips and not enough shifts, embarrassed that my father would step in to save me.

I was weighed weekly from the time I was seven until I was thirteen. My father presented the scale with flourish: a fun activity and opportunity to calm his anxiety that I wasn't getting enough to eat for a growing kid.

He took it as a personal insult when I flirted with vegetarianism in my early 20s and rejected his mouth-watering fare: bacon, lamb, veal, pork chops, steak. I was casting aspersions on his ability to parent.

We quarreled. He insisted I knew nothing about suffering because I'd had a roof over my head and food on the table. He took my complaints about my less-than-idyllic childhood hard.

I argued some elements went unnourished in both of us. My dad countered that the essentials were taken care of, the parts that fortified stomachs and built muscle. I had the basics I needed to survive. *Tutto fa brodo*—every little bit helps.

We still argue about foodstuff. I honour his age-old hunger every time I quietly accept the groceries.

Eufemia Fantetti is a graduate of the Writer's Studio at SFU and the University of Guelph's MFA in Creative Writing. Her first book, *A Recipe for Disaster & Other Unlikely Tales of Love* (Mother Tongue Publishing) was runner up for the Danuta Gleed Literary Award and won a Bressani Prize.

Recipe for Greatness

LOOKS BOTH WAYS WOMAN

From nine to thirteen-years-old, I ate burnt food, lumpy tasteless food, curdled and sour milk, mildewed bread, stale and hard. One day the principal of the residential school announced that if anyone joined the track and field team, they would be treated special and fed well—bacon and eggs for breakfast. Bacon and eggs motivated me. Blessed good bacon and eggs, what a blessing! We started training for various events from March to June. Because of bacon and eggs I became a very good athlete. I won seven firsts in seven events every year for three years, savouring bacon and eggs every morning. I couldn't compete in the 4th year because I sprained my ankle at the beginning of the track meet. And you know what —I hated every second, minute and hour of it but I loved the bacon and eggs.

Bacon and Eggs
Ready in 60 minutes
Serves 30 students

INGREDIENTS
· 5 dozen free-range chicken eggs picked fresh every day
· 6 lbs of bacon
· 5 loaves of white bread
· 1 litre of margarine
· 4 gallons of fresh cows milk

DIRECTIONS
· Preheat 2 grills (big industrial)
· Ready when grill sizzles with water
· Pour oil on grill as needed ~ 6 tbsp
· Place strips of bacon on one and crack the eggs on the other
· Put bread in industrial toaster and butter as they fall
· Turn bacon until brown on both sides
· Turn over eggs until medium well done
· Serve to track and field team

Looks Both Ways Woman is of the *Kainai* tribe of the Blackfoot Confederacy.

Yemeni Soup

AYELET TSABARI

At thirty-five, I learned how to make Yemeni soup.

It was winter in Vancouver, dreary and cold, and my naturopath advised me to eat more soups.

I never liked Yemeni soup as a child, hated how turmeric stained my fingers yellow, scowled at the wilted cilantro, despised *hilbe*, a ground fenugreek paste that clouded the clear soup the way water fogged Arak. *Hilbe* emanated from your pores the following day, a tang Yemenis were often mocked for. Whenever Yemeni soup was served at my grandmother's house, I sulked, refused to eat it, and left to play outside.

Yemeni soup was one of the dishes my mother had learned from her mother after she got married. It was a recipe my grandmother had learned from her aunt who raised her in Yemen, a recipe that made it through the desert and across the sea, surviving for decades, never written down.

When my mother grew up, this soup constituted their weekly serving of meat. My grandmother gave the wings to the girls so they could fly away, marry off, and the legs to the boys, so they could form the foundation of the house.

My mother and I met in Los Angeles for one week in November, where my sister and her family were living at the time. "I'm making Yemeni soup," my mother said. "I even brought *hawayij*."

I opened the brown paper bag and sniffed it, the blend of spices instantly transporting me into her kitchen.

This time I got to watch as she prepared the soup, scribbling the steps on the back of a used envelope. We stood side by side, shoulders touching, gazing into the pot, waiting for the water to boil. She added chicken drumsticks and thighs and dished the excess fat out with a spoon. She dropped in a full onion, which would later disintegrate into translucent rings, and chunks of tomato, pepper, potatoes and carrots. She sliced garlic straight into the pot, and finally, threw in an entire bouquet of cilantro. While she poured *hawayij* into the soup, I stirred the yellow into the water with a wooden spoon.

The aroma of Yemeni soup lingers in my kitchen for days after I cook it. I grew up trying to shake this smell off me. Now it lives in my house, a permanent stamp on my walls, a pungent greeting that welcomes my guests. When the *hawayij* my mother had given me in Los Angeles was finished I started making my own: grinding cardamom, cumin, turmeric, chillies and coriander in a mortar and pestle, the way my grandmother and great grandmother had done before me. When I stand by my electric stove and pour *hawayij* into the pot, I'm a Jewish Yemeni woman making soup. I forget I live in a cold and strange city, ten timezones away from my family. I belong.

This piece was originally published online at www.themagazineschool.ca and is forthcoming in Tsabari's next book.

Ayelet Tsabari's book *The Best Place on Earth* won the Sami Rohr Prize for Jewish literature and the Edward Lewis Wallant Award. The book was a New York Times' editors' choice and has been published internationally.

A Fish Camp Story from My Childhood

T'UY'T'TANAT-CECILIA "CEASE" WYSS

From my earliest memories of my childhood, I always remember the fish camp stories as being amongst my favourite times. I grew up with my parents and siblings living in several rental homes and a couple of different homes we owned.

Because my mother is of two Coast Salish cultures, *Sto:Lo* from her mother's side and *Skwxwu7mesh* from her father's side of the family, we were always travelling throughout my grandparents' traditional villages gathering and trading for our traditional foods. My favourite foods are still wild berries and wild salmon.

My father, who was of European culture, specifically Swiss, was always questioned why he, being "white" (as he was referred to mainly by settlers and specifically, the police), was travelling with "Indians"—also mostly references made by police.

We had to travel long distances between my grandparents' homes, which were located several miles between each community. My grandmother's community is where the Fraser and Harrison Rivers meet and my grandfather's community is comprised of the City of Vancouver, the districts of North and West Vancouver, the towns of Squamish and Whistler and the southern part of the Sunshine Coast including all of Howe Sound. His family's winter home was in North

Vancouver and the family's summer home was north of the town of Brackendale. So I grew up doing various road trips with our family. Sometimes cousins, aunts and uncles travelled with us in our vehicle, or by mini convoy. We would go set up fish camps and spend a day or two setting nets and then checking them.

Our fish camps could be in the Fraser and Harrison Rivers or in the Squamish River. It always depended where my grandparents chose to go. We would alternate, mainly out of respect for the salmon stocks. And it was a seasonal choice, too. Whatever was running at the time was a big deciding factor.

We always had to time it so as to try to avoid being pulled over by the authorities. The local police and the RCMP were always watching for the native folks driving about during fishing seasons, especially with non-native passengers.

My dad was always made to pull over. Then they forced him to open the trunk and then we waited while they looked through the trunk of the car. Our salmon would get seized every time. The police always gave fines to my parents for bringing our salmon off the reserves. They would claim they had a law for us to follow. They were always stating we were breaking these laws by driving from the rivers to our homes, as "this was not reserve land anymore." They always gave him a fine for "buying salmon from the natives," even though he was simply driving his mixed-blood family home. My parents did equal time in court defending our rights to cultural food fishing, to the hours we spent in the river catching salmon in our nets.

One time my mom decided to leave the fish camp super early, like 4:30 a.m., because it was going to be really hot that day. It was in Yale, just a little north of the community of *Sts'ailes*, also known as Chehalis. She actually made it home to North Vancouver without being stopped once by any authorities! My dad stayed behind with us three kids and our grandparents, and they caught a few more salmon before we left. We cleaned up the camp and loaded up the car. Just as we were leaving the forest road by the river the police stopped us. They asked my grandparents why "the white guy was driving" them out of the forest. They said he was their son-in-law, but the police didn't believe us. They made him open the trunk and removed our salmon, accusing him of "illegally purchasing fish from the Indians."

When he went to court and was questioned about this by the judge, he explained his situation and then it came to light in court, as it often did, that he was in fact, married to the family he was with, and his wife was indeed, an indigenous woman. So the charges were thrown out that day. We didn't get all charges removed every time, but that day was a day of victory!

The amount of salmon taken from us over many years is a high number. We are a family that spent our seasons gathering, fishing, hunting and trading for our cultural foods. We were never given anything back through the many court cases we attended and the fines were only sometimes dropped. But we never stopped trying to get our salmon home. We never bowed down to the authorities. My parents and grandparents always taught me that I have inherent rights to hunt, fish, gather and trade for our cultural foods.

I cannot imagine what the future will be like if we do not protect our natural world that has gifted us so many endless treasures in the way of traditional foods. This past year I received two small salmon, two jars of salmon and some smoked and wind dried salmon. That was all I managed to store for my winter supply in my home in over a year. I cannot really go fishing because of climate change and the levels of water dropping which are killing our salmon.

The temperatures are higher now than when I was younger and the laws have been more in favour of commercial and sport fishermen than indigenous peoples. The water levels are lower and it's becoming too hot for salmon to properly run in rivers and creeks except when it's cooler out or at night when the water temperature is also cooler. There is an alarming increase in fish farms which have added health risks to wild salmon due to the fact the salmon are forced to be confined in pools in the ocean water, and swim in their own feces. There a number of other factors that contribute to health issues that affect the farmed salmon and the wild salmon they encounter. They also carry and spread sea lice that feed off salmon fry and young wild salmon.

The fact that I grew up watching my parents fill big American car trunks with salmon, which equals about a couple of hundred pounds of salmon every year, and despite the fact that it was often confiscated from us, we had enough salmon to feed my mom's eight siblings and their children, plus ourselves and my grandparents every year. In more recent years, and to be honest, our worst years, we always had at least twenty good-sized salmon each, in our communities.

I now dedicate my time throughout the year, every year for several years now, to helping with efforts to protect our wild salmon and their natural habitats. I love salmon and I feel better when I get to eat wild salmon. It is heartbreaking to be witness to the extreme decline in salmon stocks, and to grow up being accused of contributing to the decline in salmon stocks, too. The fact that indigenous people have always sustained our traditional resources in our respectful way of living in harmony with the natural world for thousands of years, and in less than 100 years seeing one of many natural resources disappear before our eyes, with our hands tied, is nothing short of devastating. I ask of everyone I meet and know, please help save the natural world beings and their environments. Human beings owe everything to the natural world. Everything.

Photograph by Derek von Essen.

T'uy't'tanat-Cecilia "Cease" Wyss is an interdisciplinary artist who works with new media, is an ethnobotanist and more recently has returned to her textiles art practice through learning Coast Salish weaving techniques. She is a member of the Aboriginal Writers Collective West Coast and lives in East Vancouver. She is a beekeeper and community engaged gardener.

Overfishing

CALEB HADDON and SAM

All around Canada and the rest of the world many types of fish are being endangered by overfishing. Fish like the blobfish are almost extinct because of deep sea trawling. As well, the rockfish, whose species was fished so much that fishing for it was outlawed. The sushi industry is also growing rapidly and with it the fish population declining. Fish farms are using GMOs on fish to make them grow larger and faster and large fishing industries use deep sea trawling to get more fish but lots of what they catch is inedible such as the above mentioned blobfish.

Jellyfish blooms are clogging nets so much that a machine has been invented for the sole purpose of shredding jellyfish. If we stopped fishing in the summer or winter to let fish populations replenish we could eat more fish during the other seasons or if we ate less fish all the time we could get the same result. In conclusion, we would like to say that large scale fishing such as deep sea trawling is appalling and in our opinion, we should do everything within our power to stop it.

Photograph by Derek von Essen.

Caleb is twelve years old and goes to Charles Dickens Elementary. He likes card games such as MTG, the ocean and burgers. He hopes to one day become a marine biologist or play in the Magic: The Gathering pro tour. He has two dogs and his favourite animal is the blobfish.

Sam is twelve years old and goes to Charles Dickens Elementary. Sam enjoys card and tabletop games. He also likes pizza and chocolate. He would like to be a Warhammer model designer. He would also like to play in the Magic: The Gathering pro tour. Favourite animal: Pufferfish.

The Carnegie Kitchen Interviews 2017

JAMES WITWICKI and JESSICA LEE

The Carnegie Community Centre at the corner of Hastings and Main Street is the beating heart of Vancouver's Downtown Eastside. This "heart" has achieved an almost mythical quality in our neighbourhood. The Carnegie was almost demolished in the 1970s. Activism saved it. There was a plan to connect the Georgia and Dunsmuir Viaducts to the Trans Canada Highway, a move which would have virtually wiped out Strathcona (an alternate name for this neighbourhood) in the same way that the viaducts themselves eliminated the vibrant Hogan's Alley community.

Certainly, a number of local legends have worked in and around the Carnegie Centre, including poets Bud Osborn and Evelyn Lau and activists Jim Green, Wendy Pedersen and Jean Swanson. These and innumerable others have looked to Carnegie as a source of ideas, inspiration and incredible food! Included in this group are upwards of one hundred volunteers who help out in many areas including in the kitchen. Volunteers are rewarded with meal tickets (of course!) which are valid at the Carnegie Cafeteria. The cafeteria has become so popular that the former long-time director, Ethel Whitty, was forced to ask non-residents to stay away if they could afford to eat elsewhere (a strategy that worked!).

Jessica Lee is a newcomer to the DTES who is quickly finding herself at home among the quirky and beautiful people she meets. I asked Jess to seek out a different point of view about the Carnegie, and she connected with Bill (not his real name) who has eaten at least one meal here every day, for more than fifteen years.

Jess: What do you like about eating at Carnegie?

Bill: Eating at the Carnegie is like having a personal chef. At $2.25 you can't beat the price. I could never afford these ingredients on my own.

Jess: You said "personal chef."

Bill: Yes. Because I'm good friends with the cooks! Diane Brown (Assistant to the Food Services Coordinator) makes mind blowing food. I mean it's just astounding. She does a Moroccan chicken dish that is unbelievably tasty. I call it Mo-rockin' Chicken. In a hushed voice he adds, "I think the staff get irritated with her since her dishes are on the more expensive side..."

Jess: Is there a dish you would say represents the Carnegie?

Bill: Yeah. Chicken! They serve it about eight times a week. Jambalaya, Moroccan, Butter Chicken, Tandoori, Ethiopian...and their chicken soup! You could build a whole chicken out of the bits." He leans in and adds with a wink, "especially if you've got a buddy behind the counter. Oh, and Carnegie's known throughout the land for their granola. They make it themselves. It's a secret recipe. They're also known for their date and raspberry squares." A friend chimes in, "at other places these would cost you $10. Here they're a buck."

Jess: Have you seen the prices go up in the last ten years?

Bill: No, I don't think so. Except the soup. It used to be seventy-five cents. Now it is eighty.

We pause to notice someone behind us offering free oranges. Brian notes that there is a lot of food swapping here, then adds that Carnegie provides a lot of employment in the community.

The first of my interviews with the kitchen team was with Diane Brown (mentioned above) who shares crucial decisions with Steve McKinley (Carnegie Food Services Coordinator since 2011). Diane does a good job of highlighting the benefits of serving food that is of very high quality, but not quite gourmet.

"Sometimes we look at a dish and wish that we could add a little red wine...or serve lamb once in a while."

But that is as close as she gets to defensive. Like Steve and Chef Shawn, Diane is proud of the work that gets done here and enjoys the connection to the customers. Shawn, a big genial man, stresses how Carnegie strives to serve a wide variety of groups, both regarding dietary restrictions (diabetes, lactose intolerance and celiac disease are very common here) and with respect to cultural sensitivities.

"So one day we have a sale on eggplant, and so we'll do an eggplant stew," says Shawn, "Fresh. Local. What's on sale." These are themes that are repeated in our interviews.

Of course food security is front and centre among the people we talked to. Steve mentioned the advantage of being a city employee. It means that staff have a high degree of job security, not always shared by employees of high-end kitchens. Diane has been with the team for twenty-one years, Shawn for thirteen and Steve for six. I believe that this sense of security among the staff contributes to the overall feeling of home that many of us rely on, especially when mental illness and poverty push us out of the mainstream. Carnegie and its sensitive, dedicated staff, volunteers and patrons provide this community with a continually available platform to draw us back in.

Jessica Lee is a newcomer to the DTES who enjoys writing with her creative companions at Thursdays Writing Collective at the Carnegie and worshipping her creator with her Vineyard family Sundays at Strathcona Community Centre.

James Witwicki has lived in Vancouver's Downtown Eastside since 2010 and has been writing about this community for all of that time. He is a *Megaphone/Hope in Shadows* vendor, his work appears often in *Megaphone Magazine* and *Megaphone's* Voices of the Street. He is a member of Thursdays Writing Collective and a member of Strathcona Vineyard Church.

Grandmother, Cleaning a Rabbit

SAMUEL GREEN

I shot this one by the upper pond of the farm
after watching the rings trout made rising
to flies, watching small birds pace the backs
of cows, hoping all the time it would run.
My grandmother told me they damaged her garden.
I think it was a way to make the killing
lighter. She never let me clean them, only asked
I bring them headless to her. I bring this one
to the fir block near the house, use the single-
bitted axe with the nick in the lower crescent
of the blade, smell the slow fire
in the smokehouse, salmon changing
to something sweet & dark. A fly turns
in a bead of blood on my boot. I tuck
the head in a hole beside the dusty globes
of ripened currants, talk quiet to the barn cat.
In her kitchen my grandmother whets the thin blade
of her Barlow, makes a sequence of quick, clever cuts, then tugs
off the skin like a child's sweater. This one was
pregnant. She pulls out a row of unborn rabbits
like the sleeve of a shirt with a series of knots.
The offal is dropped in a bucket. Each joint gives way
beneath her knife as though it wants
to come undone, as though she knows some secret
about how things fit together. I have killed
a hundred rabbits since I was eight.
This will be the last.
I am twenty, & about to go back
to the war that killed my cousin in *Kien Hoa*,
which is one more name she can't pronounce.
I haven't told her about the dead
& she won't ask. She rolls the meat
in flour & pepper & salt & lays it
in a skillet of oil that spits like a cat.
She cannot save a single boy who carries a gun.
All she can do is feed this one.

Samuel Green was born in Sedro-Woolley, Washington, and raised in the nearby fishing and mill town of Anacortes. A forty plus year veteran as a Poet-in-the-Schools, he has taught in hundreds of classrooms around Washington State and in Wyoming. Among his eleven collections of poems are *Vertebrae: Poems 1972-1994* (Eastern Washington University Press), *The Grace of Necessity* (Carnegie-Mellon University Press), which won the 2008 *Washington State Book Award for Poetry*, and his newest book, *All That Might Be Done*, also from Carnegie Mellon.

Cooking Your Life

KATE MCCANDLESS

Long ago I had a farm—one hundred acres on the Bay of Fundy, with a run-down farmhouse, barn and assorted outbuildings. With my then-partner, I had left my country-of-origin, which was perpetrating a brutal, racist war in Vietnam. I was nineteen and could not see how to take my place in a world so full of cruelty and injustice. I wanted to learn how to take direct responsibility for my basic needs without, as I thought of it then, exploiting others or being exploited by others.

We learned to garden organically, and to tend the beings who provided us with food: chickens, geese, goats, sheep and bees. We had a roadside stand, sold produce, eggs, butter and cheese and made a very marginal living. But we raised the sweetest, crunchiest carrots I've ever eaten. And our homemade wild strawberry ice cream, honey-sweetened, was the closest thing to ambrosia I'll ever know. We grew our own buckwheat and oats for animal feed. We epitomized the "self-sufficiency" our back-to-the-land cohorts aspired to.

In those seven years I learned that growing, cooking and preserving food with care and gratitude was a template for how to live. I even imagined writing a book, that would be titled *Cooking Your Life*. I also learned that there is no such thing as self-sufficiency. That we were part of a fossil-fuel based economy, and social/political/industrial/military systems that stretched around the world. I came to realize that I needed to learn more survival skills for times to come: like how to mentor others, deal with conflict, come together in community in times of sorrow, re-claim language, writing, song... This education would take me far beyond the farm.

Some years later, living in Japan and beginning to practice Zen meditation I read a translation of the thirteenth century Japanese Zen Master Dogen's "Instructions to the Cook," with a commentary by Uchiyama Roshi, called *How to Cook Your Life*. My response was: Oh, this is what I wanted to say! About food, gardening, cooking and paying attention to every aspect of daily life. Dogen gives detailed descriptions of the way a Zen cook should plan and prepare meals, handling ingredients, pots and utensils with the utmost attention and care. "Handle even a single leaf of green in such a way that it manifests the body of the Buddha." He tells us not just how to cook meals, but how to cook our lives, continuously open, observant, creative in meeting the ever-changing circumstances of our environment.

At Zen meditation retreats we encourage the kitchen and serving crews to practice mindful awareness as they chop carrots, or stir oatmeal, or pour tea. Traditional Zen meals are a ceremony for eating with simplicity and care. Before we begin we chant, "May we realize the emptiness of the three wheels: giver, receiver and gift." "Emptiness" is perhaps a poor translation of the Buddhist concept of boundless interconnection. Giver, receiver and gift—farmer and cook, cauliflower and squash, earthworms, sun, soil and rain, and we who receive their gifts, all inextricably linked in the matrix of being.

To this day, decades past my farming days, working in the garden, enjoying and sharing its gifts restores and sustains me in these troubled times, and continues to teach me how to pay attention.

Kate McCandless is a Guiding Teacher of the Mountain Rain Zen Community in Vancouver. She lives and gardens on Blue Mountain in Mission, BC.

Untitled

ANAS ATAKORA

Translated from the French by Hodna Nuernberg

Je marche
Soulève les pas
Plus lent que des nuages d'hiver
Sur la rue *GoDream*
Il fait avril mais le temps est encore froid—sans honte !
Dans ma tête se bousculent quelques rêveries...
Je pense à Malik dont je voudrais taper l'épaule
En guise de fraternité
Mais l'exil a scié les frères en deux douleurs éloignées
Lui est à l'Est
Moi à l'Ouest
Chaque soir
Quand je finis de manger à la maison communautaire
Je marche vers l'Est
Comme pour humer dans le levant
L'odeur absente du frère
Manger est ma grande souffrance d'exilé
Non pas qu'il manque un pain
Ou que la soupe soit insipide
Ou que la maison communautaire me ferme la porte
Non
Manger est le moment où me manque plus
Ma famille
Le moment où je brûle d'envie
De sentir la main de Malik
Caresser le bol de riz
Que nous partageons toujours ensemble
Avec des cuillères qui s'entrecroisent
Pour laisser entendre de petites notes précises
Les seules à faire bruit quand nous mangeons
Au pays
On mange en silence
La parole est impolie à table
Et Grand-Mère disait que la salive ne prévient pas
Avant de s'échapper d'une bouche qui bavarde
Et que personne ne veut de l'autre
Recevoir une goutte de salive
Comme assaisonnement du diner
Et pourtant il faut toujours manger ensemble
Là-bas

Au pays de Grand-Mère
On dit que manger est une manière
De faire confiance aux connections des sens
On dit aussi que c'est un moment de silence
En l'honneur des ustensiles qu'on a bousculés avant le repas
Et qu'on bousculera au moment de la vaisselle
Au pays de Grand-Mère
Là-bas
Un monde s'est installé dans ma tête
Un monde fleuri
De repas
De silence d'hommes
De musique des cuillères
Et de la main de Malik
Qui toujours caresse les bols
Comme une main aime un chat
Les saisons de l'exil
Ont rasé ce monde
Ici
On parle quand on mange
On socialise à coup d'anecdotes
De secrets ou d'un rien de paroles
Qui vous garde en conversation
Pour que naisse la chaleur
Capable de tacler les dieux froids d'Amérique
Chaque soir donc
Quand je finis de manger à la maison communautaire
Je marche en direction de l'Est
Pour ne pas oublier mon monde d'avant
Je marche et digère en solitaire
Convaincu que Grand-Mère et Malik
Sont là près de moi
En terre canadienne où j'entre
Dans une nouvelle rumeur du monde.

I walk
Raising footsteps
Slower than winter clouds
Along *GoDream* Street
It's already April but the weather is still cold—shameless!
Daydreams jostle in my mind
I think of Malik whose shoulder I'd like to tap
A brotherly gesture
But exile sawed brothers into two distant aches
Him in the East
Me in the West
Every evening
When I finish eating at the Community House
I walk eastward
As if to inhale the Orient
The brother's absent perfume
Eating is an exile's greatest torment
Not because the bread is lacking
Or the soup bland
Or that the Community House's door slams in my face
No
Eating is the moment I miss the most
My family
The moment when I long
To feel Malik's hand
Skimming the rice bowl
We always shared
Our spoons crisscrossing
Chiming small crisp notes
The only sounds that accompany our eating
Back home
We eat in silence
Speech at the table is impolite
And Grandmother says saliva gives no notice
Before escaping from a talkative tongue
And that no one wants
A drop of another's saliva
To season his meal
And yet we always eat together
Back there
In Grandmother's country
We say eating is a way
Of trusting the connectedness of senses
We say, too, that it's a moment of silence
In honor of the utensils we've jostled before the meal
And the ones we'll jostle when washing up

Back there
In Grandmother's country
A world has settled in my mind
A world garnished
With meals
And men's silences
The songs of spoons
And Malik's hand
Brushing against bowls
Like a hand loving a cat
Seasons of exile
Demolished that world
Here
We talk when we eat
Socializing, offering anecdotes
Secrets or empty words
To keep the conversation going
To give rise to warmth
Capable of tackling America's cold gods
So each evening
When I finish eating at the Community House
I walk toward the East
So I won't forget my first world
I walk and digest alone
Convinced Grandmother and Malik
Are there beside me
In the Canadian landscape where I step
Into the whispering of a new world.

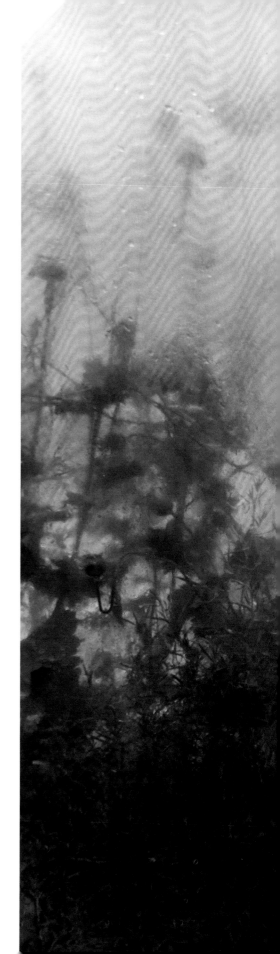

Anas Atakora is a writer from Togo. He is the author
of three poetry books, one book of essays and one
forthcoming collection of short stories. He lives in
Nova Scotia, and was a 2015 fellow at the University
of Iowa's International Writing Program.

Hodna Bentali Gharsallah Nuernberg holds both a
Master's in Francophone Studies and an MFA in
Literary Translation from the University of Iowa.
Nuernberg translates from French, Spanish, and
Arabic; her work has appeared or is forthcoming
with *QLRS*, *Two Lines*, *Asymptote*, *Poet Lore*,
Drunken Boat, and elsewhere.

Dharma Food

VENERABLE CHANG WU
Head of Dharma Drum Mountain Temple, Richmond

My dad had a very special talent and love for food. He would only have to eat a dish once and he would know how to cook it. He would only cook on special occasions, such as Chinese New Year. He would start to shop for food a few days before and then spend the whole day cooking in the kitchen. I was always the helper, washing and cutting vegetables and fetching things for him, and couldn't help wondering when I could get a break to sit down for a while. I was always amazed how he endured standing long hours cooking in a hot and steamy kitchen. Often in the end he lost his appetite for the dinner. Then I saw his face gleaming in a smile as he watched us eating, and I realized that every bite of food emanated his love for his family and friends. That smile still nourishes me, thirty-three years after his passing.

After joining the Dharma Drum monastic community, I learned to cook in simple styles and appreciate vegetarian meals with few condiments. One of the principles of cooking is to make use of the vegetables that are available, to bring out their natural flavors, and to create a delicious and healthy dish in a simple way. One of the dishes that tastes like home to me is an ordinary soup which is well liked by many monks and nuns. It is cooked with cabbage, potatoes, carrots, dried mushrooms, and sometimes with burdock on medium heat for thirty or forty minutes. It can be served for breakfast, lunch and dinner. It is most welcome at major events when we need an energy boost. The cabbage soup soothes our body and mind.

Food provides sustenance for our body, and Buddhist teachings nourish our mind. We advocate eating healthy vegetarian meals, not to take away lives; learning to cook with what is available and seasonal; and eating the whole food. This is a good way to cultivate our mind to accept all things and to reduce our attachment to certain ingredients or specific way of cooking. It also helps us to develop creativity. Many new recipes are created in this circumstance. Since there is a piece of farmland behind the Centre, we grow organic vegetables and fruits that usually sustain our food supply from late spring to fall. Members come to work in the orchard and vegetable garden and enjoy the company of one another. While eating the meals cooked by some other members with the food they grow, everyone seems to be quite joyful. Perhaps that is why we are adding more and more vegetable areas.

Opposite are two recipes for the dishes that we eat at the centre. They are easy to prepare and very wholesome.

Cooked Kale Salad

INGREDIENTS:

· 1 bunch kale
· 1 avocado
· ½ small box grape tomatoes
· 1 teaspoon raw sugar

SAUCE INGREDIENTS:

· 2 tablespoons almond butter
· 1 tablespoon soy sauce
· pinch of salt
· 4 teaspoons hot water

DIRECTIONS:

· Mix the sauce ingredients (not too watery)
· Tear kale into small pieces (use leaves only)
· Boil kale leaves; drain water.
· Mix sauce into drained kale.
· Dice avocado and spread on top of kale.
· Cut grape tomatoes in half, pan-fry cut side down with small amount of oil for one to two minutes, then sprinkle with raw sugar.
· Spread tomatoes on top of kale.

Steamed Kabocha Squash & Tofu

INGREDIENTS:

· Medium firm tofu, cut into 1" x 2" pieces
· ½ Kabocha Squash
· 2 tablespoon green peas
· 3 tablespoons cooking oil
· ½ teaspoon salt
· ⅓ to ½ cup water
· pinch of white pepper
· ½ teaspoon sugar

DIRECTIONS:

· Steam and mash Kabocha squash
· Add cooking oil, salt, water, white pepper, sugar into mashed squash then bring to a boil. Make sure it is not too watery.
· Boil tofu in water, then drain.
· Boil snow peas in water, then drain.
· Place tofu on serving plate, spread mashed kabocha squash on top, then sprinkle with shredded snow peas.

Photographs by Jacky Zhou.

Venerable Chang Wu, a Buddhist monastic in the Chan (Zen) tradition, is currently the Abbess of Dharma Drum Vancouver Center in Richmond, BC. For almost fifteen years, she has been teaching classes in Buddhist philosophy and meditation to people of widely different backgrounds and age groups. She also leads meditation retreats around the world.

Photography by Emily White of Lachlan and Emily Photography.

Tayybeh: A Culinary Expedition

DIMA YASSINE and NIHAL ELWAN

The old Middle Eastern story goes something like this: Once upon a time a wealthy merchant got separated from his caravans and lost his way in the desert. He walked for a very long time and was on the verge of giving up out of thirst and hunger, when he spotted a simple Bedouin tent. The family living in the tent took the strange man in, they gave him clean clothes, water, and they cooked a huge meal for him. As the man sat down to eat, he noticed that no member of the family, not even the children were eating with him. He grew suspicious of the food and decided to invite them to eat with him. They refused which made him even more worried, he demanded an answer. After a lot of back and forth, and noticing that their guest was getting agitated, the father of the family told the strange man they had one goat which gave them milk every morning and that's how they fed their children. But since they had him as a guest, they weren't going to only feed him milk so they slaughtered the goat and cooked it for him. And they had to make sure that their guest had enough food and he was completely satisfied before they could start eating. The story goes on to give a happy ending for all, as the wealthy merchant, touched by the generosity of that poor family, sends them money and cattle that would leave them fed and comfortable for a very long time. The story, however, is not only about trust and rewards. It's also about kindness, generosity and respect. It was expressed by offering food.

Food in most societies is people's way of showing love and care. We cook for our loved ones, we share the tastes we like with the people we like. It means warmth and intimacy. In the Middle East it's all of that and more. It is a culture. Whether they invite someone to their house, have a surprise guest or they have a plumber or someone doing some repairs in their place, it is only fit to offer whomever is in your house a meal as a token of respect and appreciation. It is *Wajib*, or duty, to show your *Karam*/generosity (Arabic), to whomever in your house. So when some Syrian refugee families arrived to Canada and, as most of them needed help not only from the government but also the community, one Arab Vancouverite woman stepped in. Her idea was to create a channel to connect the newcomer families to the new place they settled in while helping them in the process. Nihal Elwan, who has also worked in international development for over ten years focusing on women's empowerment in the Middle East and North Africa, decided to use her skills and she started seeking refugee women to create pop-up Syrian dinners where these women could introduce their culture and appreciation to the new community they settled in and also help them earn an income in the process. Starting with only a five-hundred dollar community grant in hand, a few months later Elwan found herself creating a movement of not only food but also culture, community and generosity. This left many people in the city of Vancouver eagerly looking forward to these monthly pop-up dinners. The city and the media began to rave about them. Elwan called the enterprise *Tayybeh* meaning kind in Arabic and delicious in the Levantine dialect.

Dima: Why food in particular? Why not crafts, for example? How did the idea come to be?

Nihal: Let me start with the last question, I arrived in Vancouver three years ago after having worked for over a decade on gender and women's issues in the Middle East. Upon arriving, I volunteered with an organization working on supporting the Syrian newly-arrived families through various info sessions. I got to know many families closely and became all the more attuned to the various linguistic, cultural, and limited network obstacles they faced when landing here and trying to start a life; with the women often bearing the brunt of these obstacles given their lack of professional experience and limited avenues to generate income. I felt I needed to do something to try and support some of these families. Given my professional background, I was of course even more inclined to start working with women. Why food? Well across the Middle East, Syrians have the reputation of being by far the best and most sophisticated cooks and their cuisine has rarely been commercialized. Good food is one of the few things in life that can get a group of people from different political, ethnic, religious backgrounds, different walks of life, speaking different languages to sit around a table, enjoy themselves immensely, and can sometimes get them to transcend their differences and barriers. In my mind, the formula of good Syrian food, working with women, and supporting newly arrived families seemed like an amazing project.

Dima: When and where was the first *Tayybeh* dinner held?

Nihal: It was held at Tamam Fine Palestinian Cuisine Restaurant on the 24th of October 2016. The wonderful owners, whom I am proud to call friends of mine, were immediately supportive of the event and generously provided us with the space for the ladies to cook up a storm, free of charge. At the time we were working with four chefs who cooked up a delightful menu each bringing in a specialty of her hometown or her family that reminded them of home.

Dima: How did people respond to it? And most importantly how did the *Tayybeh* women feel about it?

Nihal: The first event was generously funded by Vancouver Foundation's Small Neighbourhood Grant. The grant was exclusively used to cover the cost of food, so we had no funds allocated to advertising the event. We basically created an invitation on Facebook describing the event, the date and time, and just left it out there in virtual space.

We were delighted to see that all fifty tickets sold out in a little over a day! On the day of the event we saw guests serving themselves twice and three times and the food received rave reviews. The ladies were absolutely thrilled and incredibly moved by the reactions, praise and appreciation expressed by the guests. When all the invitees left, the women broke out into spontaneous tearful song and applause. For most of them, this was the first time they had earned an income and the happiest moment since the war raged in their countries. It was at this very moment that we knew this project had to continue… to empower these women, to give them a source of income, a sense of community, but most of all to give them something to celebrate.

Dima: Tayybeh is a very young initiative, yet it really got a lot of attention from the local, and recently international, media as well, were you surprised?

Nihal: Honestly, I was very surprised by both the community's embracement of *Tayybeh*, the women chefs, their families and Syrian food. The kindness people have showed us was remarkable. But I think the media attention is really a result of the food being brilliant. As they say, when it comes to cooking, ultimately, the proof is in the pudding! And in this case, the food is absolutely delectable. The media came when the events took. We could not have anticipated this reaction and we are still trying to pace ourselves given all the attention we are getting. With each pop-up dinner, the tickets sold out faster, the food got better, and the press took an interest. In the end, we are proud of the chefs of *Tayybeh* and what they have accomplished in such a short time.

Dima: Were there any challenges or difficulties starting up this project?

Nihal: The difficulties we face are mostly logistical. Our ladies live in different parts of Vancouver and Surrey, they attend English school, and some of them have small children so we have to work around their schedules and availability. That said, our ladies are so diligent and hardworking that they always do their best to be available for our pop-up and catering work that is at the moment growing very steadily as the demand for their delicious food increases. Also getting a commercial kitchen is complicated and costly, and getting the women certified with the Food Safe courses was tricky as the course was not available in English. However, five months into this project, we were able to overcome these challenges.

Dima: Tayybeh's team of chefs now includes about seven women and their families, do you see it growing to reach more refugee women, men and their families in Vancouver?

Nihal: Our mission at *Tayybeh* is to support as many Syrian newly arrived women and families as we can. We have grown from four to seven chefs in only six months as our pop-up events are becoming more popular. If you were to attend several dinners in a row, you will note that very few items are repeated. Syrian cuisine is so rich, complex and diverse that each women brings at least one new dish to every dinner that is reminiscent of her home town and family that she has perfected. Given how popular the dinners are, and that we are also getting more requests to cater various events around the city we definitely foresee the opportunity to introduce more Syrian ladies with *Tayybeh.*

Dima: Do you see it growing out to other cities and provinces?

Nihal: In the long run we certainly hope so but at the moment we are getting so much love from Vancouver and BC that we would love to focus on showcasing our cuisine across the province first.

Dima: You have a job of your own and are raising a young family as well, how are you dividing your time and energy amongst all these demanding things?

Nihal: Well, women have been doing this from time immemorial. I try my best to balance my work life with my family life in the same way that the amazing Syrian ladies of *Tayybeh* do their best to balance working hard and still make sure they are taking care of their families and children. Luckily *Tayybeh* itself is the sort of endeavor that allows one to work while having one's family around. Indeed a large part of our success is due to the incredible hard work put in by the husbands, sons and brothers of the women and we are always delighted to have the children of the ladies around during the cooking and throughout our *Tayybeh* soirées. My son for one is always around while I work or throughout the *Tayybeh* evenings.

Dima: Where do you see *Tayybeh* going in the future what are your hopes for it?

Nihal: Our hope for *Tayybeh* is to continue to grow and introduce support to as many Syrian women and families as we can. At the moment our *Tayybeh* pop-up dinners are organized every four to five weeks and we would like to keep them going on a regular basis. We are launching our catering arm and soon we would like to make many of our start items available through retailers across the province to be able to offer our delicious food on a regular basis to a wider audience. For the further future, who knows, maybe a restaurant, the world is our oyster and there are so many ideas we are thinking of so, stay tuned!

Dima: What are your favourite reactions you got so far from people who attended *Tayybeh* dinners?

Nihal: My favourite moment is always when we invite the ladies to go up on stage, introduce themselves to the guests, share their stories and invite them to speak to the guests.

They are also met with a standing ovation by the guests and I always absolutely love seeing the looks of joy, pride and achievement on the ladies' faces (sometimes mixed with some tears) but it is the sheer happiness on their and their families' faces that warm my heart and always remind us that we are on the right track.

Photography by Dima Yassine.

Nihal Elwan is the founder of *Tayybeh*, a Vancouver-based food company that aims to provide Syrian women chefs with the opportunity to generate an income and integrate into their new communities through doing something they love—cooking delectable home-style Syrian food! Nihal's professional background is in the area of international development where she has worked for over a decade in programs focusing on women and youth for local non-profits throughout the Middle East as well as United Nations agencies (including UNDP, UNICEF, and ILO). Through *Tayybeh*, Nihal is fulfilling her lifelong dream of supporting women from the Middle East and building community while being surrounded by delicious food all the time!

Dima Yassine was born in Beirut, Lebanon, grew up in Baghdad, Iraq, lived in different Middle Eastern countries and has been calling Vancouver home since 2004. She obtained a Creative Writing Diploma (2008) and MA in Liberal Studies (2015) from Simon Fraser University. She is a published poet, writer, photographer, filmmaker and researcher in women's art in the Middle East.

Every Dish is Unique

BODHI CUTLER and GUS JACKSON

Every dish is unique because every Vancouverite makes it a tiny bit different. We all have our styles and our ingredients, our suppliers and our equipment. There are restaurants who will probably make great pasta with the best calamari. Your mom can make a great homemade meal she invented herself. No two meals taste the same because they are like humans, unique and great.

Bodhi Cutler is a ten-year-old boy going to Charles Dickens Elementary. His favourite colour is multichrome and he loves music.

Gus Jackson is ten years old and goes to Charles Dickens. He is in grade five and loves animals. His favourite food is burgers and he also loves skateboarding.

Making Marmalade

KATHRYN ALEXANDER

This Sunday I made marmalade
with the oh so anticipated
bitter oranges of January.
I look out on the bleak landscape of grey
and contemplate Seville oranges;
defiantly tough, brilliantly inedible,
how they remind me of my grandmother.

The diversity of Aggie's marmalades:
Seville, three fruit, apricot, ginger.
Always a touch of something extra
almond slivers, crabapple with clove,
sadness.
A little something that lingers
on the tongue and is swallowed
into the dark velvet of experience.

When I make marmalade, her cells
claim me from those things that belonged to her;
the colour of my hair, a particular slant of the eye,
the telling of stories from tea leaves.
Bereft or full, I never left her table
empty handed.

The recipe:
Boil a pot of bitterness until tender
add the blood of ruby grapefruit
and set with lemons grated to the quick.
Into these women fruits
pour pounds and pounds of sugar,
so much sugar you won't believe
it takes such sweetness to cover up
the bitter tongues of memory.
Stir the bitter stories
until they froth and rise like fruity lava
to set like jewels on a cold spoon.

Now I make marmalade to evoke the grate
of your wisdom, the ferocious containment of your life
Wax seals over the topaz bitter-sweetness
and every morning I savour memories
eaten on bread made by strangers.

Kathryn Alexander makes marmalade, gardens, walks trails, and writes poetry in Port Moody. Her grandparents came to Canada in the early 1900s from Scotland and Ireland and settled in East Vancouver. Kathryn has a PhD from SFU and teaches various writing and education courses whenever they let her.

Adventure and Comfort:

RACHEL ROSE talks with FRANK PABST, Executive Chef of Blue Water Café

Photo Credit: Toptable Group

Rachel Rose: Could you share some of your early food influences?

Frank Pabst: I was born in Germany, but spent the first ten years of my life in Belgium. My parents had four sons. Both my parents worked, but no matter how long my mother worked, she'd always take care to make a hot meal for us. That's something that nowadays I appreciate even more then when I was a kid. Now that I am a professional chef, I see how much effort and time it takes to actually do the cooking, besides working and running the household as well. That certainly influenced me, seeing my mother taking the time and making the effort. That's something that I have in my memories, over all those years. Obviously I'd like to pass on the love and adventure of food to our family as well. Unfortunately, it's not as easy. We had a grocery store across the street—nowadays with a car or public transit, shopping is a little different. The weekends are a sacred time for me. During the week I don't see the family that much. I come home late and everybody's sleeping. But during the weekend I stay close to home and cook dinners and try to pass on those experiences and adventures.

Rachel Rose: Could you describe a weekend at home cooking with the family?

Frank Pabst: I have twin daughters. They are both now thirteen. We started when the kids were eating solid food. We tried to introduce them to new things. Sometimes it was a little challenging! You think you are a chef, so they should be eating everything, but they have their own palates. Sophia has Autism, so every time she tries something new we applaud. Tatjana, she tries everything. We have an open kitchen, so they smell what I'm cooking. I don't force them to help, but at least we are in the same room, and when cooking goes on, they comment, "Do you cook with garlic? Is there some thyme in there?" We have dinner all around the kitchen island together. I always make plenty, so we have leftovers for warming up. We got Tatjana used to wine pretty early on, she would get a sip from my glass to get the flavors in her mouth. I think this is very important.

Rachel Rose: My French in-laws did this with our kids! It was a shock for me; this is not a North American approach at all.

Frank Pabst: Exactly! We had a little beer, a little sip of wine here and there. You learn so much as a child having those food and culinary experiences as well. I think it is very important. It forms you. You are more comfortable when you go to a restaurant, less intimidated around food and wine from a young age. Tatjana likes *foie gras*—she likes all the expensive foods—and both girls enjoy caviar!

Rachel Rose: How did you decide to become a chef?

Frank Pabst: Once you finish high school, in Germany, you have to decide on what you want to do in your life, if you want to go into an apprenticeship or university. For me, I always liked the hands-on work. Because of the influences of my mother cooking all the time, and me mucking around sometimes with the food she was making, and doing my own little twists on the finished product, I thought maybe a chef would be something nice. I wanted to travel and learn languages, meet other people that way. I took an apprenticeship in the French restaurant in the city where I grew up, and then I went to the South of France, where I lived for four years. I left home and never came back.

When I started at Blue Water Café, the Oceanwise program wasn't started yet, We found out only through the newspapers which species were endangered and which were sustainable, just like the broader public. Now it's much easier to tell what's good and not good.

We promote sustainable seafood, mostly local seafood. We have lots of guests coming in every night, so we have to cater to those who don't eat fish. We have a few vegetarian and meat items. We work with Oceanwise from the Vancouver Aquarium to figure out what is sustainable, what we should and should not have on the menu. Once a year, now, in February, I create a special menu, the Unsung Heroes. It is eleven or twelve items, which we have all year but never all together. These are species that seem to be underappreciated, mostly because they are too adventurous for lots of people—sea cucumber, limpet, jellyfish, whelk, octopus, mackerel, herring, sea urchin, items that are more pronounced in flavor. We promote these dishes for people to try out so they realize you don't always have to go for halibut or salmon. It's to share an experience too, from our point of view. We donate 10% to the Oceanwise program at the Vancouver Aquarium.

Rachel Rose: What informs your cooking; what is your food philosophy?

Frank Pabst: I always cook by the seasons, based on what's fresh, what's available. When halibut season is on, when spot prawn season is on, that's what I serve. We are seasonally driven, with fresh and mostly local ingredients. Obviously in a restaurant, you cook for guests who are paying money to have a nice dinner. We can offer either new experiences for the adventurous, like the Unsung Heroes menu, or established favorites that offer comfort, like the food I had growing up.

Rachel Rose: Thank you! Both experiences sound lovely.

Sugar Added

NANCY MEAGHER

Added sugar: I have strong beliefs about the importance of limiting it for my children for health and well-being reasons, and have been known to bluster about it from time to time, yet, I frequently falter. It is as though there are two angels from each end of the sugar spectrum, rattling on in alternate ears at decisions involving sugar.

The sugar angel delights in the moment of peace and contentment that surrounds the sharing of sweets. The expression of love in the gingersnaps Nana makes or the apple caramel confection that completes the birthday. The signal of celebration in shortbread, candy canes, chocolate eggs and pumpkin pie. It cradles our hearts with a warm fuzzy blanket that feels like belonging and contentment. Ah, this is nice.

The shrill tweet of the health angel's whistle stops the reverie. I am reminded of the adverse health and behavioural effects of sugar in children that imprints forward to adulthood—obesity, diabetes, hormone disruption, heart disease, insulin resistance, mood swings. Organizations such as the American Heart Association and the World Health Organization are now setting recommendations for the maximum daily added sugars, four to seven teaspoons for kids under eighteen, way below the current estimated average of nineteen teaspoons. A single soda at nine teaspoons far exceeds this target, not to mention what we accumulate in the blueberry yogurt, bran muffin, granola bar, pasta sauce, and even bread.

The sugar angel pivots towards the flow of current norms: Life is short. We can't control our kids forever. Enjoy while you can. It isn't that big a deal. It is a fact of life. These were vivid memories for you as a child, are you going to prevent your own children from the same joy? Don't be such a downer! You're making people feel so judged when you talk about sugar.

Health angel puts aside the facts and figures and urges me to remember the post-euphoria raggedness that the children so readily demonstrate, bringing out their worst.

Back and forth, back and forth, at any of the myriad decision points in a given day—the beseeching eyes of my children at a birthday party hoping to get a nod for a taste of Coke; the blue freezies at the school fundraiser; the desire for strawberry yogurt rather than plain. It is unrelenting.

Ultimately, while I don't want to make sugar the forbidden fruit, the sugar angel has the decided home turf advantage, and we need a plan to support our resolve to reduce sugar. Education and reminders help, like through the documentaries *Sugar Coated* or *Forks Over Knives*, or Jamie Oliver's recent work. I'd love to see a bigger role in schools, even to go sugar free. Involving the children in learning about added sugar helps them start to develop their own personal compass towards intentional consumption. Can we decide as a family on a sugar budget for the week, and how we spend it? Rituals are important to me, especially as a foodie, but we can replace some of the good stuff with other good stuff (to avoid a feeling of deprivation): swap in non-food elements like a Valentine's poem, or an Easter treasure hunt. When mindless consumption is curbed, the actual treat is that much sweeter.

Nancy Meagher's love of food and cooking started as a young child, making her first bread at eight years old. She was heavily influenced by the natural foods philosophy of her parents, as well as by her older sibling's covert fudge making enterprise. She lives with her two sons in Vancouver.

Jack's Restaurant

HENRY RAPAPPORT

I thought the endless dripping
Coffee cup on the façade
And the stained floors
And the shaky counter stools
Meant love gone stale in the place
We ran from Independence
To Labour Day from one season
To another's exhausted end
But when I was there again
It was me asking if the building
Was for sale and me proposing
We could fix it up and renovate
Our hapless livelihood
And even though she was brittle
As before I found myself wondering
How to shim the wobble
And make things better for her
And that gave credence to elbow
Grease and what dreams could do.

Henry Rappaport's fifth book of poems, *Loose to the World*, is available from Ronsdale Press. He likes presenting his work. Catch him if you can.

stir / fry

DAPHNE MARLATT

noodling who loved that phrase among the knotted past acoustic
memory toss from char qua as what tag ends unscrolling dense
savours stress or pitch like garlic fried in that particular oil's not
palm illumined rank of puja jugs in light off harbour quay the jetty
shrine's small candle float hiatus in the stroll each phrase unwinds
no chopstick comma interrupts the noodle line but teow distinct
unreplica'd prawncurl but leave tail ends intact no small cockles
here yes beansprouts high-five Keefer's supermart had chives
long flower budded green and gone with highrise sprout deleting
kampong style but chili yes char kway teow sliced lap cheong
for spice hold sprouts hold chives til last black skillet bounce on
open flame it's eye size plus practice years all ears for sizzle tag
ends memory stirs to deftly tip the mound on plate

Acclaimed poet (*Steveston, Liquidities*) and novelist (*Ana Historic, Taken*), Daphne
Marlatt's most recent title, *Reading Sveva*, features a series of poems in response to
the life and work of the Italian Canadian painter Sveva Caetani. *Intertidal*, her collected
earlier poetry, edited by Susan Holbrook, is forthcoming from Talonbooks, fall 2017.

Recipes of a Kitchen God

ELEE KRALJII GARDINER and ANDREW McEWAN

Revolve the wintermelon. A cranium, a soul.
Deseed it of desire. Slice it thinly.
Let it weep on paper towels
while you cast rocksalt into spitting oil.
Decant tequila in an espresso cup and sip while eyeing
the knives. Huck in roots of ginger, then cover
yourself by the corner of the fridge. Things are about to explode.
Blister a week of elementary school until "golden"
is a long gone memory. Char it. Burn the sunset right out
of young love. Smoke mustard seeds until the firefighters come.
Wave the crew away to other homes worth prolonging.
Let cruelty crust the pan. Juggle six eggs near the ceiling fan.
Get the blender going, feed it silverware. Boil hairbrushes
and throw them in the coffee pot. Brew. Cleave
a chicken breast, splintering bones as needed. Cut
cooking time in half by gassing the stove and igniting an addiction.
Get ready to deliver the work of a lifetime prematurely.

Set the table with ringlets of fear. Each place deserves
a surprise, a lost hope, some curdled affection.
The guest of honour gets her illness.

They think they have ordered their lives but you hold the die
in this aleatory cuisine. The next course is coming and it is best
served cold, in thick slabs. Mutton should have the colour
of an endless workday and a whinge of despair.
Clear. They are ageing. Ash-ripened cheeses. Approach
the table with a tray of diamanté strawberries and pop one
in each mouth. No sweeter choir
than unknowingness of what is to come;
they are dazed and glutted. Cut them off. Pick one and lead her
back to the kitchen. While you pull up a stool and drain a glass
have her lift 100 lb flour sacks. Get her baking. Watch blisters
rise on her forearms and collapse like soufflé. Reach
for the zester. Apply it to the wounds mercilessly. Once
she is trained, you can exit.

Elee Kraljii Gardiner (*serpentine loop*, Anvil Press, 2016; *Tunica Intima*, forthcoming Anvil Press, 2018) and Andrew McEwan (*Repeater*, Book Thug, 2013; *If Pressed*, BookThug 2017; *Tours, Variously*, forthcoming Talonbooks, 2018) are collaborating on the poetry project *Nature Building*.

Fair Trade

MEREDITH QUARTERMAIN

In 1958, Mom ordered a year's supply of food for our family of four, and shipped it to Frobisher Bay (now Iqaluit). Government rations for northern workers did not meet her standards as a dietician. She ordered cases of powdered eggs, powdered milk, dehydrated orange juice, dried Chinese vegetables, rice, dried apricots, prunes, raisins, dried beans, whole grain flour, rolled oats, safflower oil. She packed codliver oil for vitamin D during months of little daylight. Strapped to a few seats in the hold of a freight plane, we flew north so my father could teach carpentry in the Rehab Centre for Inuit returning from southern TB sanatoriums. The Centre taught typing, sewing, carving, carpentry and cooking.

Kabloona. That's what we were. An Inuit word for white government personnel who depended on wages and manufactured food. In our case, Mom was the manufacturer. In between boiling water, running the wringer washer and filling the 512-square-foot house with racks of wet clothes and bedding, she baked bread and cookies, invented stews from dehydrated vegetables, and cooked porridge, rice and reconstituted scrambled eggs. Every few days she would start a new batch of bean sprouts between dampened dishtowels housed in white enamel containers she'd salvaged from a lab.

I will never forget eating some of the gifts from Inuit friends: fresh arctic char, caribou and seal. Never forget seeing a *kamatik* just back from a hunt, loaded with seal. Even as an eight-year-old I knew this was good because it meant Inuit people were getting food to eat. Good food, not the white flour and sugar the government handed out.

At school I sat in rows of desks with Inuit kids and thought they liked school as much as I did. But I noticed they had rotten teeth and teeth coming out in weird places, and they scrapped a lot in the school yard. Martha, a super unhappy kid, beat me up one day; she had extra fangs on top of her other teeth and couldn't close her mouth properly.

My parents explained that these kids were survivors of famine and starvation (widespread in 1947 and through the 1950s) that had killed their parents and relatives. Their families didn't want to be here. They wanted to be out hunting and following their traditional way of life. But there were hardly any caribou. The Inuit were forced into white settlements to get government rations that were bad for them, little more than a diet of white bread. They crowded a dozen people into tiny government prefabs. They got diseases like TB that normally they'd be immune to.

To remain healthy, Inuit must eat meat and fat from red meat. Fish lacks enough fat. But white colonizers destroyed Inuit food sources through excessive butchery. Trading posts urged Inuit to slaughter caribou for the meat trade and depend on flour and fish. Sealing ships ravaged the seal population. RCMP and missionaries destroyed walruses for unneeded dog teams. White hunting parties killed whales, shipping the meat south to feed fox ranches. How I loved to run my hand over the bales of fox furs in the sewing classroom. Not knowing how Inuit came to depend on trading fox furs for food that would kill them.

Mom, being the scientist she was, tried to do something about the malnutrition she saw. She invented the most nutritious thing you could make out of Hudson Bay Co. and government rations for the Inuit: muffins made with lots of powdered eggs, rolled oats, fat, and raisins. She made charts in syllabics and showed Inuit women how to make them. It was all she could do. Her heart was in the right place but in the end, Inuit needed caribou, whale and seal, not *kabloona* food.

Meredith Quartermain's *Vancouver Walking* won a BC Book Prize for Poetry; *Nightmarker* was a finalist for a Vancouver Book Award. Other books include: *Recipes from the Red Planet; Rupert's Land: a novel; I, Bartleby: short stories*; and *U Girl: a novel*. She was SFU Writer's Studio Poetry Mentor 2014-2016.

New Growth

CHELENE KNIGHT

a small black pot on the back of the stove mama
says the well's run dry someone has leaned on
the ocean the way teeth bleed an apple
face down in a seashell while three mothers
pray for full bellies and clean brown hair
she plants her seeds at night but fruit don't grow
in winter dirt rims her fingernails push
the roots deep ground-buried secrets
whisper recipes of warm bread chicken
pot pies crust curves jagged edges she weeps
when nothing comes, hollow here in this field
cut the ends gently—a sprout slices soil

Chelene Knight is the Managing Editor and Executive Director at *Room* magazine. She is the author of *Braided Skin* (Mother Tongue Publishing) and *Dear Current Occupant* (forthcoming with BookThug, 2018). She's currently working on a novel set in Vancouver's 1930s-50s Hogan's Alley.

Motor Meat or How My Mom Fed Our Family Off the Car

SHARON KALLIS

When I think about the word sustenance, it seems to encompass so much more than just food for eating; it speaks of food for the soul, the body, the brain, and even a community.

Mulling on this for a while, a story from my own life kept coming back. It's the quirky story of my 10th birthday celebration. But before I can tell that story, I have to go back to age six, and tell you about my family's road trips.

Growing up in Ontario we went camping—east coast one summer, west the next—visiting the family diaspora with our pop-up trailer towed behind our eight cylinder Oldsmobile sedan.

On one such summer vacation, when I was six, we rolled into a filling station for some gas. Resting her hand on the hood while filling the tank, my mom declared, "The engine is hot enough to cook a roast!" Being who she is, our next stop was the grocery store, where she convinced my dad it was worth the expensive experiment of $6 for a roast, a roll of heavy duty tinfoil, and a packet of onion soup mix.

Out in the parking lot, the roast and mix got rolled together in foil while my mom found the perfect hot spot above the engine block. Back on the road, my job in the back seat was to keep a vigilant watch for a little silver bundle bouncing down the road behind us. Over the course of that summer it was determined that the car could cook a roast at the rate of one pound an hour at sixty miles per hour. Based on this, we experimented with everything from heating the contents of cans to baking fresh fish, timing things to be ready for arrival at camp by day's end.

At various times we travelled with friends: aunt Maggie, a sister's boyfriend. Or, when my older sisters became "too old" for such things as family vacations, my parents' friends. We would rotate the task of meal planning with a $2 budget max among the group of six. The cast iron engine block became a regular kitchen appliance for our travels.

My birthday is in August near the long weekend. Some years this meant we were away, and I missed having the typical birthday party. In particular, my mom

felt bad that we would be away for my 10th. I remember her asking me what I would like as a special meal on my birthday. I aspired to the height of fine dining: roast beef and cheese fondue. I remember her thinking on that for just a few beats, then saying, "OK, I can do that." I am still not sure how she managed the cheese fondue on the engine block alongside the roast, but I do remember arriving at the campground in Northern Quebec at dinner time, driving slowly over the bumpy road with the trailer behind, and passing our soon-to-be-neighbours all in various states of cooking over hibachis. We did our usual time-trial camp set-up. Everyone has a teammate and a task, from unpacking the car to setting the table to getting the trailer ready for the night. And within twelve minutes, we were sitting for dinner, with a real tablecloth, real wine glasses, and lit candles—even though it was still light. My mom served up a roast beef and cheese fondue, much to the shock and amazement of our camping neighbours. I can still hear their exclaiming in awe in a language I didn't understand.

My mom's ability to deliver such a splendorous dinner party of ridiculous pomp and ceremony after hours in the car has stuck with me. That feeling of being loved, of being honoured, and having not just my belly filled, but of our working as a group to make it happen. And my mom, using the available resources—even a hot engine block—to feed her family and bring us together for special meals. That is what sustenance means to me.

Based in Vancouver BC, eco-artist, Sharon Kallis discovers the inherent potential in a landscape with a "one mile diet" approach to sourcing art materials. Her book, *Common Threads: weaving community through eco-art* (New Society Publishers) is a field guide to making with others with what is found close at hand.

Three Short Poems About Sticky Things

CARLEIGH BAKER

1.
Jug's no stranger to violence.
We work alone
together in the honey house
on Coldwater road.
I bottle honey and
he works the DECAPPER.
DE
CAPS frames of thick
comb. Frame after frame
pass through the machine,
with the honey, the wax
and the bees who won't be
persuaded to leave. Chains
rip the caps off the cells,
and the bees limb
from limb, pieces
of bodies collect on the floor with
splintered wood, and wax. Christ,
the noise that thing makes.

2.
Jug knows how to case a joint.
He takes a lot of breaks,
so he has a lot of time
to appraise the beekeeper's
John Deere ride-a-mower,
his Craftsman tools,
even the DECAPPER itself.
How much you think I could get for this?
he asks me, seventeen year old
eyes wide with possibility.
If he fences the John Deere
before the end of the summer
he'll be mowing fourteen acres of lawn
with the goddamn push mower.

3.
Street kids are all entrepreneurs.
Jug has a home
based business now. Sells drugs
from his room
at the Double D motel—says he'll get me
anything I want.
Most clients pay in shoplifted steak,
but he doesn't mind cash.
Says he's done a little time inside.
Says he moved to the Interior
to get away from the crime.
Says if you do enough blow you lose your
appetite for steak.

Carleigh Baker is a Cree-Métis/Icelandic writer who lives as a guest on the traditional, ancestral, unceded territories of the Musqueam, Squamish, and Tsleil-Waututh peoples. Her work has appeared in *Best Canadian Essays* and *The Journey Prize Anthology.* Her debut story collection, *Bad Endings (*Anvil, *2017)* is now available.

Homemade Pie

BEVERLEY O'NEIL

"Want a pumpkin pie?" I asked my buddy Michael.

"Yes!" he said, "and not because it's free, but there's something that goes into homemade pie that isn't in store bought. Only homemade pies are made with memories."

Mom taught me how to make pies.

I was around five when I began watching her from a kitchen chair I pulled up to the counter. My siblings disappeared when it came to cooking, so this was the rare 'just mom and me time.'

Mom would drop a pound of Crisco into the big orange Tupperware bowl she used only for making dough. Then by hand she broke the lard into small bits to combine it with five cups of Robin Hood All Purpose Flour, one tablespoon baking powder, a teaspoon salt, and a tablespoon brown sugar, which Mom informed, "would help the pastry brown." She blended these ingredients with her hands, while I watched white fat ooze between her fingers till she squeezed and pushed everything into a sticky, grey blob.

I couldn't wait to see it transform into the pumpkin pie we'd enjoy at dinner when our house overflowed with laughter of family friends who didn't have a home for Christmas. Mom said, "There's lots of food. Everyone's welcome."

She didn't think people should be alone during the holidays.

In a separate measuring cup, she beat a large egg, then added a dash of white vinegar before filling the vessel with cold water till it reached the one cup mark. She stirred the liquids furiously with a fork until it turned milky white, contents escaped over the cup's edge. Next, she poured the mixture on top of the flour ball, and began kneading them together.

I listened to the juices squelch, watched the fluids spill over Mom's fingers, as she massaged the ingredients into one another until they were as smooth as Play Dough. Then, she stopped and wiped her hands on the floral apron wrapped around her. I savoured the pastry's aroma, which smelled like the putty Dad spread around the bathtub rim.

"So water won't leak into the wall," he explained.

I thought of the times I practiced making pastry using the garden hose and dirt in the back yard where the dogs did their business. Mud squished the same as dough, though smelled like our pets, a scent I knew as 'the floral of spring.'

"Can I try?" I asked Mom, my hands already wildly squashing and punching the dough the way I practiced with mud.

"Don't!" she panicked.

I looked at her confused.

"What?"

"If you mix it too much, you'll make it hard to chew."

I stopped pounding. Mom yanked the bowl away, removed a part of the dough and dusted it with flour, sprinkled more flour onto the counter and rolling pin, and rocked the pastry into a ball before flattening it. She applied the rolling pin to its centre and pushed outward several times till a perfect circle was formed, then gently lifted it into the glass pie plate.

When Beverley O'Neil (*Ktunaxa* Nation) pens her stories, she aspires to paint a picture with words that moves people to tears or laughter or both. A former columnist in Indigenous newspapers and magazines, Beverley converts her life and humour to short stories and emerging novels.

Suppose You Were an Orange

MARK HOADLEY

You couldn't ride a bicycle
or get on the bus. You couldn't
ride a skateboard or ski or skate.
You could roll down hill
but not far up.
If it was windy you wouldn't
have to put on a jacket.
If it rained you wouldn't
need an umbrella or boots.
You'd never catch a cold.
You'd never sneeze or cough.
Your brothers would be oranges.
Your mom and dad and cousins—
all oranges. Your grandma and
your grandad, even your cat—
oranges, oranges,
oranges!
Sometimes you'd remember
being small and hanging
from a tree. Green leaves
rubbing against you and shadows
and sun on your bumpy skin.
You swinging back
and forth in the wind.
Now you sit in supermarkets
and lunch boxes. You wait.
People pick you up. They squeeze
and poke you and turn you
round and round. They study you
from top to bottom. Are you
the one for me? they think.
Are you good enough to eat?

Photograph by Derek von Essen.

Mark Hoadley writes poetry, fiction, and memoir. His
work has appeared in *Word Riot, Tin House's Open Bar,
The Guardian*, and *KYSO Flash*. He lives beside a forest
in Vancouver with his wife Sarah and is currently writing
a space opera with multi-media artist Matthew Barnard.

Queuing for Food

PETER QUARTERMAIN

(1941) Mum had sent you out with the ration books, "Don't forget to ask the butcher if he's got any lamb, tell him who it's for and don't let him take too many points or charge you too much. If he hasn't got lamb try and get a bit of brisket," or "Make sure you speak to Mr. Harding when you get the potatoes, he knows who we are and he's got a new girl who doesn't, you don't want to get potatoes with wireworm or with a lot of mud on them. I don't want to pay for three pounds of dirt," not that I'd dare say anything if there was, you just had to take what he gave you. Shopkeepers, especially butchers, had enormous power, you had to keep on the right side of *them*, everybody wanted a roast for Sunday, you'd eat it cold on Monday which was washing day, Shepherd's Pie on Tuesday, leftovers on Wednesday, spin the food out make it last, rissoles perhaps sausages if there were any for Thursday, fish on Friday, whatever you could scrape together on Saturday, and, on Sunday, start again. So you didn't want the butcher to give you a bit of tough old mutton full of fat and gristle that you couldn't eat, and you had to make friends with the butcher and the grocer, that's who you'd registered your ration book with and you couldn't shop anywhere else for meat and what Mum called staples. Some things, like tinned fruit, used up points in your ration book, you could get that sort of stuff anywhere provided they had some and you'd got the points. But you had to be careful, you didn't dare offend the butcher or the grocer, you'd be standing in line at Jones's and someone in the queue would say, "Didn't I see you in Smith's yesterday when I walked by?" they'd likely been in there themselves for that matter, but they'd got their oar in first, and you had to ingratiate yourself with the shopkeeper all over again or, even if you had been in Smith's, lie about it. But you'd better not get caught, lying was a tricky business. If one person in the queue had seen you then so had somebody else, denial was no good, so you acquired a repertoire of strategies, "I went to ask about young Millie's mother, I heard she'd been poorly" or "I heard he'd got some Kolynos toothpaste, *you* don't have any do you Mr. Jones?" knowing full well nobody had seen any of that stuff for months and you hated it anyway. Everybody knew what was going on but your status with the shop would be safe and your dignity more or less intact. Tobacconists had the same sort of power, *and* their favourite customers, but they weren't so possessive, cigarettes weren't rationed just in short supply, and sometimes you'd see people going from shop to shop looking more and more despondent as they tried to get hold of a packet of ten or even a packet of five, they'd take *any* brand, it didn't matter, you learned not to be fussy. You learned quickly, too, not to be la-di-dah about anything, but to chat with other people in the queue about where you'd found things, or who hadn't got any what and how much you missed it. If a posh person came in, excessive politeness lording it over everybody *Aym not at all suah you will hev what aym lookin for, would you be so kaind as to see?* there'd be a lot of loud remarks as soon as they left about how they'd been seen popping in and out of shops all over the place looking for stuff like anchovies or "Gentleman's Relish" whatever *that* might be, "You can't expect those sort of people to pay attention to the likes of us and Mr. Jones, that you can't, can you?" and heads would nod and wag under the bandanas. It wasn't just buildings that the War leveled.

Peter Quartermain is the author of two books of critical essays: *Stubborn Poetries* and *Disjunctive Poetics*. He edited the award winning two-volume *Collected Poems and Plays* of Robert Duncan, and co-edited two other collections. *Growing Dumb*, his memoir about boyhood in wartime England, is nearing completion. "Queuing for Food" is a selection from that memoir.

Hunger

JAMI MACARTY

1
Giving, then refusing him
the text of my mouth
I wrote my voracity
onto the world's
crowded page—a sentence
left hanging
from lover's ledge. Falling
from what was
into what I want it to be—
rapture's net:
dazzling, plausible,
relished on the tongue.

2
Ghosting me via satellite TV
during breakfast:
        a woman and her pact
        to weigh forty-
        nine pounds.
She aimed to attain
weight perfect
        as this egg's shell.
She wants only water:
        calorieless, colorless—
Sheer as veil
between now and eternity:
        food, she said,
        detains her.

Jami Macarty is the author of two chapbooks: *Landscape of The Wait* (Finishing Line Press, June 2017) and *Mind of Spring,* winner of the 2017 Vallum Chapbook Award (forthcoming, fall 2017). She teaches creative writing at Simon Fraser University, edits the online poetry journal *The Maynard,* writes *Peerings & Hearings–Occasional Musings on Arts in the City of Glass* for *Drunken Boat,* and serves as a Poetry Ambassador for Vancouver's Poet Laureate, Rachel Rose, and a Fresh Local Poet for Vancouver Park Board.

Sustenance: Food, Basic Needs, and School

HARTLEY BANACK

Through patterns of connection of shared basic needs (air, water, food), school "sustenance" is explored. For humans, our basic necessities are our roots. We cannot wander too far from Earth's surface without rather specialized care (under sea or off in space), and if Earth's atmospheric conditions change too dramatically, too quickly, humans perish. We are tethered to Earth through our basic needs. One might even be so brazen as to conjecture that doctrines of sustenance ought to undergird education, reminding us of concern and care for our needs.

Considering patterns around our daily decisions regarding these needs, we seem to prefer one against others. Many humans now live in polluted cities and subdivisions, drive cars, smoke, and work in indoor spaces that do not really deem quality of air too highly. The bottled water and sugary drink industries have demonstrated much greater success (financial and in practice) over water purification or access to local clean, fresh water. Wholesale privatizations of national water resources to corporate interests offer yet another example. It is food we seem to praise highest. We have fancy eateries, and treat our cooks as celebrities. We pit organic and ethical versus mass-produced food. Food is touted as the most important of our rudimentary needs. However, we must remember that food is beyond any instrumentality or representation in its affective power between and beyond (spiritually, physically, and inter-creature) humans. Historically, the fire and kitchen have often been the most social place in a home: to cook, to eat, to talk, to gather, to keep warm, and to laugh. Over millennia, humans have adopted practices and habits that have given rise to food ceremonies and acknowledgements to specific foods, seasons, and places.

How does school consider food? Most of us attended school, particularly between the ages of five to thirteen years old. These were also the years of basic habit formation, when many of our lifelong values were developed. Reflecting on my experiences growing up with food in school, I recall cafeterias, sandwiches, juice boxes, vending machines, apples, pudding, trash... lots of trash. Only a few eating experiences happened in class, mostly birthday cakes and treats (Halloween, Valentine's Day). Generally, we were not allowed to eat or drink in my classrooms.

Curiously, integral human relationships to food and eating have become decoupled from school and learning. Food at school, as lunch or snacks brought from home, is most commonly consumed during non-instructional periods (lunch and recess). Generally, everyone fashions their own food. Students and teachers eat apart. Students eat amongst lunch monitors, who do not eat, while trying to ensure a *just* eating experience for all. Limited time is given to eating, and this time has shortened in recent years at the schools my children attend as a cost-saving response to reduce school budgets and in connection to an ever-increasing emphasis on academic outputs.

The fact that eating and learning became, and continue to be, isolated in the K-12 school experience has lasting impacts on how we are human and how we understand and practice our sustenance. But what a student (or teacher) eats (or does not eat) for breakfast, lunch, or snack impacts class climate and learning, the research is clear. Food, regardless of being consumed together or not, plays integral roles in what happens at school, as do air and water. This decoupling of vital, essential, indispensible needs has become, and continues to be, a damaged and damaging pattern. In part, as a result of schooling practices, we remain disconnected and reproduce disconnection from food and each other. We might ask, "how inalienable are our inalienable rights?" with respect to school and our basic needs. Perhaps in our zeal to visit the depths of the sea or the planets of TRAPPIST-1, we fail more basic tenets?

Humans do not eat to merely survive, or to out or over live some extreme life, but rather to *vive* in our quotidian life... to harmoniously move in/with life, as living creatures, connected through our basic needs. We do not hold to "over hold" (sus-tener), but rather hold as we move with life, ensemble. This is a mutually emergent and shared experience, a pattern of human existence. Air, water, food, human connection, land, non-human creatures, and spirituality hold (sustain) us and we hold (sustain) these, sympathetically. And while we continue with marvel at how adeptly we move through uncharted territories (celestial to cybernetic), or the fabulous new dishes we create by combining exotic foods, we remain rooted to our terrestrial home through our basic needs, tethered, as muscle and bone, to land.

Might we be so unabashed as to demand that our educational (and more broadly, our societal) doctrines of sustenance ought to teach and remind us of concern and care of our basic needs?

Hartley Banack is a lecturer and the coordinator of the Outdoor Environmental Education programs with the Department of Curriculum and Pedagogy in the Faculty of Education at the University of British Columbia, Vancouver, Canada. He works with pre- and in-service teachers on how to increase the amount of time spent outdoors during instructional times. Hartley met Rachel Rose when she was invited to write a poem for Wild About Vancouver (WAV). WAV is an outdoor education festival spreading around the Lower Mainland of Vancouver which encourages more outdoor time. Rachel's poem, *Song Dogs*, can be read here:
www.wildaboutvancouver.com/song-dogs/

A Most Memorable Meal

KARENZA T WALL

i have eaten an average of three meals a day
including snacks
in one week, seven days
i have eaten
about twenty-one meals
including snacks
in one year, fifty-two weeks
i have eaten about
one thousand and ninety-two meals
including snacks
in the seventy years that i have lived
i have eaten about
seventy-six thousand, four hundred and forty meals
including snacks
how the fuck do i choose one

karenza t wall is an anglo indian from india. for the past fifty or so years she has been squatting on coast salish lands in the area known as vancouver.

Some Green Onions

LYDIA KWA

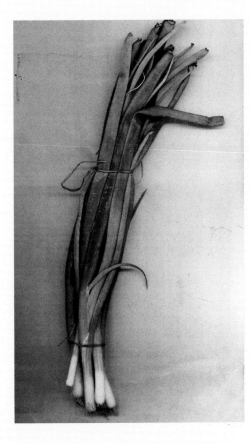

minus the guise of romance
they found themselves uprooted
then bound together
you'd feel tight
discomfort if bunched with
the lumpenproletariat
of vegetables
cheap, common
taken for granted
buddies in bad times
a gang of deviant
lightweights and
extravagant scrappers
possessed of unkempt 'dos
and tattooed stalks
they unfurl a pungent whiteness
with lean, green
unpredictability

Photography by Rita O'Grady

Lydia Kwa has called Vancouver home since 1992.
She has published three novels and two books of
poetry. Her first novel *This Place Called Absence*
(Winnipeg: Turnstone Press, 2000) was nominated
for several awards, including the Books in Canada
First Novel Award, and the Lambda Literary Prize.
She has several projects on the go, including a
chapbook project with poems as companion pieces
to artist Rita O'Grady's photocopied images.

Rita O'Grady is an artist living and working in
Vancouver, BC. Her print-based practice investigates
the tension between object and image, means of
production, the archive, and sometimes, futility.
Her work comprises traditional printmaking
methods as well as alternative photographic
processes such as cyanotypes, photograms, and
photocopies. Rita graduated from Emily Carr
University of Art & Design in 2011 and has exhibited
work at Malaspina Printmakers, Winsor Gallery, VSA
Gallery and the Port Moody Arts Centre. This is her
first ekphrastic collaboration.

Poem

KARA-LEE MACDONALD

eating
no longer about sustenance
or joy, but a struggle
for control—her image, her emotions, her
impulses, impulse
to consume, to be consumed

>   and on the seventh day
>   her body gave her a complex

she wants to decide
her weight, how others see her
she wants to be in the world, be present
have a presence, instead—
she slowly disappears
the question remains—how
can she hold on to her sense
of self while so preoccupied
with evacuation

Kara-lee MacDonald is the author of *Eating Matters* (Caitlin Press, 2016). She teaches English for Northern Lights College and has a BA and MA in English from UNBC. She is co-editor of *Thimbleberry Magazine* and has been previously published in *Dreamland Magazine*. She is a lifelong resident of Northern BC.

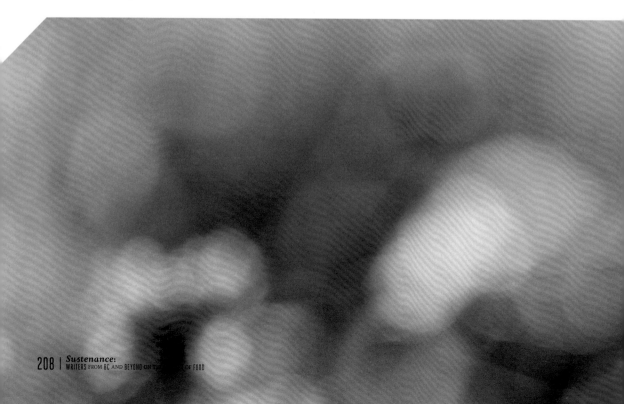

Tallest Objects

ELENA JOHNSON

Wildflowers one knuckle high.
Mammals the width of a hand
gather bouquets in their mouths,
pile them in havens under stones.
Each human gesture
weighted with layers of fleece and wool,
zippers and eiderdown.
A kilometre above sea-level,
we are the tallest objects
bent by the wind.
Wide-legged gait
of researchers. The hunch
at day's end, over a kitchen table
that is a series of planks.
On evenings that aren't wind and rain,
we form a loose circle. Chew false tobacco,
spit it red onto the rocks
outside the cook-tent's silvery dome.

Elena Johnson is the author of *Field Notes for the Alpine Tundra* (Gaspereau, 2015), a collection of poetry written at a remote ecology research station in the Yukon. Her work is featured in *Lemon Hound's* New Vancouver Poets folio and has appeared in numerous journals and anthologies, including *The Fiddlehead, ARC* and *Best Canadian Poetry in English 2015*. Born in New Brunswick, she has lived in many parts of Canada, as well as abroad. She currently resides in Vancouver.

Recipe

JEFF STEUDEL

The laundry sink overflowing with hockey
equipment, robots on the floor, we cook later
these days to saxophones like incandescent bulbs
lighting snooker tables in a basement pool hall.
We read out the ingredients and improvise:
plums and brandy for lemon; coriander, cumin,
and cayenne for a curry. Chorizo, garlic, cream,
and chives already on the stovetop, I read out
the steps. You flip the snapper. The steam rises
into the hood fan. I get mint from the garden.
Is this sex?   I read...   You...
          Yes dear...
read. Dear?   Yes. Soft lips of oysters
on the countertop. I cup your nipples. Bounce.

From *Foreign Park*, 2015 (Anvil Press). Used with permission of the publisher.

Jeff Steudel's poetry has appeared in publications across Canada, including, *PRISM international*, *CV2*, *The Fiddlehead*, *subTerrain*, and *Canadian Literature*. He received the Ralph Gustafson Poetry Prize, and his work was chosen as a finalist for the both the CBC Literary Awards and the Montreal International Poetry Prize. His first book, *Foreign Park*, was short-listed for the Dorothy Livesay Poetry Prize. He lives in East Vancouver.

Ballad in Crazy Quilts

KEVIN SPENST

In the beginning,
the Tree of Knowledge was in
a vending machine. Adam
borrowed two-bits
from that nice Norse fellow
named Buri. The fruit
fell halfway, jammed
behind the glass. Adam
snatched the snake
from under Vishnu's
dream, piped it through
the opening. Whit-
chamacallits and thing-
amajigs blocked its throat so it could
only fang the fruit. Mean-
while Buri needed
money to buy a thank-you
card for the cow
that had licked him
free from the ginnungagap
ice, so he moseyed
back to Adam's.
The snake was stuck.
Adam asked Eve
to use her little hands
to get in there. *Who's been*
tampering with
my vending machine?
God asked. Adam blamed
everybody, even Vishnu
who just kept snoring
(hence the eviction and a lot of bad
blood between everyone).

Kevin Spenst, a Pushcart Poetry nominee, is the author of *Ignite, Jabbering with Bing Bong,* (both with *Anvil Press*), and over a dozen chapbooks. His work has won the Lush Triumphant Award for Poetry, been nominated for both the Alfred G. Bailey Prize and the Robert Kroetsch Award for Innovative Poetry, and has appeared in dozens of publications including *subTerrain, Prairie Fire, CV2, the Rusty Toque, BafterC, Lemon Hound, Poetry is Dead,* and the anthology *Best Canadian Poetry 2014.*

Recipe

SHELAGH ROGERS

I confess to being addicted to maple syrup. My favourite thing is a maple syrup on snow (or *tire sur la neige*—literally a draw on the snow). Fresh snow and maple syrup heated to 240 degrees F, drizzled on snow and then rolled to form candy. I would go to sugar shacks, *cabanes à sucre* in the Ottawa/Gatineau area as a kid and watch sap boiled down to that luxurious elixir that is maple syrup. When I go to visit my godmother in Montreal in winter, I insist we go to a market where a *tire* is possible.

No snow (or at least not often enough, if you ask me) here on the west coast, and so I offer you my 3-Zeds Salad Dressing (the Zed being the hand motion as you drizzle it on to the greens).

Good fresh greens with some kind of peppery lettuce like arugula
1 Zed of extra-virgin olive oil
1 Zed of balsamic vinegar
1 Zed of maple syrup
A pinch of Maldon salt

Toss salad.

Shelagh Rogers, O.C., is a veteran broadcast-journalist with CBC Radio. From working alongside Peter Gzowski on *Morningside*, to hosting *Sounds Like Canada*, Shelagh is a familiar Canadian voice. Currently, she hosts and co-produces *The Next Chapter*, the program devoted to writing in Canada. When not on the air, Shelagh travels the land as a mental health advocate, and speaks about her time as an Honourary Witness to the work of the Truth and Reconciliation Commission. She is the co-editor of the book *Speaking My Truth: Reflections on Reconciliation and Residential School* and is the recipient of five honourary doctorates.

Cabbie with Pips

SHAZIA HAFIZ RAMJI

I almost forgot about the cabbie
who offered me cherries as soon
as I sat inside, before I could
tell him where we were going.
My reflex was to say "no
thank you," but it was 4 a.m.,
I was thirsty, made a quick
judgment and made it right
saying "yes," until he started singing
about home and love and I thought
he was readying to launch
full-force into his divorce or
some other matter, but he said:
"You haven't told me
where home is." He gave me
a Ziploc baggie and said,
"save your pips, you'll need them
when you get there."

Shazia Hafiz Ramji lives in Vancouver, BC
where she writes stories, poems, and works
as the poetry editor at *PRISM international*.
Her writing has been shortlisted for the
2017 Robert Kroetsch Award for Innovative
Poetry, the 2016 National Magazine
Awards, and has recently appeared in
Canadian Literature.

Seven Weeks

ROB TAYLOR

Each year, Thanksgiving and Christmas,
I make the cranberry sauce. Everyone
around the table agrees it's the best
they've ever had, even those
who used to swear by the canned stuff.
I used to swear by the canned stuff.
At first everyone assumed your mother
made it, but she would always clarify.
Now they ask how I do it and I say
I follow the instructions on the bag.
They ask what I put in it and I say
water and sugar and cranberries.
Every Thanksgiving it's the same,
then, amazingly, again each Christmas—
something to fill the spaces between mouthfuls.
When we tell them about you this Christmas
they're going to lose their minds. Then once
they've calmed down we'll go back to eating
and maybe later they'll ask about the cranberry sauce
and I'll say Instructions Water Sugar Cranberries.
Or maybe we'll just keep talking about you
until it seems we've conjured you from our dreams
and you're there, flesh and blood, in the room,
which of course you will be.

from *The News* (Gaspereau Press, 2016)

Rob Taylor is the author of the poetry collections *The Other Side of Ourselves* (Cormorant Books, 2011) and *The News* (Gaspereau Press, 2016), which was a finalist for the 2017 Dorothy Livesay Prize. In 2014 he was named one of the inaugural writers-in-residence at the Al Purdy A-frame, and in 2015 he received the City of Vancouver's Mayor's Arts Award for the Literary Arts, as an emerging artist. He lives in Vancouver with his family, where he makes cranberry sauce and coordinates the Dead Poets Reading Series.

Fresh meat on the edge of a knife

Food I ate in the Torngat Mountains

by Sarah Leavitt

Last summer I was lucky enough to go to Torngat Mountains National Park in the far north of Labrador. The park was so remote that I knew I would probably never get to go there again, so I was determined to say yes to every opportunity. So I did things like flying in a helicopter three times even though it terrified me, and got to look down from the sky on supernaturally green lakes and turquoise fjords, skim over the tops of glaciers and swoop between towering mountains.

I also said yes to food I had never eaten before. One day our group went along on a hunting expedition. After one of the hunters shot a caribou, everyone was helping with the carving up, and one of the hunters came around and offered each of us a small bit of raw meat on the edge of his sharp knife. He was smiling like he knew it would be one of the best things we'd ever tasted. The small soft red bit of meat tasted delicate but also powerfully alive. It was perfect and the sky over our heads was gigantic and bright blue.

On the way back to base camp we stopped at an island to cook some of the caribou meat. One of the hunters, Maria, was cutting up the meat and I heard her mutter, "I asked him to bring me a hind leg and he brought me a front leg." I laughed to myself because I thought I probably would never hear anyone say that again and I couldn't believe where I was. Maria cut up the meat and we took turns cooking it over a fire on flat rocks coated with a bit of margarine ("the traditional Inuit way," laughed one of the men). The meat was seared on the outside and juicy on the inside and had an incredibly dark, rich, concentrated flavour. We ate it with our fingers.

Later that evening back at the camp I ran into Maria in the women's bathroom. She said she wished we'd gotten a seal because she likes to eat the brains right after the seal is killed, while they're still warm.

I did try seal meat another day, boiled, but it tasted like liver and tuna mixed together and I didn't like it. Someone said you shouldn't try to eat it plain. You should cook a pork roast, then cook the seal meat in the pan that the pork was in so that it is flavoured with the pork fat.

On an overnight camping trip, Robert, one of the hunters, wrapped a fresh-caught Arctic char in tinfoil and cooked it in the flames of a big fire. When he unwrapped it there were strips of bacon laid across the fish. "Look," he said, "it's one of those Arctic bacon char." Beneath the blackened skin, the fish was sweet and oceany.

The next morning, one of the park staff, Mary, cooked us scrambled eggs and fry bread on a Coleman stove inside a white canvas tent. It was cold and the inside of the tent was very warm and the eggs and bread were some of the best food I have ever tasted. Of course I had eaten eggs and bread before, but never like that, never at the edge of a fjord on a rocky beach that I'd flown to in a helicopter.

Sarah Leavitt's first book, *Tangles: A Story About Alzheimer's, My Mother, and Me*, a graphic memoir, has been published in Canada, the US, UK, Germany, France and Korea to international critical acclaim. A feature-length animation based on *Tangles* is currently in development. Sarah is also working on a second book, *Agnes, Murderess*, a graphic novel set in nineteenth-century British Columbia, forthcoming from Freehand Books.

Apples and Honey

MARK L. WINSTON and RENÉE SAROJINI SAKLIKAR

September and October are important months for honeybees and beekeepers, their final opportunity to bring in the last dribs and drabs of fall honey, and ours to prepare hives for the long winter ahead. But fall beekeeping and winter colony survival are dependent on spring bloom, because it's those nectar-producing flowers of spring from which we harvest honey in the fall, and it's the honey we leave for the honeybees each fall on which they survive until the next spring.

The Jewish New Year, *Rosh Hashanah*, also happens in September or early October, a festival of renewal and reflection where bees and honey play a prominent role. We dip slices of apple into honey and recite: "May it be your will, Lord our God and God of our ancestors, to renew this year for us with sweetness and happiness."

The simple rhythm of blessing, dipping and merging apple and honey holistically unites my own disparate identities of beekeeper, scientist, teacher, writer and Jew. It is at these moments that I feel most whole, and at these times of celebration that I most deeply understand the role of bees in nature and in my own life.

Apples would not exist were it not for the pollinating influence of the bees, which transfer pollen between flowers every spring, setting the seed for the apple fruit. The apples, for their part, produce sweet nectar in their flowers, which attracts the bees to dip their tongues deep into the flower, knocking pollen off the flower and onto their hairy bodies in the process of imbibing.

The pollen rubs off on subsequent floral visits, fertilizing the flowers, and the life and growth of the new apple fruit begins. The nectar from the apple flowers is carried back to the bees' nest, turned into honey and stored for the winter, providing honeybee colonies with food to survive until the next spring, when the cycle is renewed as the bees pollinate again.

We celebrate this annual cycle by joining the apple and honey together to renew the sweetness of the seasons. But this closely intertwined relationship has deeper meaning, because the quality of the apple depends on the number of bee visits. The more bees that visit each flower, the larger and rounder the fruit. The quality of the fruit is further enhanced when the donor and recipient trees are different varieties, yet another celebration of diversity's inherent value.

Quality also has to do with the diversity of bee species that visit the blossoms, with many dozens of wild species attending to apple pollination in addition to the managed honeybees. Each bee species works the flower differently, transferring pollen in various ways, thereby contributing their own unique style to the critical task of pollination.

So it is with human societies. It is through the cross-fertilization of ideas and talents that we express our best communal selves. We derive strength and wisdom from our mutual visions, just as the apples are improved by the visits of diverse bees to set fruit.

The feel and smell of the bee yard are right there with me during our holiday celebrations, connected with the cycles of the seasons and the profound beliefs and history from which my own rituals descended and my descendants will learn from and enjoy.

Yes, there is much that can be revealed when the taste of crunchy apple is mixed with the sweetness of honey. But isn't it always like that, with wonder all around us when we open our eyes to the profound insights imbedded in the simplest of pleasures?

Mark L. Winston is the recipient of the 2015 Governor General's Literary Award for Nonfiction for his book *Bee Time: Lessons From the Hive.* One of the world's leading experts on bees and pollination, Dr. Winston is also an internationally recognized researcher, teacher and writer.

Renée Sarojini Saklikar writes *thecanadaproject,* a life-long poem chronicle, volume one of which is the award-winning *children of air india, un/authorized exhibits and interjections* (Nightwood Editions, 2013). Renée is the Poet Laureate for the City of Surrey and is currently working on the long poem, THOT-J-BAP. She collects poems about bees and is working on a series of bee poems for a collaborative work with bee scientist and author, Dr. Mark Winston.

Sustenance (from *THE BOOK OF SMALLER*)

rob mclennan

The days prolong, in fragments. First thing. Children banter. Cereal, milk. Preschooler's laugh. Devoured by what separates, combines. Coffee, doesn't. Are we out of? Newspaper, moments. Rose, a wish to water seedlings. Sprout. All we've managed to garden. Where's her schoolbag? Put your socks on. Chew. Beyond the frame: Christine's work-prep. Liner notes. An ache, to dispatch. Empty driveway bins they feel such rain. Banana handful to the baby's mouth.

Born in Ottawa, Canada's glorious capital city, rob mclennan currently lives in Ottawa, where he is home full-time with the two wee girls he shares with Christine McNair. The author of more than thirty trade books of poetry, fiction and non-fiction, he won the John Newlove Poetry Award in 2010, the Council for the Arts in Ottawa Mid-Career Award in 2014, and was longlisted for the CBC Poetry Prize in 2012. He regularly posts reviews, essays, interviews and other notices at robmclennan.blogspot.com

No. 6

KERRY GILBERT

the 737-pound woman on display was a slender child—the kind that sucks on a springy auburn curl while carefully pushing peas with her finger to a designated spot on her plate—leaving the mashed potatoes untouched—mount vesuvius heavy with thick sauce. but then, when she was five, she witnessed a girl crawl into a backyard snow fort with a man at recess. and in the swiftest of moments, faster than melting butter on warm bread, she ate the child all up—wiping the last curl from her drippy wet mouth before anyone could guess what had happened. and as the years passed, she grew with different versions of the same girl over and over and over until now, up on a dimly lit stage, she sits on an ornate tapestry sofa, in a soft pink baby doll dress—her curls pinned too high with a doubled-up silk ribbon.

Kerry Gilbert teaches Creative Writing at Okanagan College. Her first book of poetry, *(kerplnk): a verse novel of development*, was published in 2005 with Kalamalka Press and her second book of poetry, *Tight Wire*, was published in 2016 with Mother Tongue Publishing.

The Seven Best Places to Eat in Canada

J.B. MacKINNON

1. The simple table of the German-Canadian farmer I used to work for, planting seedlings maybe, or shovelling the steaming funk of the compost pile, until the cold rain came hammers and nails, and he called lunch early and we went inside to spread strong garlic and thick yoghurt on homemade bread while he cooked a soup called "one pot" because everything in the kitchen—apples, onions, cauliflower, herbs, mustard—got cooked up in just one pot, and then afterward we would have schnapps, and maybe a beer, and never would get back to working the fields.

2. My mother's house, at the table her father made, which is nothing special, really, just benches and a butter-yellow table like you'd find in a children's book, on the day that the orderly mind that is necessary for cooking somehow emerges from the wilderness of her dementia, and I arrive for a visit to find good fish, good rice, good broccoli, a warm bun, a salad, a small miracle, really, waiting for me to witness it.

3. In a tent in the middle of Labrador, in winter, at -40 Celsius, which is so cold that you can hear your teeth squeak as they expand and contract with each hot breath out, each frozen breath in, eating bun-less hotdogs with my friend Jerry, twenty years my senior, and the steam fills the tent (it will freeze and in the morning we will sweep it up with a whisk broom, like dust), so much like smoke that we begin to hold the hotdogs between the fingers of our gloves in the manner of rich men, or gangsters, and take to calling the tent the Cigar Lounge, and laughing until tears freeze onto our eyelashes.

4. Any riverbank, beach, shore, sheet of ice, campsite or cabin where you cook over an open fire a fish that you have caught, having first humbled yourself before the fact that we all feast on the death of living things.

5. My own kitchen on those rare days when I bump into friends on the street, and the weather is fine and time feels limitless, and so we agree to eat together, not a "dinner party" with its elaborate modern scheduling dance and gift bottles of wine and performance anxiety around puff pastry, but a coming together for whatever can be made of that moment, say, omelettes with cheese and sage, fried potatoes, frozen peas, two sweet-sharp apples broken into quarters.

6. Along the Nass Highway, where you might taste salmon, opened up like a butterfly and dried, and then heated again on a fire until the jerky drips with its own fat, or then again you might taste pickled bull kelp, or the grease extracted from *oolichan* smelt, which have fermented in open bins for nine days, or then again you might taste sea-lion stew, as rich as anything you will ever put in your mouth, unless you keep going north until you taste whale blubber, and any or all of it will remind you that in this place that we call Canada, the familiar can always turn strange, the strange always turn familiar.

7. There are some excellent restaurants, too.

J.B. MacKinnon is a journalist and author of the bestsellers *The 100-Mile Diet* (with Alisa Smith) and *The Once and Future World*. He lives in Vancouver and online at jbmackinnon.com and @JB_MacKinnon (Twitter).

In Autumn Garden

JOANNE ARNOTT

in October fields
I sit
all around me
the summer fruits
were plucked
and hauled away
their residual greens
of leaf and stalk and vine
become yellow
brown
black
and die away
in October fields
I sit
slow I ripen
on the vine
my colours deepen
my fruit
thickens to round
as the gardens
quiet around me
and the gardeners
put each plot to bed
then turn themselves
away
with thoughts of tea
in winter kitchens
in October fields
I sit
a harvest moon
on a frosty day

First published in *Mother Time* (Ronsdale, 2007).

Joanne Arnott is a Canadian Métis/mixed-blood writer
& arts activist, originally from Manitoba, at home on
the west coast. *Wiles of Girlhood* won the League of
Canadian Poets' Gerald Lampert Award (best first book,
1992). She has published essays and poetry in many
anthologies, and eight further books. She is currently
the Poetry Editor for *EVENT* magazine.

Making Pies with Sylvia Plath

LORNA CROZIER

We both insist on lard. Even here with me,
in the kitchen and so long after, she wears lipstick
bright as poppies, and a kerchief on her head
as if she's just come in from riding
in a roadster along the coast.
I've misplaced my rolling pin so we use
a bottle of pinot grigio cold from the fridge.
Is there milk for the children? Yes, yes.
My oven is electric. It's heating up.
So much taller, she can reach the pie tins
on the highest shelf. Side by side
in the bottom shell, she lines up rooks,
five of them black with rain, dabbed with butter,
stiff feet holding up the top. You make good pastry
only if you're in love, she says. The magic's in
the hands, their faith in never-after. By the time
the pie is done, she's gone, I don't know where.
I set the pie on the windowsill to cool
and alone in the kitchen, in the warmth and dark,
I wait till dawn for the birds to sing.

First published in *What the Soul Doesn't Want* (Freehand, 2017)

Lorna Crozier's *The Wrong Cat* received both the Raymond Souster and Pat Lowther
Awards in 2016. She lives, gardens and cooks with fellow writer Patrick Lane on
Vancouver Island.

Crabapple Jelly 1

MAUREEN HYNES

Two bulging bags of crabapples—not so welcome a gift.
Hundreds, each the size of a pituitary gland, a small red egg.
Chopped, the white flesh yellows in the pot as the pile
so slowly accumulates. Notice your forearm ache
from slicing off the stem and blossom ends.
The occasional worm on your cutting board.
Don't discard the peels or seeds or cores, cook them in,
the pectin closest to the peel. Feel your silver bracelet heat
alarmingly as you stir and stir. The apples turning into a mash
of yellow, red, pink. Worry: how cloudy
the mixture is. Wait for the full rolling boil,
the boil that doesn't go away.
Lay the steaming fruit on four layers of damp cheesecloth,
tie thick wet knots and suspend the parcel
over the bowl on a broomstick between two chairs overnight.
Let the mixture drip.
The next morning bring precisely five cups
of strained liquid back to a full rolling boil. Add
an appalling amount of sugar. The first
sign of clarifying: relief. Pour the hot coral syrup
into eight small jars, immerse them in a canning bath,
cover with two inches of boiling water. The slight pop
as the last jar seals, cooling on your counter.
Contemplate precision. The goal of clarity.
The principle of reduction. Take clean and tender care of your pots,
your spoons and jars, your muslin and wide-mouthed funnel,
your friends who leave fruit on your porch.
Accept imperfection, the *wabi*
of unskimmed flecks.
What substance will thicken your work
like pectin, give it form?
Persistence
and the small result.
Patience
and the small audience.
The sweetening, how necessary it sometimes is.
The gleaming.

"Crabapple Jelly 1" was first published in *Marrow, Willow* (Pedlar Press, 2011).

Maureen Hynes's poetry collection, *Rough Skin*, won the League of Canadian Poets' Gerald Lampert Award. Her most recent book, *The Poison Colour*, was nominated in 2016 for both the Pat Lowther and Raymond Souster Awards. Her poetry has been included in over twenty anthologies, including *Best Canadian Poems in English 2010* and *2016*. Maureen teaches creative writing at the University of Toronto, and is poetry editor for *Our Times* magazine. www.maureenhynes.com

A Small Prayer

RUSSELL THORNTON

Two days and nights
after your heart attack,
you asked for a first meal,
a sip of raspberry Boost,
a mouthful of Cream of Wheat.
We propped you up,
held your head for you,
put a straw then a teaspoon
to your elderly lips,
delicate and eager
as some tiny infant animal's.
You were so grateful,
and managed "Delicious"
and "Thank you," and lay back.
It was a last supper,
that first, last meal,
during which the betrayer, Time,
sat next to you.
You were already empty space
pouring into us
and starving us
who knew you would be gone
before morning,
nothing to remember you by
but our solitary selves.
Oh my holy one, my grandmother.
The hospital room
is a dark garden,
the avenues are winding streets
where Time skulks, damned.
The world you tasted
separates you from us.
Oh my raspberry and milk.
Oh my broken one.

Printed with permission from Harbour Publishing from *House Built of Rain* (Harbour Publishing)

Russell Thornton's *The Hundred Lives* was shortlisted for the 2015 Griffin Poetry Prize.
His *Birds, Metals, Stones & Rain* was shortlisted for the 2013 Governor General's Award
for Poetry, the Raymond Souster Award and the Dorothy Livesay BC Book Prize.
Thornton's poems have appeared recently in translation in Greek, Romanian, and
Ukrainian. He lives in North Vancouver, BC.

Wild Plum

SALLY ITO

Her soccer practice cancelled,
we walk to the woods instead
to pick wild plums.
Leave some for the squirrels
the daughter says absently
while minding the dog.
Each plum in the tree dangles
like a jewel from a lobe,
and like some matronly monarch
from yore, I finger them like
treasure. The treasure is time,
you see, spent with the daughter
in a careless hour of foraging
just before dusk. Soon
she will disappear like the moon
into a brooding cloud of dismay
and disappointment in me, her mother
who knows only greediness
for these scant occasions when
the fruit is ripe and ready
for the plucking.

Sally Ito is a writer and translator who lives in Winnipeg. Her latest poetry book, *Alert to Glory* was published in 2011, and a recent poem, 'Idle' was selected this year for the *Best Canadian Poetry 2016* anthology.

Tomatoes on the Windowsill After Rain

and bread by the woodstove
waiting to be punched down again.
I step out into the dark
morning, find the last white flowers
in a Mason jar by the door
and a note from a friend saying
he would call again later. I go back
into the kitchen, tomatoes
on the windowsill after rain,
small things but vast
if you desire them.

The deep fresh red.
This life rushing towards me.

Susan Musgrave has published more than thirty books and received awards in six
categories—poetry, novels, non-fiction, food writing, editing and books for children.
She lives on Haida Gwaii where she owns and manages Copper Beech Guest House, and
teaches poetry in UBC's Optional Residency MFA in Creative Writing Program. Her
most recent book, *A Taste of Haida Gwaii: Food Gathering and Feasting at the Edge of
the World,* won the Bill Duthie Bookseller's Choice Award at the 2016 BC Book Prizes,
and was the gold winner in the regional cookbook category at the Taste Canada
Awards, November 2016.

Apple Picking

SUSAN OLDING

It started before we even left
the house—her anger, my lecture,
the usual clenched teeth and reddened
cheeks, eyes hard as apple seeds—
and this time we almost cancelled
our outing. But our friends were waiting,
and without a purpose, the day would stretch so long
and I wanted the fruit
so in the end, we came to some settlement,
and pulled on our shoes
to go picking.

The girls fought
all the way to the ferry.
Mine making furious faces,
the other whining and telling tales,
the seemingly endless round of passing
the blame. Still guilty about my lecture,
I tried coaching and other sleights
of hand. But my daughter is too smart
for that. She only sneered at me and turned
away. "Mrs. Change the Subject!"

As we crossed the narrow channel from mainland
to island, it poured.
We scanned the sky and reassured ourselves
that it couldn't last. But it did last. Of course it did,
and when we reached the trees, the rain
renewed itself. All afternoon, the girls sniped
and parried, throwing burrs and hoping they'd stick,
pointing out the deer shit wedged
to the other's shoe,
warning about the worm in the apple
already eaten.

Later, we picnicked near the pier. The shoreline melted
like a Monet as the clouds
parted. For at least an hour,
the girls fought imaginary pirates
instead of each other,
then mine collected
wildflowers and offered
herself, nestling under the crook of my arm
for a kiss.

Irene, the orchard owner, complained
about the work. The endless lawn that takes hours
to cut, the marauding deer that must be stopped,
the need to be constantly on duty
during the season.
Sometimes, it feels like too much, tending
my child. Grafted from another place,
she'll need so much sun,
such delicate pruning and solid
buttressing to ripen.

She and I are the same
species. Hard on the outside.
Stubborn clingers, who don't want to let
go. And both of us fallen—
fallen and bruised—
yet sweet at the core
for anyone brave enough
to taste us.

Susan Olding is the author of *Pathologies: A Life in Essays*. Her writing has won a National
Magazine Award (Canada), and has appeared in *The Bellingham Review, The L.A. Review
of Books, Maisonneuve, The Malahat Review, The New Quarterly*, and the *Utne Reader*,
and in anthologies including *Best Canadian Essays 2016* and *In Fine Form, 2nd Edition*.

Chocolate Sparkle Cookies

THOMAS HAAS

"You only have one life, and every day is precious. If there's one question in life it's who you are and what makes you happy. If you have a positive attitude you will get closer to the answer. What makes me happy? Harmony and honesty and genuine success in the big picture. Being right is not what I want. It's being better. Life is a lot about heavily embracing compromise, sacrifice and tolerance. I want to grow old with an amazing feeling of not having regrets."
—Thomas Haas

(as quoted from "Thomas and Lisa Haas: Sweet Success, Their Way" in an article by Martha Perkins in the WestEnder, February 14, 2014 http://www.westender.com/news-issues/thomas-and-lisa-haas-sweet-success-their-way-1.878998)

Makes 20 cookies (recommended: make one batch at a time)

INGREDIENTS:

· ½ lb semisweet chocolate, chopped
· 3 tbsp. butter, at room temperature
· 2 eggs
· ⅓ cup sugar
· 1 tbsp. honey
· ¾ cup ground almonds
· 2 tsp. cocoa
· pinch of kosher salt
· coarse sugar or granulated sugar for rolling

METHOD:

1. Melt chocolate in a bowl set over simmering water. Stir in butter.
2. With a mixer, beat eggs and gradually beat in sugar and honey. Continue beating until eggs are light and form ribbons (5 minutes). Fold in chocolate/butter mixture. Combine almonds, cocoa and salt. Gently combine with egg mixture. Cover and refrigerate 4 hours to overnight.
3. Form batter into approximately 1" balls. Roll in sugar and place on a baking sheet lined with parchment paper. Press cookies down slightly.
4. Bake in a preheated 325F/160C oven 10 to 12 minutes until firm but still chewy inside. Cool on wire racks.

Thomas Haas is an internationally acclaimed, fourth-generation *pâtissier*. He first gained experience in his family's café in Germany before apprenticing and working in Michelin-starred restaurants in Europe and North America, and earning his stripes as *Konditormeister* or Master Pastry Chef.

Lured by the beauty of Canada's West Coast, Haas settled in Vancouver, opening two eponymous cafés and launching a line of hand-crafted chocolates and confections available in leading hotels, retailers and restaurants across North America. Using only the finest raw ingredients, Haas eschews the notion of assembly lines and mass production techniques—rather, he leads a talented team of pastry chefs and chocolatiers whose finesse and sensitivity, like his, is lovingly expressed in every hand-spun confection.

Thomas Haas Chocolates & Pâtisserie
North Vancouver | 998 Harbourside Drive
Kitsilano | 2539 West Broadway
Twitter: @thaaschocolates
Instagram: @thaaschocolates
Facebook: /thaaschocolates
Web: www.thomashaas.com

A Grain of Rice

EVELYN LAU

My father once plucked a grain of rice
from his porcelain bowl, suspended it
between wooden chopsticks—
this pale nub like a cell, a sickly
white worm, grub. His instruction
was to chew it slowly, savour it,
let the starch release and dissolve—
he wanted to teach the child
that even a grain of rice
could yield a store of sweetness
if you were starving. I tasted syrup,
molasses, a lash of vinegar.
Perhaps the body holds a genetic memory
of hunger, lack and privation
stamped into its neurons—
peasants starving to death in the parched
countryside, stuffing their mouths
with seeds, grass, hissing insects.
In my twenties, in the plenitude
of the western world, locked
in self-imposed starvation, I would reel
down the too-bright street in a daze,
gaze at anyone with food in their hands—
molecules of salt and grease and sugar
exploding like dandelions in the breeze,

I breathed and breathed,
wanting to claw their fat-smeared faces
like a wild beast after a trek through frozen tundra.
My mother's family in China shared a single
scrawny chicken on feast day,
hacked into bony pieces,
feeding two adults and twelve children.
Once I devoured a whole chicken in the bathtub—
slimy skin, rich barbecued flesh,
bitter hidden innards—
tearing it apart with my hands,
tossing the bones overboard.
Vomiting a village's dinner into the toilet.

Evelyn Lau is the author of four volumes of poetry, two works of nonfiction, two short story collections and a novel. *Runaway: Diary of a Street Kid*, published when she was eighteen, was a Canadian best seller and was made into a CBC movie starring Sandra Oh in her first major role. Lau's prose books have been translated into a dozen languages worldwide. *You Are Not Who You Claim* won the Milton Acorn People's Poetry Award; *Oedipal Dreams* was nominated for the Governor-General's Award. Her work has appeared in over a hundred literary magazines, garnering four Western Magazine Awards and a National Magazine Award. Her poems have been included in the *Best American Poetry* and *Best Canadian Poetry* series. She presently freelances as a mentor to aspiring writers through UBC's booming Ground and SFU's Writing and Publishing Program.

Kidney Beans and Rice (*Rajma Chawal*)

MEERU DHALWALA and VIKRAM VIJ

When we were growing up, *rajma chawal* was one of our favourite meals, and when we became parents, we introduced it very early into Nanaki and Shanik's diet. It is the one meal that all Indian kids learn how to make when they leave home for good; in fact, as a twenty-year-old student in hotel management in Austria, the one dish that Vikram and his friends could afford to make, and always enjoyed, was *rajma chawal*. On Sunday afternoons they downed bowls of it along with glasses of cheap whisky. Meeru's sister, Ritu, didn't put much effort into cooking until her twins got off baby food. At the time the only dish she knew how to make was *rajma chawal*, so the twins were eating it two to three times a week. Even today all of her recipes are descended from *rajma chawal*.

When Nanaki was five and Shanik was three, they had some friends over for lunch and wanted to serve *rajma chawal*. One of the friends saw the kidney beans and said, "Eew, what's that?" Shanik was genuinely bewildered that these kids didn't like this dish. For Nanaki, it was a disappointing moment. It wasn't just that her friends had insulted her favourite food—this meal represented who her family was. For all of Nanaki's pickiness when it comes to Indian food, *rajma chawal* is still the one she likes most.

From what we've observed, for non-Indian diners kidney beans aren't exactly at the top of the list. In India kidney beans are a staple food item and mightily enjoyed. They're a high source of iron and protein for a vegetarian society. Kidney beans and rice *(rajma chawal)* is as common a combination in India as macaroni and cheese is in North America, and although we speak English at home, we always say *rajma chawal* (pronounced "chavel"), never kidney beans and rice.

It may seem silly to write down a *rajma chawal* recipe for Indians, because most Indians already know how to make it. In our version we add mild Mexican chili powder and less cumin and coriander. In Ritu's version, there are no onions but an abundance of garlic. Ritu and the twins are so hardcore about their *rajma* that sometimes theirs has only garlic, tomatoes, turmeric, salt and black pepper. If you want to experience the comfort of this dish but really don't like kidney beans, you can also use pinto beans.

To make this recipe quick and easy, we suggest you use canned kidney beans. If you are using soaked dried kidney beans, you will need to boil them on medium heat, covered, for one hour. If you are using a pressure cooker to make this dish with dried beans, you will need to cook the beans for twenty-two to twenty-five minutes. If you're concerned about having gas at work the next day, there's ginger in the recipe; as long as you chew properly, you'll be fine. For a heartier meal, serve *rajma chawal* with yogurt or a side salad.

Serves 6
Prep & cooking time: 30 minutes (if you have already cooked the rice)

- ½ cup cooking oil
- 2 cups chopped onion (1 large)
- 2 tbsp. finely chopped garlic (6 medium cloves)
- 2 tbsp. finely chopped ginger
- 1½ cups chopped tomatoes (3 medium)
- 1½ tbsp. mild Mexican chili powder
- 1 tsp. turmeric
- 1 tbsp. ground cumin
- 1 tbsp. ground coriander
- 1½ tsp. salt
- 1 tsp. black pepper (optional)
- 1 tsp. ground cayenne pepper (optional)
- ½ cup plain yogurt, stirred (optional)
- 5 to 6 cups water (6 for a soupier curry)
- 3 14-oz cans kidney beans, drained and rinsed
- 5 to 6 cups cooked white or brown basmati rice

Heat oil in a medium pot on medium-high for 30 seconds. Add onion and sauté for 8 minutes, or until slightly dark brown. Add garlic and sauté for 2 minutes, then stir in ginger and tomatoes. Add chili powder, turmeric, cumin, coriander, salt, black pepper and cayenne and sauté this masala for 5 to 8 minutes, or until oil glistens on top.

Place yogurt in a small bowl. To prevent curdling, spoon about 3 tbsp. of the hot masala into the yogurt. Stir well, then pour yogurt into the pot of masala. Sauté for 2 minutes, or until oil glistens again.

Add water, stir and bring to a boil on high heat. Add kidney beans, stir and bring to a boil again. Reduce the heat to medium and cook for 3 minutes. (If you are using a pressure cooker, you can make the masala in the cooker and then add the dried kidney beans and water.) Serve the rice and beans buffet-style in separate bowls.

Photograph courtesy of John Sherlock (with permission)

Meeru Dhalwala was born in India and grew up in the Washington, DC area. In DC, she worked with various organizations on human rights and economic development projects. Meeru moved to Vancouver in February 1995 and has since been cooking and running the kitchens at Vij's and Rangoli restaurants. Vij's has been hailed by the *New York Times* as "easily among the finest Indian restaurants in the world." Meeru works closely with her all-female, Punjabi kitchen staff to experiment with cooking techniques and spice combinations.

Meeru penned the three Vij's cookbooks: *Vij's—Elegant and Inspired Indian Cuisine*, which won Cuisine Canada's 2007 Gold Award for Best Cookbook, and *Vij's at Home: Relax, Honey*, which placed second in the Best Indian Cuisine Book in the World category at the 2010 Gourmand International World Cookbook Awards. The third cookbook, *Vij's Indian: Cherished Recipes*, with Penguin-Random House was released in October 2016.

Chef Vikram Vij moved to Canada in 1989. He owns three award-winning Indian restaurants: Vij's, Rangoli and My Shanti. He created a line of frozen meals, Vij's At Home, sold across Canada. He launched a food truck in 2012, Vij's Railway Express, and his foods are sold at BC Place stadium, Whistler/Blackcomb and Loblaws. In 2014, Vikram debuted as the first Indo-Canadian Dragon on CBC's Dragons' Den. He is a recipient of honourary doctorates from Simon Fraser University and the University of British Columbia. He is co-author of *Vij's: Elegant & Inspired Indian Cuisine*, *Vij's At Home: Relax, Honey* and *Vij's Indian: Our Stories, Spices and Cherished Recipes*.

Omelet

FIONA TINWEI LAM

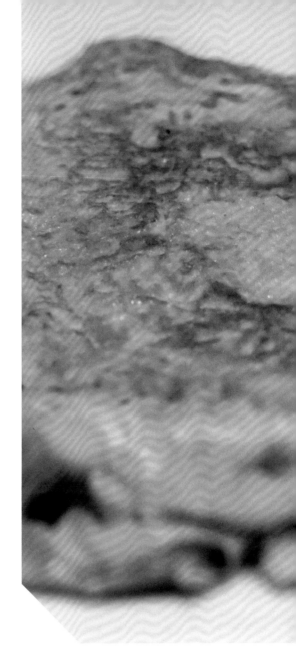

First, the egg.
I teach him the way I taught myself,
food group by food group
through the tattered cookbook.
I break the eggs; he stirs them.
A flick of salt, a few drops of cream.
I heat the pan, grate the cheese.
He pours the eggs in. Opacity
spreads from the edges inward:
an ocean sizzles into land.
Perched on the countertop,
he observes me like the scientist
he might become.
I flip one side over. *Voila!*
Last night, we played a game
and pulled a card. What would the world
come to in a hundred years?
I feared a polluted war zone
unless humankind changed.
He said we'd live on Mars.
I pour the claret tea as fragrant
as a berry patch into the good cups.
Warming his hands, he wiggles his fingers
through the prospect of clouds.
He stirs in the honey, licks the spoon,
says *Thank you bees*.
White cyclamen on the table. Blaze of winter
sun through trees. A plate
of simple food. Beside us,
the ones we love.

"Omelet" was first published in *Enter the Chrysanthemum* (Caitlin Press, 2009) reprinted
with permission from Caitlin Press and the author.

Author of two poetry books and a children's book, Fiona
Tinwei Lam's works appears in over twenty-four anthologies.
She co-edited the creative nonfiction anthology, *Double Lives:
Writing and Motherhood*, and edited *The Bright Well: Contem-
porary Canadian Poetry about Facing Cancer*. She currently
teaches at SFU Continuing Studies. www.fionalam.net

NOTE: See animated video recording of poem at https://vimeo.com/48603178

Ponytail Wealth
Feedback Mechanism

KYLA JAMIESON

if there is fate
i think it favours girls
with good hair
the thick shiny kind
is it money or genetics
that gives vancouver
its ponytails?
in line at whole foods
among the impulse
purchase bottles of soap
and loofahs to exfoliate
our idleness
under the banners
that say alleviating
global poverty
the corners of my mouth
are sycophants
deferring to gravity.
i am not free
to consider the children
nearby or the helium
in their foil balloons.
i fixate on the numbers
above registers
and not being
the men ahead of me
oblivious to their turns
when they come. i am
docile in the gears
of consumerism.
i am saccharin
ready to dissolve

Kyla Jamieson is a nonfiction writer, poet, and editor
who lives and relies on unceded Coast Salish territory.
Her poetry has appeared as part of *Room Magazine's*
"No Comment" project and in *Poetry is Dead*.

They Eat Dogs

ELAINE WOO

The Chinese eat dogs
don't they? my friend asks,
her eyes round
as peppermints.
Heat infuses my face
pomegranate red.
What can I say?
My dad, from Canton,
confirmed that some Chinese
do eat canines
when I was no taller
than a St. Bernard.
I look at my friend's bacon-pink
T-shirt. *Don't you eat pork chops*
every Saturday night? I quiz,
my vision narrowed
licorice strings.
Only plant foods
pass through my lips.

NO DOGS AND CHINESE ALLOWED

Those legendary words
framed the entrance to
a park in British-ruled Hong Kong.
Perhaps that's why
some Chinese eat dogs.

Elaine Woo is a poet, graphic comics artist/writer, librettist, non-fiction writer, and video-maker. Author of *Cycling with the Dragon,* she only eats modest amounts of traditionally farmed animals. Caught in a Western cultural dietary stereotype of the Chinese, she addresses this and other social/political issues throughout her debut book and in *Veils, Halos & Shackles, Grain Magazine, NationalPoetryMonth.ca 2017, The Ottawa Poetry Newsletter, h& (handandpoetry), The Literary Commune,* and *Uut Poetry.*

Sitter

MALLORY TATER

My parents are out teaching marriage,
my mother in a wrinkled blouse.
Before leaving the house, she picked
at a grocery store chicken and I picture
her fingers glistening with oil as she lifts
the mic to her mouth, shares pretty foolproof
vows at Immaculate Conception Church.
My sisters and I watch Blair Witch Project
and whine over a bowl of salt-less pretzels,
Meredith sick in the sitter's arms. Brenna feeds
her fruit lozenges, tucks all of us into bed
before the witch appears. My mind barely leaves
that forest in Maryland, those three lost teens
finding fistfuls of branches, baskets of fingers.
From my room, door open, I listen to my sitter
stick her fingers down her throat after licking
frosting off a knife. Brenna flushes and enters
our room, reties her hair in the mirror,
smoothes my sister's bangs. Meredith lies
one bunk down, coughing out all that is left
of a flu so grape-flavoured, so unforgivable.
Brenna unwraps two lozenges, feeds one
to my sister, swallows the other herself.
Horror is not how to coach a body.
Horror is that I was listening. And I fall
asleep, so far from dying. The moon,
a lemon, rots in the sky.

Mallory Tater is a writer from the traditional, unceded territories of the *Algonquin Anishnaabeg* Nation (Ottawa). Her poetry & fiction have been published in literary magazines across Canada. She was shortlisted for *Arc Magazine*'s 2015 Poem of The Year Contest, *The Malahat Review*'s 2016 Far Horizon's Contest and *Room Magazine*'s 2016 Fiction and Poetry Prizes. She was the recipient of *CV2*'s 2016 Young Buck Poetry Prize. Her first book of poetry *This Will Be Good* is forthcoming with BookThug Press in 2018.

Akinsdale Arena

CURTIS LEBLANC

Before the first cold white cuts mark the face
of the ice at Akinsdale, the rink attendant, stubble-jawed
forty-something in jeans and corduroy jacket,
uses the flattop grill in the concession kitchen
where I work during my first year out of one school
and into another. He brings three brown eggs in half a carton,
a ziplock of Montreal steak spice, a skinny cut of bright red beef
sealed beneath cellophane in its Styrofoam casket, so cheap
it has no marbling, no grey fat to keep it from drying out
on the grill. I do the day's prep, count cans of soft drinks,
KitKats and Twix bars and bags of chips, replace the previous
night's thick brown fryer oil with a new jug of Golden Canola,
while the attendant cooks breakfast—only enough for himself.
He eats like he works: speechless and alone, with the stale gestures
of a person who knows what to expect of any given day.

All glazed over, eighteen and at work, I split stacks
of frozen patties, leave hotdogs to burst and shrivel
on the roller, pour water-thin hot chocolates
for hockey parents as the day's games play out—
novice to atom, bantam to midget, the Junior Bs asking
a toonie at the door. I was a leftwing once, rubbed shoulders
with Plexiglas from end to dead end, watched teammates
pot hat-tricks from the stained-wood bench. Now I'm fixed
on the pop and sizzle of that round cut on the grill, the tinny smell
of blood turned to steam. Even the permanent stench of sweat
and black rubber flooring laid to forgive steel-bladed steps
is not enough to make me forget the peppercorns, coriander,
dried garlic, coarse salt, hanging on with each quick flip.

During these morning shift hours, when sleep clings
like static to the corners of my eyes and the cold follows
me in from the outside, I want another man's simple breakfast
more than the minimum wage I make or the youth
I've been charged with. More than the icy sheet of time
and potential that has been cleared for me. But only that. Never
his laps and laps with frigid hands on the Zamboni's vinyl wheel,
those last heavy shovelfuls of wet snow over the lip
of the gate, left to melt through the drain on the floor,
or each mandatory inspection of another surface restored.

Curtis LeBlanc was born and raised in St. Albert, Alberta. He is the author of *Good for Nothing* (Anstruther Press, 2017) and *Little Wild* (Nightwood Editions, forthcoming 2018).

Poets and Cheese

ERIN FLEGG

Cheese is, by weight, the most oft-pilfered item in most grocery stores, and I have a theory (backed by personal anecdotal evidence) that the key culprit here is poets. Writers are excellent at rendering obscure the line between things we want and things we need, and nowhere is this more evident than in a poet's love of good cheese and their willingness to go to great shady lengths to get it.

Poets are denied so much. Their books are typically expected to make so little money as to make the authorial convention of securing an agent a financially counterproductive endeavour. Even the more widely read poets I know have full-time day jobs to pay the rent, and these are often teaching jobs since a master's degree in creative writing doesn't prepare you for much else (at least according to most of the people who have ever read my own resume). The trope of the bad poet, the sad sack poet, permeate pop culture from Joss Whedon's William the Bloody to Connor in the recent Netflix comedy *Chewing Gum*. To call yourself a poet in public is to risk association with that lineage, unless you're one of the lucky few with a shiny round badge on the cover of your already-published book and job in a prestigious English department.

Other kinds of writers, fiction writers but especially journalists, have always been unmitigated vagabonds. My electrical engineer father once told me he would never be able to approach work the way that I do (which is to say casually, a freelance journalist who takes on side gigs to my side gigs to fill the gaps writing leaves open) because he likes cheese too much. A kind of vagabond himself, (and one who has worked in high tech since the early eighties) I suppose it hasn't occurred to him in his adult life to commit theft to maintain his lifestyle. Fair enough.

But poets are different. They have always been painted with at least a veneer of gentility and sophistication, expected to show up in nice shoes and demonstrate

good taste in the finer things despite the runs in their stockings. And maybe those things went deeper in bygone days, but as a culture, we have long failed to put our money where our collective mouth is when it comes to giving poets the support they require to maintain our own image of them.

So we have a façade of the high brow covering up a distinct lack of buying power, and what better place to play out this dichotomy than the cheese aisle? After all, what's an afternoon salon without goat's cheese and crackers? Or a dinner party without baguette and brie? Cheese is both elegant and filling, even offering a modicum of nutritional value via a few grams of protein. Not quite a luxury but not a necessity either. And cheap—the good stuff at least—it is not. Here's where the romance takes over. There is a sense that good cheese is owed poets, both an entitlement and a deprivation. In many ways it's the essence of class struggle: guerrilla redistribution of resources as a way to disrupt power.

Crossing thresholds both figurative and literal, cheese thievery also provides entry into privileged spaces, spaces like Whole Foods. A little ironically, it's in this fancy place that poets are safest, since it's unlikely the Vancouver yuppies handling $13 loaves of gluten-free bread are going to give a fuck about a sad-looking ginger in a dirty raincoat pretending to belong before walking right out the front door with a backpack full of nice haloumi.

Erin Flegg is an Ontario-born, BC-dwelling writer and journalist. She likes hiking, hanging with the neighbour's cat and seeking out the most expensive block of cheese in the store.

Project Chef: Something's Cooking in the Classroom
Recipe for Afghan Bolani Katchalu

FIONA TINWEI LAM

Imagine elementary school kids preparing meals of golden-crusted macaroni and cheese casseroles made with homemade béchamel and whole wheat rotini; fragrant pots of minestrone soup with fresh herbs and over half a dozen different local vegetables; a vibrantly coloured stir-fry with tofu in a savoury sauce; or steaming bowls of creamy breakfast porridge loaded with oats, millet, amaranth and quinoa, flavoured with cinnamon, honey and dried fruits, and topped with chunky homemade applesauce.

The award-winning Project Chef program, developed and run by Barbara Finley, is teaching students in public elementary schools across Vancouver how to make these and other delicious and healthy dishes for themselves and their families. Finley has developed a fun and mobile curriculum that covers food and kitchen safety, the origin and nature of food, good nutrition, culinary techniques, the significance of local farms and producers, as well as the pleasures of sharing homemade food and good conversation at a sit-down meal with people you care about. Depending on funding (the program relies on private donors, with no public funding), the program can occasionally organize field trips to farms, grocery stores, and public markets, or go behind the scenes to a kitchen in a local restaurant.

During the period 2007-2017, the program taught over 13,500 children in 509 classrooms from kindergarten to grade seven in schools throughout Vancouver about healthy food choices and how to prepare food for themselves, directly involving over 7000 parent and community volunteers and working with over 800 teachers and school staff members. There is a huge demand and long waiting list for the program, which was awarded the Governor General of Canada's Meritorious Service Medal (2017), the Maple Leaf Foods Feed it Forward Award (2016), and the Canadian Association of Food Service Professionals Community Leadership Award (2016).

Finley inherited her passion for food and cooking from her mother. "My mom was an amazing cook. Our year was built around food, whether it was picking berries, canning salmon or peaches, making Christmas cake." She was a teacher for over twenty-five years, working in Langley before completing her master's in education at the University of British Columbia. She also studied at the Dubrulle Culinary School, where she developed a kids cooking program. She then taught in the professional culinary and pastry programs at Northwest Culinary Academy of Vancouver while conducting various kids cooking programs around town.

Since starting Project Chef in 2007, Finley has been immensely gratified by her experiences. Some classes have explored other cultures through food: one year a grade six class at Grenfell made Afghan *bolani*, and grade six and seven students studying ancient Rome at Bayview Elementary School dressed in togas or as gladiators and prepared food based on fourth century Roman recipes, including omelets with honey and cinnamon, "must" bread, spiced grape juice, poached pears and roasted spiced squash. Other children have cooked for and with their families for the first time.

Finley wants to make an impact, especially among kids of the working poor. "They are the most vulnerable. Both parents are working and aren't home a lot. There aren't the school programs after school. It's the grey zone where there isn't the funding and there aren't the support systems—these are the kids that are often most in need." She noted that seventy per cent of children don't eat meals regularly with their families around the table, which is linked to rising rates of childhood obesity and related learning and health problems.

Finley recalls a particular day as a highlight one year when the Project Chef program celebrated the exuberant finale of its program at one school in the morning, followed in the afternoon by an enthusiastic school reception at another school. She wrote: "If we could bottle the energy and enthusiasm around food that was created... we could remedy our society's disconnection with the food we eat....It was an overwhelming day that demonstrated the importance of food in our lives: nutritionally, socially, culturally, environmentally and emotionally."

See http://www.projectchef.ca/
This piece is an updated excerpt from "Something's Cooking in the Classroom" written by Fiona Tinwei Lam and published in *The Tyee* https://thetyee.ca/Life/2013/12/07/Project-Chef-Vancouver/

Afghan *Bolani Katchalu* (Potato Filled Turnovers):

Bolani is a traditional Afghani flatbread stuffed with potato, spinach or lentils. It is usually served warm as an appetizer, side dish or even a main dish.

Yield: Serves 8
Preparation Time: About 60 minutes
Cooking Time: 20 minutes

EQUIPMENT:
· measuring cups and spoons
· 2 medium-sized bowls
· pot
· potato masher or fork
· small sharp knife
· rubber spatula
· rolling pin
· spatula or pancake flipper
· frying pan

INGREDIENTS:

Dough:
- 3 ½ cups all purpose flour
- 1 tsp. salt
- 1 cup water
- 1 tsp. olive oil

Dip:
- ½ cup plain yogurt

Filling:
- 4 medium potatoes, cooked
- ½ cup chopped cilantro
- 2 or 3 green onions,
  cut into 1 cm sized pieces
- 2 tbsp. olive oil
- ½ tsp. salt
- freshly cracked pepper, to taste

Method:
- Mix flour and salt together.
- Add water and oil. Mix until dough starts to form. If dough seems a little dry, add a tbsp. or 2 of water.
- Knead dough for about ten minutes, until smooth.
- Place dough in lightly oiled bowl. Cover with clean tea towel or plastic wrap. Let rest for about an hour.
- Wash potatoes. Cook in pot of salted water until knife or skewer slides in and out when poked. Drain and let potatoes cool.
- In a medium-sized bowl, mash potatoes. Add olive oil, salt and pepper and mash together until smooth.
- Using a small, sharp knife, cut the hairy root end off of the green onion, then slice into pinky-wide slices. Add to the potato bowl.
- Roughly chop the leaves and upper stem of the cilantro. Add to the bowl. Mix the potato mixture together.
- Cut the dough into 4 equal sized pieces. Take a piece of dough and roll into a smooth ball.
- Flour work surface then roll out dough as thin as a tortilla.
- Spread about ¼ cup of the filling on one half of the dough. Leave a 2 cm border around the rim.
- Fold the dough in half over the filling and press to seal. Press and flatten the *bolani* to remove air from inside the pocket.
- Place frying pan on heat. Turn on to medium. Add 2 tbsp. olive oil and let heat up. Cook *bolani* until golden, about two minutes, then flip over. Both sides should be browned and crispy.
- Place on paper towel or plate.
- Repeat to cook other *bolani*.
- Slice into wedges and serve warm with yogurt for dipping.

Tasty Tip:
- You can add ¼ cup chopped cooked spinach to the potato mixture for colour, flavour and nutrition.

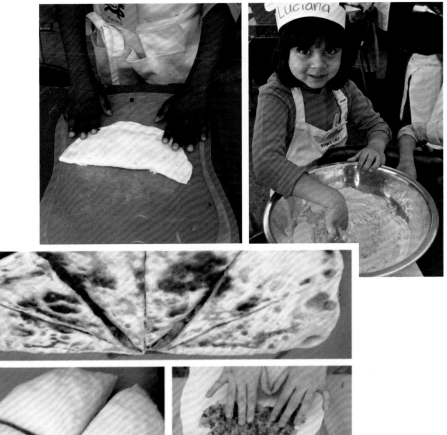

Interview with Paw Thi Blay

RACHEL ROSE

Rachel: Paw Thi Blay, you and your family came to Canada after living in a refugee camp in Thailand for years. Would you please tell me about how you prepared food in the camp?

Paw Thi Blay: In the camp, we made a stove with mud, and did our cooking with wood or charcoal. They gave us a place behind our house to grow vegetables. We used behind the house, in front, everywhere that we could, to plant vegetables.

Rachel: Could you tell me about when you left Burma and had to move into the camps?

Paw Thi Blay: I left Burma when I was around two years old. We tried to escape from the Burmese soldiers, because we couldn't live in that country any longer—we had to escape with our lives. My parents tried to carry me on their backs.

Most of the families struggled with many difficulties when they were living in the *Karen* state (region of Burma). They had to hide in the jungle, build a small house for two or three days, then move to another place. There were soldiers and there were deaths—our people were killed. So finally the people gave up and moved to a refugee camp.

My older sister, she was hiding so many nights in the jungle. My father tried to cook rice for us, but we sometimes had to leave before it was ready because of the soldiers. My mother and father always tried to find food for us. My father and my mother went back to the house in the middle of the night and got rice. If the soldiers heard any babies cry, they would find us and catch us all, so we had to be separated in the jungle.

Rachel: A long time ago, I spoke to some older *Karen* men and they told me about hunting porcupines and wild pigs while hiding in the jungle during the escape to the refugee camps.

Paw Thi Blay: Yes. My father was a very good hunter.

Rachel: He had a gun?

Paw Thi Blay: Yes, but it is not like guns here, we made it ourselves. All of us walked more than fourteen days and nights to arrive to the *Karen* state. But we weren't refugees right away. We became refugees when I was about sixteen years old.

Rachel: When you were living in the refugee camp, did you have enough to eat?

Paw Thi Blay: My family had enough. We received food from the NGOs—rice, cooking oil, fish paste, yellow beans, all dry food—but there was not enough for the large families. My husband and I only had two kids, so we were okay.

Rachel: How long did you live in the refugee camp altogether?

Paw Thi Blay: After I escaped from Burma, altogether about thirty years. I went to high school in the refugee camp, and I graduated there in the camp. My whole life was in the refugee camp. I grew up in the Salween river side of the camp. The other side was the *Karen* state, in Burma. I lived in the Thai side. Sometimes we could cross, sometimes not—the Burmese soldiers can't come to the Thai side. We got all our water from the Salween river. We drank from it, and we carried the water to the camp. I carried it in a bucket. Most women put the bucket on top of their heads to carry it. They were very good at carrying water, but I was no good at it! They put a towel on top of their heads and then a big bucket of water— but I had to carry it on my back.

Rachel: When I first met you, you and your family and many other families had just arrived. What was it like eating Canadian food?

Paw Thi Blay: The first year that we settled in Canada, we were not used to the food. Most of the Canadian food is not spicy, not tasty and salty like our back-home food. Canadian food is more healthy but not spicy. The first Canadian food I ate, I remember that day! I ate boiled pasta with tomato sauce, and I didn't like it. Even the noodle here is not like our back-home noodle.

Wah de Pah and Palace love Canadian food, they love bread and especially McDonalds. I know it's not healthy so we try to make food at home. Now we love Canadian food.

Rachel: What *Karen* foods do you like best?

Paw Thi Blay: My favorite food is noodle soup, homemade with chicken or eggs, onion, garlic, yellow beans, sometimes coconut milk. We also have papaya salad. It's very spicy. We mix papaya with crab paste, lime and tomato and green beans, peanuts and also dry shrimp. Then we mix with some salt and cilantro, and cooked onion and garlic.

Niġipiaqtaviin? / Do You Eat Real Food?

JOAN KANE

I have no brothers and my husband is not a hunter. I have held a gun once and only with great reluctance, during a backcountry clamber up the slopes of Grand Singatook on the Seward Peninsula. My father had accoutered himself with a weapon in case we encountered bears or wolverines or worse: we were not hunting. Rather, I was in search of perspective. My older son was a toddler and I carried my younger son in early pregnancy. At one point my father offered to pack his grandson on his back and encouraged me to switch out for his canteen and firearm. I agreed. I held the gun and regretted it, and we switched back. We saw no mammals that day, but happened upon feral reindeer (*qunŋiq*) cached in soil on our descent of the mountain.

My grandmother and her sisters were raised by my great-grandparents in a reindeer camp at Mary's Igloo until the 1918 flu pandemic left nearly every adult in the village there dead. Then, they lived at the Catholic orphanage at Pilgrim Hot Springs, where, alongside hundreds of fellow orphans, they worked the geothermal-thawed soil under the tutelage of Ursuline nuns to grow potatoes, cabbage, carrots, and other crops hardy enough to thrive in subarctic conditions.

My sons inherit my caginess around rules: they wonder if we need a permit to gather *Lottia pelta* when we chance upon an abundance of them at low tide on a recent hike near *Angagkitaqnuuq*. I didn't know. We didn't pick any. Instead, we make a snack of oyster leaf greens, sea purslane, and beach lovage to tide us over.

*

I once spoke with a Danish journalist about the relationship between language and survival, how my sons know well the Inupiaq words for airplane (*tiŋmizun*), pencil (*aglaun*), tomorrow (*ublaakun*), but how they did not know many words for traditional subsistence food or its harvest, because our lives did not include hunting. Their father is not Inupiaq. He cannot legally harvest a single seal (*niqsaq*), bearded seal (*ugruk*), or walrus (*aiviq*).

*

We have returned to Anchorage from some time away, and called my parents to tell of our adventures. My father mentions that my mother has not eaten in ten days.

She has been this way before. I had been away at *Utqiaġvik*. She became so weak and confused that I carried her to the car to bring her to hospital as instructed by her doctor ("she will be too scared by an ambulance and it will be easier to bring her yourself," he said).

She spoke only *Inupiaq*. My monolingual father couldn't communicate with her. I interpreted as she was placed on an IV and underwent CAT scans, as the doctors asked things like, "what day is it?" and "who is president?"

My older son, about to visit her this afternoon, asks, "does she have any seal meat?"

"Yes," I remind him, "she does. We stocked her freezer with *paniqtuq* and *miziġak* earlier this spring."

He looks at me apprehensively.

"Dried seal meat and seal oil," I explain.

I am not a hunter and I have no brothers.

Photography by Kim Hansen.

Joan Naviyuk Kane lives in Alaska with her husband and sons. Her books include *The Cormorant Hunter's Wife*, *Hyperboreal*, *The Straits*, and *Milk Black Carbon*. She teaches in the graduate creative writing program at the Institute of American Indian Arts and was a judge for the 2017 Griffin Poetry Prize.

Gaultheria Shallon (The Way In), Salt Spring Island

KAREN SHKLANKA

"Here by myself away from the clank of the world"
        —from Calamus [In Paths Untrodden] by Walt Whitman

On a tangled path behind the cabin, tripped up
by twisted stalks of Salal
under the Douglas firs, I escape
the habit of titrating
symptoms into bell curves,
rows of patients like jars
that must be closed,

from skirts that hide my knees,
underhanded bras, heels quick—
clicking the hall to the nurses' station in
pileated woodpecker code
for *busy,* and *working hard.*
I no longer bite my tongue into canker sores
or tear my hangnails into pink tendrils—

still, the wounded soul of a doctor calls
without words.

The reply: scent of salted forest, wrap of humidity
from logs almost returned to earth, and reassurance
from thickets of Salal flowers cupped in prayer.

Gratitude bursts from within my own secret ovals,
my pointed tips, my berries, fleshy
and ciliate, with numerous minute seeds.
I untangle myself, proceed

as the *Tsawout* women on this island before me,
to strip Salal berries from laden stems, basket them
in my long-sleeved sweater, tumble them
into the cast iron pot filled with stones
glowing red from the bonfire on the driveway.

I boil water and berries with the stones,
mash them into a purple mixture,
which I pour onto skunk cabbage leaves in cedar boxes.

I clear the dead wood
from under the power lines, burn
the alder branches, dry the mixture over embers.
I am preparing.

I cut the dried mixture into Salal-squares
to be stored until the feast.

I am by myself.
I go through all the rooms
and remove mirrors and old clothes.

I am preparing for the ceremony
of forgiveness,
the feast of undressing,
the feast of giving away,
the feast of opening the hands.

"Gaultheria Shallon (The Way In), Salt Spring Island" was first published in *Ceremony for Touching* (Coteau Books). Photography by Derek von Essen.

Karen Shklanka, has an MFA from UBC in Creative Writing, and is a Vancouver physician who works as an addiction medicine consultant. Previously, she was a family physician in Salt Spring Island, BC, and Moose Factory, Ontario. Her first book, *Sumac's Red Arms* (Coteau, 2009), was a finalist for the Foreword Review Book of the Year prize; in 2016 she published her second poetry book, *Ceremony for Touching*, and two long poems from that manuscript were finalists for the 2012 CBC Poetry Prize.

Meeru Dhalwala, Vikram Vij and John Sherlock
(photographer) have all given permission for their work
to be published in *Sustenance*, as has Douglas & McIntyre.

Nicola Goshulak
Assistant Editor / Permissions Coordinator
Harbour Publishing Ltd. / Douglas and McIntyre (2013) Ltd.
The original was published in *Vij's at Home: Relax, Honey*
(Vancouver: Douglas & McIntyre, 2010)

Acknowledgments: *Sustenance* truly was a community effort. Without the visionary support of Yosef Wosk, this book would not exist, nor would Vancouver have a Poet Laureate position. The City of Vancouver and VPL supported *Sustenance* from the beginning throughout its long gestation, and I'd like to particularly thank Marnie Rice and Metha Brown. My cousin, Herman Rose, offered a surprise donation at just the right time, an unanticipated gift of support and belief in community building. The Vancouver International Writers' Festival, particularly Hal Wake and Clea Young, generously invited us all to launch *Sustenance* in their fine company, as has Barbara Edwards and the other terrific librarians at the Vancouver Public Library. The Poetry Ambassadors each offered their support and expertise at different points of this process: Hartley Banack, Adèle Barclay, Juliane Okot Bitek, Jillian Christmas, Elee Kraljii Gardiner, Fiona Lam, Jami Macarty, Ngwatilo Mawiyoo, Lynda Prince, annie ross, Renée Sarojini Saklikar, Karen Shklanka, Kevin Spenst and RC Weslowski. Brian Kaufman continued doing the good work for which Anvil is known; he, Cara Lang, and designer Derek von Essen went far above and beyond in shaping the anthology to grow and become what it was meant to be. Derek Fu's gorgeous photographs of local food and food artisans complement the writing, and illustrate just how fortunate we are to live and eat in this place.

—Rachel Rose, Editor